Uncharted Territory

The story of Scottish devolution 1999–2009

Uncharted Territory

The story of Scottish devolution
1999–2009

Hamish Macdonell

POLITICO'S

First published in Great Britain 2009 by
Politico's Publishing, an imprint of
Methuen Publishing Ltd
8 Artillery Row
London
SW1P 1RZ

10 9 8 7 6 5 4 3 2 1

A CIP catalogue record for this book is available from the British Library.

ISBN 978-1-84275-235-7

Set in Bembo and Zapf Humanist by Methuen Publishing Ltd
Printed and bound in Great Britain by Cromwell Press Group,
Trowbridge, Wiltshire.

Contents

Key players   vii
Prologue   xi

1. The price of a deputy's badge   1
2. New game, new rules   12
3. Our friends in the south   27
4. Two First Ministers and a funeral   38
5. Foot and mouth, foxes and fish   55
6. A muddle, not a fiddle   63
7. Strangers on a train   73
8. Lucky Jack?   90
9. Free radicals and stalking horses   105
10. King over the water   115
11. Splitters and swingers   129
12. Grand designs   138
13. The harder they fall   150
14. The seven-year itch   163
15. The long walk to freedom   173
16. It's time   185
17. Going it alone   203
18. A takeaway coup and a coronation   217
19. Cheques and balances   227
20. Divide and rule   236
21. Uncharted territory   247

Epilogue   261
Appendix: Election results in Scotland 1999–2007   264
Index   266

For Ronald and Diana

Key players

Wendy Alexander Labour. Became leader of the Labour group in the Scottish Parliament in September 2007; resigned in July 2008 after an ongoing row over donations to her leadership campaign.

Tony Blair Labour. Prime Minister from 1997 to 2007, Scottish born and educated. One of the first moves he made in government was to create the Scottish Parliament.

Gordon Brown Labour. Chancellor of the Exchequer from 1997 to 2007, Scottish born and educated. Became Prime Minister in 2007.

Donald Dewar Labour. Secretary of State for Scotland in the Blair government in 1997, First Minister of Scotland in 1999. Died of a brain haemorrhage in October 2000.

Alex Fergusson Conservative. Old Etonian farmer who became the third Presiding Officer of the Scottish Parliament in 2007.

Annabel Goldie Conservative. She became the second leader of the Scottish Conservative group at Holyrood in 2005 following the resignation of David McLetchie.

Iain Gray Labour. He became leader of the Labour group in the Scottish Parliament in September 2008 following the resignation of Wendy Alexander.

Robin Harper Green. He became Scotland's first Green MSP in 1999. He was also joint leader of the Scottish Green Party and was returned as an MSP in 2003 and 2007.

Jack McConnell Labour. He became Scotland's third First Minister when he succeeded Henry McLeish in 2001, a job he held until he stood down following Labour's election defeat in 2007.

Margo MacDonald Independent. Former SNP MP and MSP, she quit the SNP in 2003 then stood, and was elected, as an independent MSP in 2003 and again in 2007.

Henry McLeish Labour. He became Scotland's second First Minister when he succeeded Donald Dewar in 2000, before resigning a year later after a controversy over his office expenses.

David McLetchie Conservative. He was the first
leader of the Scottish Conservative group in the
Scottish Parliament from 1999 but resigned as leader
in 2005 following ongoing rows over his travel
expenses.

Enric Miralles Architect. The lead architect of the
Scottish Parliament building, he died in 2000, aged
forty-five, of a brain tumour.

George Reid SNP. He became the second Presiding
Officer of the Scottish Parliament in 2003 and retired
from frontline politics in 2007.

Alex Salmond SNP. Party leader between 1990 and
2000, Salmond returned to the leadership in 2004
and led the SNP to its 2007 election victory, when
he became Scotland's fourth First Minister.

Tavish Scott Liberal Democrat. He became leader
of the Scottish Liberal Democrats in 2008 following
the resignation of Nicol Stephen.

Tommy Sheridan Scottish Socialist Party and
Solidarity. SSP MSP from 1999, re-elected in 2003
before quitting the party in 2006 and forming
Solidarity. Lost his seat in 2007 following a sensational
defamation case against the *News of the World*.

 **David Steel** Liberal Democrat. Former leader of the UK Liberal Party who was the first Presiding Officer of the Scottish Parliament between 1999 and 2003.

 Nicol Stephen Liberal Democrat. Became leader of the Scottish Liberal Democrats in 2005; resigned in 2008 to spend more time with his family.

 John Swinney SNP. A former MP, he became SNP leader in 2000 and resigned in 2004; became finance secretary in the SNP government elected in 2007.

 **Jim Wallace** Liberal Democrat. Leader of the Scottish Liberal Democrats from 1992 to 2005. He was also Deputy First Minister to three Labour First Ministers between 1999 and 2005.

Prologue

ON the bright sunny morning of 12 September 1997, Tony Blair strode around Edinburgh's old Parliament Square, smiling and shaking hands with supporters in the small but enthusiastic crowd, many of whom were waving brightly coloured 'Yes, Yes' banners. Blair had come to power promising a referendum on Scottish devolution and here he was, just five months later, celebrating its success – 74 per cent voting for a Scottish parliament and 63 per cent backing tax powers for the new institution. It was an overwhelming endorsement, capturing the spirit of change embodied in the New Labour administration and the desire for a new form of government for Scotland.

But even with the tremendous support of the Scottish people and the backing – not all of it enthusiastic – of the Blair Cabinet, opinion was still bitterly divided within the Labour Party over where devolution would take Scotland and the United Kingdom. For George Robertson, the former shadow Scottish secretary, the case was clear. 'Devolution will kill nationalism stone dead,' he declared. For Tam Dalyell, the veteran Labour MP, the opposite was true. Devolution, he warned, would be a 'motorway with no exits' to Scottish independence and the break-up of the United Kingdom.

What was clear at that time, though, was that the landscape of British politics was going to be changed forever. The referendum had already helped move on the political debate within the whole of the United Kingdom, taking the concept of Scottish independence from the fringes to the centre. It was also changing the way people throughout the United Kingdom viewed themselves, their country and their compatriots, forcing previously esoteric concepts like the 'West Lothian question' and the Barnett formula to the top of the economic and constitutional agenda.

For Scotland, the first decade of devolution, from 1999 to 2009, was to prove both dramatic and groundbreaking. There were three national elections, four First Ministers and two different types of government, one coalition and one minority. The parliament lost one First Minister to a brain haemorrhage, one to electoral defeat and one to scandal.

But this ten-year journey was also characterised by the growing maturity of the Scottish Parliament. It saw the policy differences between England and Scotland stretched to unprecedented and unexpected levels as the Scottish Executive abolished up-front student tuition fees, then brought in free care for the elderly, froze council tax bills and moved to end prescription charges. The institution also learned how to deal with the unrealistic expectations placed on it by the electorate and the unremitting scrutiny of the press. It came through these tests and marked its new-found confidence by taking on a more assured and confrontational attitude towards its parent in Westminster, asserting a small but definite role on the world stage and demanding more rights, responsibilities and freedoms for itself.

In party political terms, the parliament grew in stature as the Scottish National Party transformed itself from a loose pro-independence movement into an effective political machine capable of taking on, and beating, Labour in its traditional Scottish strongholds. But in UK terms it coincided with the Labour Party's decline as the UK's dominant political force, putting in place the ideal conditions for the SNP to capitalise in 2007.

On 12 May 1999, Winnie Ewing, the first MSP to take the Presiding Officer's chair in the new parliament, declared:'The Scottish Parliament, which adjourned on 25 March 1707, is hereby reconvened.' It was a day when all those who had campaigned for so long for 'Scottish home rule' could celebrate but it was also the day which marked an end to the decades of theorising and debating. The parliament was now a reality. The reams of paper detailing the endless deliberations over the scope of reserved powers and the rules for parliamentary committees had been replaced by the hard wood of MSPs' desks and the sharp rasp of the chamber microphones.

Many of the new MSPs thought they were merely starting on a gentle excursion to improve the lives of Scots by deliberating over simple domestic legislation. None of them foresaw quite what an extraordinary voyage they were about to embark upon, a journey which would change them and their country for ever.

1

The price of a deputy's badge

WHEN Donald Dewar and Jim Wallace put their signatures to the formal agreement creating Scotland's first government in 300 years, neither looked particularly comfortable. Dewar, the Scottish Labour leader, joked with the television crews to cover his nerves as the cameras flashed and the reporters shouted. Wallace, the Scottish Liberal Democrat leader, simply adopted a rather forced, fixed grin as he took the heavy ink pen and signed.

The final details in what had become a rather tetchy negotiating process between the two parties had only been completed late the night before. The coalition discussions had been so frenetic and intensive since the election eight days earlier that neither Dewar nor Wallace had been able to enjoy much rest before meeting once again for the official signing, which took place on 14 May 1999.

The new Royal Museum of Scotland, on the corner of Edinburgh's Chambers Street, stylish and modern with its sweeping curves of golden sandstone, had been chosen as the venue for the ceremony to echo Scotland's new, modern, style of politics. But not everyone approved of the spirit of consensus, as the *Daily Mail* demonstrated that morning with a strident front page on its Scottish edition depicting Wallace alongside a lawman's badge from the Wild West and carrying the splash headline 'Sold Out for a Deputy's Badge'.

Much to the surprise of everyone outside the negotiating teams, Wallace had secured the post of Deputy First Minister in the coalition negotiations with Labour – despite bringing only seventeen MSPs to the deal, compared with Labour's fifty-six. The news that the Liberal Democrats were to get the Deputy First Minister's job, two Cabinet posts and two junior ministerial posts had leaked out from a delighted Lib Dem MSP the night before.

By this time, senior Labour members were already grumbling about Wallace's influential new position, a concession from Dewar which irritated Labour MSPs for the next four years. But most MSPs in the smaller party had good reason to feel pleased with the coalition deal. The Liberal Democrats had studied coalition agreements in other countries and knew they should expect nothing less than the Deputy First Minister's job and much, much more in policy terms.

Indeed, when the two negotiating teams met for the first time on the top floor of the old council offices on Edinburgh's George IV Bridge on the Monday after the election, Dewar turned up with his ideas written on four sides of A4 paper, whereas Wallace arrived with a bulging ring binder full of policies, ideas and positions – all of which had been debated and agreed by the party's new MSPs over the weekend.

Wallace remembers how the two parties approached the negotiations from completely different perspectives. 'I got the impression Donald thought he could get us on board just by putting two Liberal Democrats in the Labour Cabinet but it wasn't going to work that way,' he said.

The negotiating teams were divided into pairs comprising one Liberal Democrat and one Labour member. Each pair was tasked with going through a set of party commitments to find common ground. Where there were disputes, items were put into square brackets and taken into the top-level talks, with Dewar and Wallace. On one occasion, Dewar noticed a policy in square brackets and barked: 'For God's sake, Jim, what's this piece of Liberal nonsense you've got here?' One of his officials then leaned over and told Dewar that the policy in question was actually a Labour one.

The Liberal Democrats dropped their demand for the abolition of the tolls on the Skye Bridge and the immediate lifting of the beef ban. They also agreed to set aside their commitment to proportional representation for local government elections, after being persuaded by Dewar that it would be looked into by a commission. Labour got most of its manifesto accepted but, as everyone knew they would, the negotiations came down to student tuition fees – the Liberal Democrats wanted them scrapped, Labour was in favour of retention.

In any other European country, the talks would probably have taken weeks but this was all new ground to the Scottish politicians, still working under the traditional assumptions bred through decades at Westminster. Wallace said: 'This was against the culture of the UK, where the removal vans move into Downing Street the day after the election to move the incumbent out. Even though the negotiations only took a few days, at that stage it really did appear to be taking a long time.' As a result, there was a strange, exhaustive pace to the talks, as if each party felt under enormous pressure to get them finished as soon as possible. They started early and went on late.

Much of the pressure on the teams came from the press and, with each day's negotiating session lasting well into the night, the Scottish political press pack had taken up a station, doorstepping the entrances to the old council offices. It soon became clear that the main doors could be monitored from Deacon Brodie's Tavern, a slightly soulless, touristy bar on the corner of George IV Bridge and the Royal Mile. The pub would empty within seconds if anybody from either of the negotiating parties emerged from the offices within.

John Farquhar Munro, a Gael, a crofter and a first-time MSP at the age of sixty-four, caused more false alarms than anybody else, going outside in his three-piece tweed suit for a smoke. Although he wasn't part of the official negotiating team, as an MSP he would be kept informed of any major developments but he refused to reveal anything. 'I have no idea what you are on about,' he used to say to the pleading journalists, hiding a smile beneath his pipe.

With tuition fees the last outstanding issue in square brackets, everybody from both teams was tasked with finding a solution. The compromise, when it came, was surprisingly simple: the matter would be farmed out to a review commission. It was a perfect fudge and neither side had to back down – despite pledges from both that the issue was a 'deal breaker'. The job of deciding what actually should be done with student fees, work which took several months, went to a lawyer named Andrew Cubie, a former CBI Scotland chairman with senior roles at two Edinburgh colleges.

However, as the two coalition parties started the process of forming an administration for the first time, the leader of the Scottish National Party, Alex Salmond, was trying to come to terms with a poor election result and a disastrous campaign.

The SNP emerged from Scotland's first parliamentary election with thirty-five seats, a comfortable second place to Labour but well short of party expectations. To make matters worse, it had spent heavily in the election, largely on desperate, last-minute measures to try to rescue its faltering campaign. Not only had this strategy failed, but the cost of the election was starting to bite into party finances.

The seeds of the SNP's poor performance were sown early in March 1999, at a special pre-election conference in Aberdeen. Salmond had unveiled a policy he believed would allow him to outflank Labour on the left: the 'penny for Scotland'. This was a commitment to raise the basic rate income tax in Scotland by 1p in the pound, to pay for health, education and housing.

The Scottish Parliament had been given the ability to vary income tax by up to 3p in the pound on the basic rate – the so-called 'tartan tax' – following the successful referendum in 1997 but none of the other main parties wanted to go into the election promising to put Scottish income tax at a higher level than in England. They all felt it would be electoral disaster, and so it proved. Salmond argued that he was merely cancelling out the 1p basic rate income tax cut announced by Chancellor Gordon Brown in the Budget, but that failed to register with the electorate. The overall message that went out was that the SNP would put taxes up and that hurt the party's chances.

The election was contested against the background of NATO bombing in Kosovo, a military operation agreed by Labour ministers in London in an attempt to halt the atrocities which were destroying what was left of Yugoslavia. Salmond was against the bombing and on March 29, on the eve of the campaign, he went on television to counter a national address by the Prime Minister. The SNP leader condemned the NATO bombing as a 'misguided' policy of 'dubious legality and unpardonable folly'. It was a principled stand but it allowed Robin Cook, the Foreign Secretary, to brand Salmond the 'toast of Belgrade' and it did not go down well with the voters. At the official start of the campaign a week later, only a quarter of Scots backed Salmond's stance on Kosovo, which, combined with the SNP's tax-raising agenda, put the Nationalists so firmly to the left of Labour in Scotland that they appeared dangerously out of touch.

The SNP campaign was masterminded by Michael Russell, a gregarious writer and broadcaster who was also the party's chief executive. He was behind the Nationalists' manifesto launch, an event which should have kicked off a day of positive publicity, but which bordered on disaster. With UK broadcasters and journalists from around the world present for what was seen as a major political event, Steve Goodwin, the *Independent's* Scottish correspondent, noticed that, in a list of the SNP's fourteen political priorities on page four of the manifesto, a referendum on independence was right down at the bottom at number fourteen, while in a list of ten key pledges it was down at the bottom again, at number ten. 'Why is independence at the bottom? Surely it is the SNP's top priority,' he asked.

Salmond dismissed the question by replying that everyone knew that independence was the SNP's top priority, but it couldn't be achieved by the Scottish Parliament so was not the top issue for this election. But others in the media scented a story and didn't let up. Instead of fielding questions on the intricacies of health or education policy, the increasingly angry SNP leader had to fend off repeated requests for him to explain his approach to independence and why it was last on a list of his party's priorities. That may not have been the most important part of the SNP manifesto – it may have been nothing more than a sideshow – but, as far as the press was concerned, it was the story of the day and the SNP's election campaign was off to a dreadful start.

More was to follow as the campaign developed and the Nationalists failed to eat into Labour's poll lead. Tactics became ever more desperate, culminating in an extraordinary decision by Russell to launch the SNP's own newspaper.

Convinced that the SNP was unable to get its message across because of the unionist bias of Scotland's newspapers, particularly the *Daily Record*, which Russell had described as a Labour election 'leaflet', he decided to produce his own, SNP newspaper – *Scotland's Voice*. Planned with an initial print run of 50,000 a day, and only produced for the final week of the campaign, *Scotland's Voice* was seen by almost everybody in politics – outside and inside the SNP – as one of the most foolish and misguided moves by any political party in Scotland. It made the party look churlish and added to the debts that eventually contributed to the sale of its central Edinburgh head-quarters. The paper made no impact whatever and was roundly ridiculed by the rest of the media (and not just for reasons of self-interest). SNP officials talked after the election of having to remove thousands of copies of the ill-fated newspaper from party offices, which had been produced but never distributed.

While it was clear in the run-up to polling day that the SNP had waged a very poor campaign, its election defeat was not entirely its own fault. The Nationalists were fighting a Labour machine which had become very adept at winning. It was only two years since Tony Blair had been swept into Downing Street on a wave of pro-Labour enthusiasm right across the UK, and passionately so in Scotland. Labour fought a solid, if negative, campaign warning of the dangers of independence and promoting itself as the party of devolution, and it worked. The resentment felt by many in Scotland towards the Conservatives remained live and heated and Labour was still the natural party to support for a majority of Scots.

Salmond did enjoy one particular victory over Blair, however, which was simply conceived and beautifully executed. The occasion was the grand and well-lubricated Press Fund Lunch in the banqueting hall of Glasgow's Hilton Hotel just five days before polling day. This charitable event is usually little more than an opportunity for senior press figures to network and enjoy a long and decent lunch. The guest speaker is always someone of stature but the clear expectation is for an amusing after-lunch address. Blair's advisers may have been warned to stay clear of politics but, whoever's fault it was, the Prime Minister, as guest speaker, rose to his feet at the end of this particular lunch and launched into not just a political speech but an extraordinary partisan tirade against the SNP.

It was dreadfully misjudged as a speech for this kind of gathering; moreover, such an anti-SNP address made everyone on the top table uncomfortable because there, sitting just yards from the Prime Minister, was Salmond, unable to respond or to intervene.

As Blair went on with his attack on the SNP's economic policies and guests started shifting uneasily in their seats, so Salmond began to smile and, just when the Prime Minister turned his fire on the Nationalists' plan to secure Scotland's economy on North Sea oil revenues, so Salmond reached into his pocket and, still sitting but facing most of the guests in the hall, he opened up a familiar, folded orange card with just one word inside – 'Bluff'. The card, which

Salmond had borrowed from the producers of the still popular television celebrity game show *Call My Bluff* a couple of months earlier, completely undermined the Prime Minister's speech.

Salmond held the well-known card in front of him. Slowly at first, and then with increasing speed, as the eyes of the audience were drawn towards it, laughter started and spread, followed by a ripple of applause from some parts of the hall. The worst part for Blair was that he had no idea what was going on because he couldn't see the card; all he knew was that something had gone wrong in his speech, for his audience was laughing when it shouldn't have been.

It was just the sort of guerrilla political tactic that Salmond has revelled in over the years and it helped cool his already frosty relationship with the Prime Minister still further. A clear, simple and magnificent victory, it meant little in the wider context of the SNP's election defeat five days later, but, just for a while, it humiliated and embarrassed the Prime Minister, delighting Salmond's beleaguered activists.

This was Scotland's first election as a devolved nation and, for some in the Labour Party and many across the country, it was important that it was run by those standing for the Scottish Parliament and was not merely an extension of centralised election campaigning organised from London. However, it was hardly helpful when the Chancellor of the Exchequer, Gordon Brown, intervened to significant effect in the Labour campaign, just ahead of the annual Scottish Trades Union Congress (STUC) conference.

The unions had been getting increasingly hostile to the Private Finance Initiative – the mortgage-style public expenditure model which was introduced by the Conservative government and continued by Labour. It was, on the surface, a dry and unexciting topic and not likely to enthuse the voters, but such was the extent of the unions' anger at the use of private finance in public sector building projects that they threatened to campaign against Labour in the Scottish Parliament elections.

Donald Dewar appeared powerless to do anything to head off a damaging confrontation with the unions at the STUC, until Brown came to Scotland on Sunday 18 April, sat down with the union leaders and got them to back down. Brown offered a deal of sorts, promising to protect public sector workers' rights under the private finance deals but refusing to contemplate an end to the scheme itself. Realising they would get nothing else, the unions withdrew their threat to derail the Labour campaign, once again sending out the clear message that Scotland was very much Brown's personal fiefdom and nobody else, including Dewar, was able to challenge that.

Part of the Labour strategy was to send Dewar out to meet the voters. For such an erudite and parliamentary sort of politician, Dewar was surprisingly effective on the streets. He loved Glasgow in particular and, for the most part, Glaswegians were equally affectionate towards him. He cut an awkward figure campaigning on the street, all gangly limbs, unkempt hair, big glasses and a large red rosette, but he would break into a smile at the sight of the voter. He was able to chat amiably with almost all the people he met on the campaign trail, about everything from football to potholes in the road.

Dewar was sent round the country on a campaign battlebus, spelling out the simple, if negative message that the SNP was 'simply too big a risk' and the Nationalists would sue for an 'expensive and messy divorce' if they got into power. He agreed to do what Brown had decided, even though it appeared that he was being sent out to the country to keep him away from the day-to-day decision making at Labour's headquarters in Glasgow. Despite this, Dewar joyously ignored all attempts to 'manage' him in the New Labour way. His one concession was to allow his aides to buy him an overcoat, something he had not bothered with for many, many years, and he did so only to stop the constant badgering about it.

Labour's eventual coalition partners, the Liberal Democrats, went into the 1999 campaign with the hope and expectation of ending up in government but spent the entire time trying desperately not to admit it. Under the slogan 'Raising the Standard', they promised 1,000 new nurses, 500 extra doctors and 2,000 additional teachers if elected to govern Scotland. Jim Wallace also admitted he might put a penny on income tax to fulfil his promises, although he didn't suffer as much as Salmond because he said he would do so only as a last resort.

The Liberal Democrat leadership had a simple ploy all the way through the campaign: don't commit to anything ahead of the coalition negotiations – and it almost worked. At each of the party's daily press conferences, the party leaders were asked: Was this non-negotiable? Was that non-negotiable? Was there anything the Liberal Democrats would hold out for and not compromise on? Most of these questions were aimed at the key issue of tuition fees and, for almost the entire campaign, the Liberal Democrats refused to answer, merely stating that they were standing on their manifesto policies and would hope to get elected on that basis.

Everything went well until Tuesday 4 May, two days before polling day, when for some reason, Sir David Steel, the former party leader, departed from the script. 'Whether it's a coalition or a minority government, tuition fees will go. Tuition fees are dead as of Friday,' he said. His comments astonished and infuriated party managers, who needed to go into talks with Labour able to negotiate and compromise on everything and now they couldn't. They had visions of their treasured ambition of getting into government disappearing with one unplanned comment from a former leader.

Steel's comments did make negotiations much more difficult and the delicate compromise of the Cubie inquiry had to be worked through to the satisfaction of both parties. However, this was not a mistake the Liberal Democrats – who know more about the politics of coalition negotiations than anybody else in Scotland – ever made again.

For the Conservatives, the 1999 election offered a lifeline, a second chance after the humiliation of the 1997 UK general election, when the party was wiped off the political map in Scotland, losing all ten of its MPs in a concerted effort of anti-Tory tactical voting across the country. The party had a new Scottish leader in David McLetchie, someone who came across as just what he was – a competent but rather strait-laced Edinburgh lawyer. And, in the proportional voting system being used in Scotland for the first time in the 1999 election, the Conservatives were in with a good chance of at least partly redeeming their 1997 performance.

Any sort of revival would be welcome for the Tories, who also had to cope with the uncomfortable fact that they had campaigned against the parliament itself. It was not easy for them to deflect the criticism that they were cynical opportunists, standing for an institution they did not want and had opposed in public. Near the end of the campaign, McLetchie admitted that some Conservative supporters were not going to bother voting because they did not approve of the parliament itself. Yet despite these problems, and the feel-good wave of Labour populism, which just added to the deeply entrenched anti-Tory sentiments in Scotland, the Conservatives did win 18 seats out of the 129 on offer in the new parliament.

All of these came from the fifty-six additional seats allocated on a proportional basis under the list voting system adopted for elections to the parliament, an electoral system which the Tories also opposed. The Conservatives failed to win a single one of the seventy-three constituency seats on offer, which suggests that, had the Scottish Parliament been elected under the old first-past-the-post system, they would have continued to bump along the bottom with no parliamentary elected representatives in Scotland for some time to come.

McLetchie ran a solid if unspectacular campaign, failed to make any significant gaffes and brought his party into the new parliament in third place, ahead of the Liberal Democrats. It was, though, probably more than the party dared hope for at the start of the campaign.

The proportional system, which gave every elector two votes, one for a constituency MSP and one for the party list, also succeeded in giving representatives from more fringe parties a seat in the parliament. Tommy Sheridan, the colourful anti-establishment politician and powerful street orator who had led the campaign against the poll tax in Scotland, was elected as the sole representative of the Scottish Socialist Party; Robin Harper, a middle-aged teacher with a taste for multi-coloured scarves, came to the parliament as an additional member for the Lothians region as the first Green MSP; and Dennis Canavan, the maverick left-wing former MP who left the Labour Party after it decided he was not suitable to be a Labour candidate, embarrassed Labour by taking Falkirk West on his own, as an independent.

As the politicians tore into each other on battlebuses and at hustings meetings around the country, joiners and fitters were turning the stately old Church of Scotland General Assembly Hall on The Mound in Edinburgh into a parliament chamber.

Dewar had taken the decision to build a new parliament building down the Royal Mile at Holyrood, but it would take time – and a lot of money and controversy – before it was complete. A temporary home was found for the parliament in the General Assembly Hall, a beautiful Victorian debating chamber, subtly tiered, with oak galleries above all four sides and a marbled black and white corridor behind the speaker's chair. It was a perfect venue for the new institution, particularly as it was needed for General Assembly meetings only once a year, when it could quite easily be changed back into a debating chamber for the Church of Scotland.

By the eve of the election, the chamber was ready. The MSPs' desks were arranged in a European-style semi-circle, facing the Presiding Officer's elevated position, with space for the newly commissioned debating mace just in front. Steel had emerged as the sole candidate to become the first Presiding Officer and everything was ready. The pale wood desks were highlighted by the striking bright blue carpet running down all the aisles and giving the old hall a new feel. By 14 May 1999, the Scottish Parliament, which for so long and for so many had been nothing more than an aspiration, was now a reality. It had its venue, it had its MSPs and, now – just – it had its government.

2

New game, new rules

IF Donald Dewar didn't know quite what he had taken on the
moment he became Scotland's First Minister, he certainly
understood it five months later when, on a bright cool morning
in Dublin, he emerged from a chauffeur-driven limousine onto the
steps of the Taoiseach's official residence.

Dewar was elected formally as the first First Minister of Scotland
on 13 May 1999. There was much to do and little attention had been
paid, either by him or his staff, to a date in the diary for an official
visit to Dublin in late October. The Irish, however, had paid considerable attention to the visit: it was in their interests to do so – a strong,
semi-autonomous Scotland would only help them counter the
economic might of the UK and raise the profile of small western
European states such as Ireland. More importantly, with the Good
Friday Agreement still in the balance, they wanted to use the visit of
29 October to send a vital message to Ulster Unionists that Dublin
could work with a society similar to Northern Ireland – a largely
Protestant country with a sizeable Catholic minority.

Dewar arrived expecting nothing more than the usual sort of
low-key visit he would have enjoyed as Scottish secretary, with
maybe an obligatory photocall but with most of the work done in
convivial closed-door meetings with ministers and officials. He was
not prepared for the five-car motorcade of sleek diplomatic saloons
with flashing blue lights, the half-dozen motorcycle outriders and
armed bodyguards with FBI-style earpieces – in fact just the sort of
reception more often given to visiting heads of state, not leaders of
local administrations.

Irish officials made a half-hearted attempt to play down their
extraordinary welcome as they swept a bemused Scottish First
Minister in from the airport to the Prime Minister's official residence

and then on to a formal audience with Mary McAleese, the Irish President. But it soon became clear that they were using Dewar's visit to send key political and diplomatic signals. Scotland in general and Dewar in particular were both now seen as players – albeit to a limited extent – on the European stage. Dewar had influence in his own right as Scotland's First Minister, status he certainly hadn't had before as one of Tony Blair's Cabinet ministers.

The meetings themselves produced nothing of any significance but the visit was important in other ways. In that moment when a slightly embarrassed First Minister, stood with one hand in his pocket, the other shaking the hand of Bertie Ahern on the steps of the Irish Prime Minister's residence, it was clear that he had arrived.

Dewar had started his official life as Scotland's first First Minister fairly well. He picked a ministerial team which appeared to capture a good blend of youth and experience. There were four Cabinet ministers who were also Westminster MPs: Dewar himself; Jim Wallace, the Liberal Democrat Deputy First Minister and justice minister; Henry McLeish, who was asked to look after enterprise and lifelong learning; and Sam Galbraith, the minister for children and education. They were joined by first-time public representatives Jack McConnell, the former general secretary of the Scottish Labour Party, as finance minister; Susan Deacon as health minister; Wendy Alexander, Dewar's young protégée and former special adviser, as communities minister; Sarah Boyack at transport; and Tom McCabe as minister for parliamentary business. Ross Finnie, the second Liberal Democrat in the Cabinet, was given the rural affairs brief.

But a burst of early positivity, engendered when the new Cabinet team stood on the steps of Bute House, the First Minister's grand official residence in Edinburgh's Charlotte Square, disintegrated very quickly as a mixture of unplanned events and self-created problems soon landed Dewar's team in trouble. Wallace was the first to face up to one harsh reality of life as a minister – that political success depends on how well you cope with events, not by how well you drive through your policies.

Noel Ruddle, a psychopath dubbed the 'Kalashnikov Killer' by the tabloids, was freed from the State Hospital at Carstairs on 2 August 1999 through a legal loophole. A sheriff ruled that Ruddle was not being treated for his condition so could no longer be held, even though he was 'abnormally aggressive'. It then emerged that the loophole had been known about for two years. The pressure mounted on to Wallace to explain why nothing had been done to keep Ruddle in Carstairs and there were demands to change the law immediately. Dewar and Wallace agreed to rush emergency legislation through the Scottish Parliament, which they did, in early September. But what this meant was that the first piece of legislation passed by the Scottish Parliament was not a highly significant bill designed to improve the lives of Scots, it was a quick-fix legal statute to close a loophole which many felt should have been shut months or years before. This episode helped create an impression that Dewar's administration was too reactive, that it was being swayed by events and was not leading as a new government with a clear mandate should do.

Unfortunately for Dewar, that apparent lack of strong leadership was reinforced by the so-called 'Lobbygate' affair, a crisis which gave a clear indication, not just of the extra press scrutiny which politicians would now be under in Scotland, but also of the dangers of creating a new parliament from scratch.

On Sunday 26 September, the *Observer* published the results of an undercover operation which, it claimed, showed that lobbyists were claiming privileged access to Scottish ministers. At the centre of the story were Kevin Reid, the son of the Scottish secretary, John Reid, and Alex Barr, a lobbyist and also someone with Labour connections. Both Reid and Barr worked for Beattie Media, a Scottish public relations company with a big lobbying wing.

In the newspaper sting operation, an *Observer* reporter had posed as 'Anthony James', a businessman who said he was representing American clients eager to pitch for big public sector contracts. The meeting between 'James' and the pair from Beattie Media was filmed by the *Observer* and while Reid stressed that he could not guarantee access to ministers, he made it clear that he believed he had significant influence in the Labour Party and government. 'I know the secretary of state very well because he's my father,' Reid said at one point.

The crunch came when Barr claimed that he had managed to get a diary date arranged for McConnell simply by knowing Christina Marshall, McConnell's diary secretary. 'Christina checked his [McConnell's] diary for me and said: "Consider it done,"' Barr said.

The exposé created a furore, principally because many people – inside and outside politics – had hoped that the new Scottish Parliament would herald a new beginning, that the old ways of sleaze and shady influence, which had characterised the last years of the Tory government, were in the past. The 'Lobbygate' revelations blew a hole right through that aspiration and prompted loud calls for an urgent inquiry. Dewar was caught between the demands from his own party – as well as from others – for a full inquiry on one side and the bruising John Reid on the other, someone who believed that his son had been stitched up and that no inquiry was needed.

It did not help that the *Observer* story broke just before Labour politicians gathered in Bournemouth for their annual party conference. With Reid livid at the story and a shocked and angry Dewar determined to do something about it, it was inevitable that the two would clash, and so they did, standing outside a party meeting on the Sunday night in Bournemouth, shouting at each other in full view of Labour activists, some of whom were quick to tell the press.

Dewar got his inquiry but the affair was damaging and his relationship with Reid never really recovered. The Standards Committee of the Scottish Parliament launched its investigation on 8 October, the rather limited highlight of which was the evidence given by Marshall on 27 October when, under intense pressure, she flatly denied putting a date in McConnell's diary at the request of Beattie Media. The affair petered out when the Standards Committee reported a day later, clearing McConnell of any wrongdoing but expressing concern at the conflicting evidence given by members of Beattie Media.

By the end of 1999, attention was back on tuition fees once again, as Andrew Cubie's commission was ready to report. Having provided the compromise which allowed the Liberal Democrats to join a formal coalition with Labour in the first place, the commission then came up with another perfect fudge when it reported. The Cubie report recommended that up-front tuition fees should be scrapped but it also suggested that students should pay something towards university education after they graduated and were earning enough to do so. This allowed the Scottish Executive to abolish the

£3,000 bill imposed on students when they went to university, but also gave it the chance to impose another fee on graduation. Known as the graduate endowment, it was a £2,000 levy payable when students started earning at least £10,000 a year, with the money ring-fenced for higher education.

It was another convenient compromise. The Liberal Democrats were able to claim that tuition fees had been scrapped – although they changed their approach eight years later when they went into the 2007 election demanding that the graduate endowment be scrapped as it was unfair – while Labour could insist that students would still have to contribute to the costs of their education. Dewar lived with the compromise because it gave him the chance to run a stable administration with a clear majority.

This fitted his more traditional view of government. Indeed he was very much an old-school parliamentarian, rather than a modern politician. One of his aides remarked that once, on going into the First Minister's office, he saw Dewar pointing his computer mouse at his screen, clicking it in a vain attempt to turn the machine on.

Dewar was used to the Westminster system, which had been honed by generations of politicians into one of comfort and tradition. In the Scottish Parliament, some of the methods of working were taken from Westminster but many were fresh. There was much to discover, work out and decide, and there were new demands on the politicians, not least from an intensive press corps which brought in a level of scrutiny far above that experienced in London. It didn't take long for this new, more demanding, environment to make itself felt as MSPs found themselves pilloried, first for apparently giving themselves a pay rise and then for deciding to award themselves medals, all within weeks of taking office.

The first set-piece debate in the new parliament, on 8 June 1999, allowed MSPs to discuss and vote on their allowances package. They decided to allow £46,000 per MSP for staff costs, similar to the situation in Westminster. They weren't giving themselves a pay rise as such but the decision appeared self-serving and small minded nonetheless. To use one of the first real debates of the parliament for housekeeping was practical but hardly sensible given the heavy expectations of the Scottish people for some sort of groundbreaking change.

Then, just as the parliament was recoiling from the allowances row, it emerged that MSPs had all been presented with medals to commemorate its opening. It did not seem to matter that the medals, produced at a cost of £7,000, had been commissioned by the UK government's Scottish Office before any MSPs had even been elected; the message that went out was that they had somehow awarded themselves medals on top of a pay rise and it helped depress their reputation still further.

During these difficult opening months, however, it wasn't all a damage-limitation exercise for Dewar and the Scottish Executive. One notable highlight of 1999 which showed Dewar at his best was the ceremonial royal opening of the Scottish Parliament on 1 July.

The new parliamentarians and their staff had settled in very well to their temporary home at the top of the Royal Mile. The chamber was in the General Assembly Hall while the MSPs, the parliamentary staff and the press were crammed into old council offices about 50 metres down the road, on the corner of George IV Bridge and The Mound. The various venues were temporary but, for an area so steeped in history, this early home of the parliament did carry its own, unique charm.

The MSPs had to leave their offices every time they wanted to go to the chamber and walk the short distance up the steep cobbled steps of the Royal Mile to the Assembly Hall. This allowed them to swap stories and gossip with political opponents and it gave journalists the chance to swoop, demanding responses to questions the politicians would rather not answer. It also gave the public the chance to shout their appreciation of their representatives, or not if they so chose, as the MSPs walked up and down from the chamber. It really felt as if the temporary home of the parliament was actually providing a link to eighteenth-century Edinburgh, when the parliament had last sat: the people's representatives would walk or ride up and down the Royal Mile, exposed to the views – and mostly the invective – of the bystanders.

The whole of the Royal Mile was closed off on 1 July for the grand opening, a ceremony designed to promote both the pageantry of Scotland's royal history and the aspirations of the new institution to represent Scotland's more egalitarian tradition of respect for the common man. This combination was summed up by the procession of the Queen and the Crown of Scotland, followed by a haunting and beautiful unaccompanied rendition of Robert Burns's 'A Man's a Man for A' That' by the Scottish folk singer Sheena Wellington, with the MSPs joining in spontaneously for the chorus.

The entire day was well judged and went off, almost, without problem. One demonstrator broke through the crowd crash barriers and got within a couple of feet of the Queen, who was riding up the Royal Mile in a horse-drawn carriage. But he was quickly brushed aside by a member of the Household Cavalry in full cere- monial dress with sword drawn.

The highlight of the day which will live on as a central part of Dewar's personal political legacy was the First Minister's speech to the new institution. Eight years later, when he was elected First Minister, Alex Salmond quoted from that address, praising it as the finest speech of Dewar's life. A gifted parliamentarian as well as an extremely well-read amateur historian, Dewar managed to craft a speech which conveyed the sense that while the new parliament was both fragile and modern, it was rooted in Scotland's past and that it drew Scots together, whatever their religion, background or political views.

It is worth reprising the whole of that short speech, because it gives voice to the underlying feeling, alive and well in 1999, that the Scottish Parliament meant change and change for the better.

Rising to thank the Queen for her gift of the Scottish Parliament mace, Dewar said:

> Your Majesty, on behalf of the people of Scotland, I thank you for the gift of this mace. It is a symbol of the great democratic traditions from which we draw our inspiration and our strength. At its head are inscribed the opening words of our founding statute: 'There shall be a Scottish Parliament.' Through long years, those words were first a hope, then a belief, then a promise. Now, they are a reality.
>
> This is a moment anchored in our history. Today, we reach back through the long haul to win this parliament, through the struggles of those who brought democracy to Scotland, to that other parliament dissolved in controversy nearly three centuries ago. Today, we look forward to the time when this moment will be seen as a turning point: the day when democracy was renewed

in Scotland, when we revitalised our place in this our United
Kingdom.

This is about more than politics and our laws. This is about who
we are, how we carry ourselves. In the quiet moments today, we
might hear some echoes from the past: the shout of the welder in
the din of the great Clyde shipyards; the speak of the Mearns, with
its soul in the land; the discourse of the enlightenment, when
Edinburgh and Glasgow were a light held to the intellectual life of
Europe; the wild cry of the Great Pipes; and back to the distant cries
of the battles of Bruce and Wallace.

The past is part of us. But today there is a new voice in the land,
the voice of a democratic parliament. A voice to shape Scotland, a
voice for the future.

Walter Scott wrote that only a man with a soul so dead could have
no sense, no feel of his native land. For me, for any Scot, today is a
proud moment: a new stage on a journey begun long ago and which
has no end. This is a proud day for all of us. A Scottish parliament. Not
an end: a means to greater ends. And those too are part of our mace.
Woven into its symbolic thistles are these four words: 'Wisdom,
Justice, Compassion, Integrity'.

Burns would have understood that. We have just heard –
beautifully sung – one of his most enduring works. At the heart of
that song is a very Scottish conviction: that honesty and simple
dignity are priceless virtues, not imparted by rank or birth or privilege
but part of the soul. Burns believed that sense and worth ultimately
prevail. He believed that was the core of politics, that without it,
ours would be an impoverished profession.

Wisdom, justice, compassion, integrity. Timeless values, honourable
aspirations for this new forum of democracy, born on the cusp of a
new century.

We are fallible. We will make mistakes, but we will never lose
sight of what brought us here, the striving to do right by the people
of Scotland, to respect their priorities, to better their lot and to
contribute to the commonweal.

I look forward to the days when this chamber will sound with
debate, argument and passion: when men and women from all over
Scotland will meet to work together for a future built from the first
principles of social justice. But today, we pause and reflect. It is a rare

privilege in an old nation to open a new parliament. Today is a
celebration of the principles, the traditions, the democratic imperatives
which have brought us to this point and will sustain us into the
future.

Your Majesty, we are all proud that you are here to handsel [to
give an inaugural good luck gift to] this parliament, and here with
us we dedicate ourselves to the work ahead. Your Majesty, our
thanks.

That day, and that speech, represented the high point for Dewar as
First Minister, and quite possibly for his whole political career.

He was a politician who had campaigned for a Scottish parliament
and who had sat on the opposition benches in the Commons
through the eighteen years of Conservative rule, often without the
hope of a Labour victory, let alone securing home rule for Scotland.
He became the Scottish secretary who delivered the Scottish Parliament, both through the successful referendum in 1997 and by driving
the Scotland Bill through Westminster: the parliament was very
much his creation. But the whole process only really culminated in
that speech in the chamber on 1 July 1999. It showed that Dewar had
managed to pause and consider and crystallise his thoughts into one
powerful address which put all the troubles of his government
behind him, at least for the day.

Dewar and the rest of the Scottish Executive had the summer
recess – specifically designed to be child friendly and coincide with
school holidays – to recover before the storms of politics knocked
them sideways once again. It didn't take long for that to happen and
this time it was Dewar's aides who were under fire. A catalogue of
mistakes by his advisers and spin doctors – which cost the jobs of two
close aides – left Dewar facing accusations that he was a flawed judge
of character, something he found hard to dispel.

John Rafferty had been Labour's Scottish campaigns director
before being appointed as Dewar's chief of staff when he became
First Minister. Rafferty was someone who had spent most of his
political life in the shadows, working behind the scenes to further
the Labour cause. He was very adept at the sort of devious, internal
warfare that the Scottish Labour Party was renowned for and was
said to have been instrumental in the sacking of Alex Rowley, the

Scottish Labour general secretary, in May 1999. The fact that Rowley was sacked despite being a close ally of Gordon Brown's showed the sort of influence that Rafferty – who was seen as a London appointee – could wield.

Rafferty managed to antagonise some of Dewar's parliamentary colleagues when he started sitting in on Cabinet meetings, but his hold on the First Minister was such that he only grew in influence. However, when he became Dewar's chief of staff, he took on a more public role, at least with the media, briefing journalists in what were supposed to be subtle, off-the-record guides for the press, just to help his new boss. It was when he went too far in this new, slightly greyer role that things went badly wrong.

In December 1999, the health minister, Susan Deacon, decided to take on the Catholic Church over abortion, backing the British Medical Association, which had called for more contraception to stop teenage pregnancies. The Catholic Church reacted to condemn Deacon and a routine sort of political spat ensued: except this one quickly became rather different and more sinister than anything that had gone before.

Deacon received two abusive phone calls at her home and while deplorable, these were not completely unheard of for politicians taking the sort of strong line Deacon took on contraception. But, by the time news of the phone calls reached the press, through one of Rafferty's off-the-record briefings, they had become 'death threats', while Deacon's daughter was said to have been given police protection at school.

It is very rare that newspapers 'out' a government source, particularly one who is well placed and has given briefings clearly off the record. But it soon became clear that there had been no 'death threats' and that Rafferty had deliberately exaggerated the threats made to Deacon to gain sympathy and make the pro-life lobby look bad, a very serious charge which led to calls for his sacking.

At the same time, Rafferty was involved in a bitter turf war with David Whitton, Dewar's press spokesman, whose job it was to brief the press, on and off the record. Dewar was faced with a choice and on 9 December 1999, after a week of holding onto him and trying to get him and Whitton to work together, Dewar fired Rafferty.

The Rafferty affair was damaging to Dewar because it appeared to show he was not a great judge of people, it eroded trust in the Scottish Executive because it gave the impression that special advisers were prepared to twist the truth to suit their case, and it dented Dewar's leadership because he dithered so long before firing Rafferty. Worse was to follow, however, when a second special adviser, Philip Chalmers, resigned on 25 January 2000. Twice Chalmers had been found over the drink-drive limit by police in Glasgow's red light district, once with a prostitute and heroin addict in his car. Chalmers's departure was relatively swift but it merely added to the sense of crisis at the heart of the Dewar administration, an impression Dewar tried to knock back by demanding better performances all round from his team.

Dewar's determination to make real political progress was not helped by a Westminster by-election at Hamilton South, caused by the resignation of George Robertson, the former defence secretary, who was promoted to take over as secretary general of NATO. Labour tried to outflank the SNP by calling the by-election – in a safe Labour seat – for 23 September, the second day of the SNP's annual conference in Inverness. Labour leaders hoped to win the by-election quite comfortably, undermining SNP attempts to set the political agenda that week.

But it didn't quite work out like that. Hamilton South embodied everything about Labour's traditional hegemony in the west of Scotland. It was a working-class, semi-urban seat like many in the same area and was the fifth-safest Labour constituency in the country. Robertson had won in 1997 with a majority of almost 16,000 over the SNP and, with the solid – if rather dour – local union official Bill Tynan as the candidate, Labour had little reason to worry.

But, as the campaign progressed, so it became clear that the Nationalists were eating into the Labour vote. When the SNP conference started on Wednesday 22 September, Labour still appeared in the lead but the race was heading for a much closer finish than anybody in the Labour camp had anticipated. As the first ballot boxes started to pile up after 10 p.m. on the Thursday, it became clear that the result would be very, very close. The votes were counted quickly and, just after midnight, a recount was called by the SNP because it was too close for certainty.

That in itself was an astonishing victory for the Nationalists. They had slashed Labour's 16,000 majority to almost nothing. When the final result was announced, it emerged that Tynan had scraped home by just 556 votes over the SNP's Annabelle Ewing while the Liberal Democrats were humiliated, dropping down to sixth place with only 634 votes, behind a candidate campaigning for Hamilton Academicals Football Club.

Labour's by-election woes continued with the resignation of Ian Welsh, the Labour MSP for Ayr, who had been in his job for only seven months when he quit on 20 December 1999. Welsh was having a tough time travelling to and from his constituency, where he had a disabled son, but he also said he found it difficult to adjust to a 'backbench role' in the parliament – suggesting he was disappointed at not being in the Executive.

Labour leaders had believed they could handle the by-election in Hamilton South, but that had come close to being a disaster. Ayr was anything but safe. Welsh had won the seat over Phil Gallie, the Conservative candidate, by just twenty-five votes in the May 1999 election.

Ayr became the first constituency to witness a by-election for the Scottish Parliament on 16 March 2000. The Conservatives won, giving them their first constituency success for the parliament. Their candidate, John Scott, achieved a comfortable 3,000 majority over the SNP's Jim Mather, with Labour's Rita Miller trailing in third.

However, the contest was overshadowed by the one big symbolic policy initiative which Dewar had driven forward, the scrapping of Section 28. This rather arcane section of local government legislation prevented teachers from 'promoting' homosexuality in schools. Dewar saw it as important to set a new, liberal, tone in Scotland so gave Wendy Alexander, his young special adviser turned minister, the job of scrapping the section – which had become a key issue of government attitude for the gay community.

The controversy started in a rather muted way. Alexander gave a speech to an international gay rights conference in Glasgow on 22 October 1999 in which she announced that the Scottish Executive was 'deeply uncomfortable' with Section 28. A week later she went further, using a speech at Glasgow University to unveil plans to scrap the part of the Local Government Act which had caused such anger among gay people. At this stage, Alexander had riled small sections of the religious right in Scotland, but it had gone no further than that.

Symbolically, though, the move was important, both for Alexander and for Dewar. They could be seen to be acting independently of Westminster and they could repeal Section 28 before the rest of the UK. Both saw it as a positive step, the transformation of long-held policy on inclusion into reality, but neither was prepared for the backlash the move created.

The intervention of Cardinal Thomas Winning, the powerful and vocal senior Catholic in Scotland, pushed the issue up the political agenda when he sought assurances from Dewar that the scrapping of Section 28 would not mean that homosexuality was going to be actively promoted in Scotland's schools. The First Minister gave the cardinal the assurances he wanted but that was not enough for Scotland's best-selling newspapers, the *Daily Record*, the *Sun* and the *Daily Mail*. For the first time, all three joined forces, uniting in an extraordinary and unprecedented eight-month campaign against the scrapping of Section 28.

Day after day the newspapers kept up the pressure on the Scottish Executive, printing warning after warning from anyone on the religious right in an attempt to force the First Minister to back down. It was a formidable battle but at least this was one that Dewar had initiated and it was being fought over policy, rather than providing another example of Dewar being battered by events outside his control, which had been the case up until then. For the first few weeks after Alexander's initial announcement, she and Dewar still felt able to ride out the media's opposition; that is, until Brian Souter, the Stagecoach millionaire, got involved, in January 2000.

The bus entrepreneur insisted he was intervening for democratic, not homophobic, reasons, claiming that parents should be given the right to have their views heard on the issue. He pledged an astonishing £500,000 to the campaign to halt the repeal of Section 28.

By this time, Dewar's Cabinet was starting to split on the issue, with the 'three Mcs', Henry McLeish, Tom McCabe and Jack McConnell, urging some sort of compromise to head off what was now becoming an all-consuming political row. Two days after Souter's intervention, Dewar offered a partial climb-down, agreeing to revise the guidelines for teachers on the teaching of homosexuality after the repeal of Section 28. This did little to appease the Keep the Clause campaign, the coalition of the religious right and members of the Scottish School Boards Association who believed that they would be able to win the battle completely, if they kept going.

By the end of January 2000, Dewar's Executive was on the defensive and a move which had appeared relatively uncontroversial and overwhelmingly positive back in October was now threatening to derail the administration. The row also put distance between the parliament and the public, or at least a vocal minority of the public, as Holyrood passed an initial vote to repeal Section 28, ignoring the increasingly demanding voices outside.

A month later, the Cabinet had come round to the idea of a more substantial compromise. After an angry two-hour Cabinet meeting on 22 February, Alexander and Sam Galbraith agreed that Section 28 should be scrapped only if it was then replaced with another clause, but something more acceptable to all. Only Susan Deacon and Ross Finnie, the rural affairs minister, held out against the compromise. However, by March, the plans were still on their way through the parliament, having changed little – despite the massive campaign against them. It was at this point that Souter played his trump card, offering to bankroll a nationwide referendum on the issue.

The Stagecoach co-founder put up £1 million to finance the plebiscite – the first privately funded referendum in Scottish history – to drive the Scottish Executive off course. For a country which had voted in a referendum on home rule just three years before and in which one major party was pushing for a referendum on independence, it seemed odd to have a national poll on something which seemed so ostensibly minor and intricate as a clause in a piece of local government legislation.

The results of the referendum were announced at the end of May. A total of 1.3 million ballot papers were returned, equivalent to more than 30 per cent of the electorate. Of these, 87 per cent voted to keep the clause and 13 per cent voted to scrap it.

Souter was jubilant. More than a million Scots had backed his campaign to Keep the Clause but it didn't matter. Dewar and Alexander were resolute. They were not going to be pushed around by an individual with money who was able to organise his own nationwide poll. They felt they had been elected on a mandate which included the repeal of Section 28 and they would drive it through. Dewar did offer more concessions to the Keep the Clause campaign, though. After the intervention of McCabe, he agreed to the adoption of statutory guidance for schools, compelling them to teach the importance of marriage and stable family relationships. Although this was far further than he or Alexander, bruised and battered, expected to go when they first unveiled their plans eight months previously, it allowed them to repeal Section 28 – or Section 2a, as it was properly known in Scotland – and move on.

On 22 June 2000 MSPs voted finally to repeal Section 28 and establish the new guidelines, ending the most divisive and stormy battle in Scotland's recent political history.

3

Our friends in the south

FOR someone born and schooled in Edinburgh, Tony Blair remained oddly ambivalent about Scotland throughout his political career. Indeed, he used to joke in private that his writ – like that of the Roman emperors – ended at Hadrian's Wall. It was clear that he preferred England to Scotland, London to Edinburgh and, most definitely, the UK Labour Party to its Scottish counterpart. He didn't even like going to Balmoral for his annual stay with the Queen very much.

Part of Blair's reticence came from the battle he had with the distinctly 'old Labour' Scottish party at its conference in Inverness in March 1995 over the scrapping of Clause IV of the Labour constitution. This was a key plank in Blair's modernisation of the Labour Party, dumping what he believed was the archaic pledge to retain 'common ownership of the means of production'. He succeeded in getting his plans through the conference but only thanks to Jack McConnell, then the general secretary of the Scottish Labour Party, who used all his political skills to cajole, threaten and force the party to back the New Labour line.

Above everything else, however, was Blair's abhorrence of the Scottish press corps, leading him to describe them as 'unreconstructed wankers' in one outburst.

Blair's views on the Scottish press crystallised during a campaign visit to Scotland at the start of the 1997 election campaign. Flying to Edinburgh on his chartered campaign jet on 3 April, Blair gave an interview to the *Scotsman* about his party's plans for devolution. He stressed, several times, that sovereignty would remain at Westminster – which had been the subject of debate in Scotland before he arrived.

But he then went on to explain his approach to tax-varying

powers for the Scottish Parliament. He said: 'The powers are like those of any local authority. Powers that are constitutionally there can be used, but the Scottish Labour Party has no plans to raise income tax and, once given, it's like any parish council, it's got the right to exercise it.' By the time Blair's flight touched down in Scotland, a political storm had already started to gather around his remarks. Then, the following morning, when his comments appeared in the *Scotsman*, the storm broke over his head. Blair found himself accused of denigrating devolution and of devaluing the Scottish Parliament by comparing it to a parish council.

Blair's remarks should be seen in full and his reference to a parish council, although unfortunate, was designed to make the point about Labour's reluctance to use the tax-varying powers. But that did not matter. Blair found himself unable to answer any question on anything else. Repeatedly, first on BBC Radio Scotland's *Good Morning Scotland* programme and then at a press conference in Labour's Glasgow media centre, he tried to shift the questions on to other ground, but without success. The BBC political correspondent Carole Walker reported breathlessly to *The World at One* that it was the toughest questioning Blair had faced on the whole of the campaign trail.

Michael Forsyth, the then Scottish secretary at a time when the Conservative government was vehemently opposed to devolution, seized on the parish council remark to warn that no parish council had the power to add £6 a week to the tax bill of the average family, and John Major, the Prime Minister, rewrote part of a speech for a London audience that night to attack Blair over his comments. Blair was battered and bruised by the whole experience and felt, with a little justification, that he had been pilloried for a remark taken out of context by a press pack determined to tear him to shreds.

Over the next couple of years, Blair came to Scotland on a regular, if infrequent, basis, mainly for fund-raising dinners or for campaigning events and to address the Scottish Labour Party conference, some- thing which always appeared a bit of a trial for the then Prime Minister. He did try to hold informal press conferences with senior members of the Scottish press pack but, after the second of these, in 1999, when he again faced some hard and persistent questioning, the press was not invited back until just before Blair stood down, in early

2007. It was almost as if he had tried but then decided that the
Scottish press was not worth the effort.

Gordon Brown's relationship with Scotland and the Scottish
Labour Party was the opposite. Scotland provided him with his
constituency, his home, his political allies and, most importantly, his
power base. He understood the way it worked, who was important
and how to influence it: all the things, in fact, that Blair had no idea
about.

Brown had always been a Scot at heart. He lived in Glasgow until
he was three, before the family moved to Kirkcaldy, where his father
John was a Church of Scotland minister. The ties from those early
days were so strong that many were still evident when he became
Prime Minister, in 2007. For example, the Labour adviser Murray
Elder, later a peer, met Brown when they were toddlers at a nursery
in Glasgow and the two stayed friends and political allies throughout
their careers. From nursery onwards, Brown's education was local,
Scottish and traditional – Kirkcaldy West Primary School, through
Kirkcaldy High School and on to Edinburgh University.

Brown's politics were shaped through his education and through
the views of his father. It was a typically Presbyterian, socialist and
egalitarian background – quite different from the privileged route of
Fettes College and Oxford that Blair took to get to the same desti-
nation.

Brown started delivering leaflets for the Labour Party at the age
of twelve and wrote his PhD thesis on the Labour socialist movement
in Scotland, so the Scottish Labour Party was engrained within him.
He stood for an unwinnable Edinburgh seat in 1979, when Margaret
Thatcher came to power, but succeeded in Dunfermline East in 1983
– less than 15 miles from his childhood home in Kirkcaldy.

When Labour came to power in 1997, with a pledge to create a
Scottish parliament, Blair had to decide who was best to drive
through what would be an extremely complicated piece of legislation.
George Robertson had been shadow Scottish secretary in the run-
up to the election, with mixed results. He had got himself in an
extraordinary mix-up over the issue of whether there would be one
question in a referendum, two referenda or two questions in one
referendum. This had tarnished Robertson's political reputation and
Blair needed someone who would focus on the parliamentary

minutiae, a parliamentarian and also a passionate home-ruler. Donald Dewar was the ideal choice for this role and he became Labour's Scottish secretary in 1997.

Dewar did not realise it when he took the job, but he was to become the focus for all UK–Scottish tensions over devolution for the next three years.

The Scottish Parliament became an early priority for the new Labour government and it quickly became a test of Dewar's authority, his beliefs in home rule and the power of various senior ministers in the UK Cabinet. At the heart of this process was the Devolution to Scotland, Wales and the Regions Committee (DSWR). The DSWR was a powerful Cabinet sub-committee headed by Lord Irvine of Lairg, the Lord Chancellor.

Dewar and Irvine had history, to say the least. Dewar's wife, Alison, had left him for Irvine years before and although relations between the two men remained professional, they were never more than cordial. Generally, Dewar was often great company – over dinner, say – but he could also be moody and grumpy. On one occasion, the press were invited to an evening of drinks and canapés at Labour headquarters in Glasgow. For some time, Dewar refused to join the crowd mingling in the main room and instead picked incessantly at the food laid out in an anteroom until he had calmed down enough to join the guests next door.

Dewar had to produce a relatively simple bill paving the way for a devolution referendum first, before going to work on the white paper to create the Scottish Parliament – which was dissected line by line by the DSWR. The lawyerly and rather pompous Irvine encouraged detailed debate on almost every aspect of the white paper through the summer and autumn of 1997.

Dewar's core proposal was brave and groundbreaking. Instead of the plan, established for the failed devolution scheme in 1979, for certain, named, powers to be devolved to the new Scottish Parliament and everything else to be reserved to Westminster, Dewar wanted the opposite. He wanted certain, named, powers to be reserved to Westminster and everything else to be devolved. The change in emphasis was subtle but extremely important because Dewar's plan gave much more to the Scottish Parliament than had ever been envisaged before. Some senior ministers, led by Jack Straw, then the

Home Secretary, tried everything they could to reduce the scope of Dewar's proposals.

The DSWR met over eleven weeks and considered thirty-nine policy papers in the white paper. Dewar had to fight the entire way. The big battles were fought out over tax (Dewar argued that the Scottish Parliament should have control over more than just a variation of 3p on income tax) and proportional representation, which had been promised to the Liberal Democrats in the Scottish Constitutional Convention but was still treated suspiciously by some UK ministers. But there were other, much smaller, battles which were fought just as keenly. One of these was over abortion, which Dewar wanted devolved, but he was overruled by the Prime Minister, who did not want to see cross-border trade in this practice.

Henry McLeish was the Scottish Office minister responsible for taking the Scotland Bill through the Commons. Writing just after Dewar's death, he remembered the trials of the DSWR. It became clear very quickly that not everyone on the Labour benches was in favour of devolution for Scotland: 'In a secret ballot in a dark room, a lot of them would not have supported devolution and the Scottish Parliament.' he said.

The DSWR was the key, particularly as it contained such Cabinet heavyweights as David Blunkett, the education secretary, John Prescott, the Deputy Prime Minister, Straw and Irvine, as well as two more junior Scots in Alistair Darling, then chief secretary to the Treasury and Helen Liddell, the economic secretary to the Treasury. McLeish said:

> Donald Dewar was joined in battle sometimes twice a week, fighting Scotland's corner with the other Cabinet ministers. He would often come back dispirited and discouraged after these long and tiring sessions, saying in his usual unassuming fashion that it had been tough and he felt he had not got what he wanted or made the points effectively. Civil servants would tell us privately that Donald had argued brilliantly and wiped the floor with those who wanted to weaken the devolution settlement. He made sure that nearly everything in our initial submission was either retained or improved.
>
> Derry Irvine was forensic in his approach. After sessions with him, Donald could come back despondent, limp and wrung out like

a wet rag. The then Lord Chancellor is an exceptional personality and, having been on sub-committees chaired by him, it is not an experience for the faint hearted. Their personal history is well known but there was never any sign of animosity between the two men.

McLeish pointed out that the stakes on both sides were extremely high, with Irvine the custodian of the UK constitution and Dewar trying to secure a new future for Scotland. 'Our strength was that we had powerful allies in the Cabinet, the Prime Minister and the Chancellor,' he said.[*]

While Brown, then the Chancellor of the Exchequer, was a strong supporter of the devolution settlement, McLeish's warm enthusiasm for the way the Prime Minister supported Dewar may be a little charitable. There is evidence from other sources that Blair was uneasy about parts of the devolution project and he used Irvine to push this scepticism to the limit during the DSWR meetings.

Irvine himself said, in a book of biographical essays about Dewar: 'DSWR was determined that the Scots could not proceed as if their lucky number had come up and what they wanted they could demand.' And he added: 'For Donald, DSWR was onerous in the extreme. There was constant sniping – entirely legitimate – from those whose enthusiasm for the Scottish project was somewhat behind Donald's.'[†]

When the white paper was eventually published, on 24 July, Dewar had most of what he wanted. Several core functions were reserved: foreign affairs, defence, macro-economics, benefits and immigration, but everything else was devolved: health, education, housing, transport and rural affairs. There were odd exceptions. Health was devolved but abortion stayed with Westminster; crime was devolved but firearms legislation stayed with the UK government. For the most part, though, Dewar had succeeded in securing the sort of settlement he wanted. There was a sense, however, that the devolution agreement had been wrenched out of the Westminster

---

[*] Henry McLeish, 'Delivering devolution: Dewar's finest hour', *Daily Record*, 24 February 2004.

[†] Lord Irvine of Lairg, 'A Skilful Advocate', in Wendy Alexander (ed.), *Donald Dewar: Scotland's First First Minister* (Edinburgh: Mainstream, 2005).

government, a feeling which was to cloud relations between the two administrations for years to come.

The toll on Dewar had been considerable. His close friend, the broadcaster Fiona Ross, writing an essay on the former Scottish secretary some years later, recalled just how much the battles at Westminster had taken out of him:

> Donald felt he was being bullied by everyone, but instead of confronting these people, he cowered in a corner. The personal attacks . . . caused him to slide into what I can only describe as a serious depression. He was paralysed by indecision, totally convinced that everyone was against him – government colleagues at Westminster, activists in Scotland, the media and even his closest friends. In my house, he was talking of resigning...
>
> Donald was exhausted and said on several occasions, 'I can't go on like this. This constant grind. On an endless treadmill.' The discussion of resignation was serious. He considered not standing for the Scottish Parliament and remaining at Westminster, where he would doubtless have been given another Cabinet position. However, the option he favoured was to resign from the Cabinet and simply retire from politics at the next election. 'If I gave up this job,' he said, 'I would miss it, but not much.'*

Dewar knew the DSWR was crucial because of its role in forming what was effectively a new constitution for Scotland. But he was also aware that it exemplified the divisions in the new Labour government over this central part of Labour Party policy.

As the devolved settlement matured, so Scottish ministers returned again and again to the original agreement, arguing for changes – big and small – to help the Scottish Parliament do its job better. For years, many politicians, including senior Labour figures, quoted Dewar as saying that devolution was 'a process, not an event' but there is no evidence that he actually said it. The phrase became so widely attributed to Dewar that it was assumed he had said it, and although Dewar acknowledged that the devolution settlement he crafted had to be flexible, there is no record of him going quite that

---

* Fiona Ross, 'As a Friend', in Alexander, *Donald Dewar*.

far. He did say, in one of his last public set-piece speeches before his death in 2000, that devolution was 'stable', before adding that it was 'stable but not rigid'. That was how Dewar viewed it. He had crafted a settlement which he believed gave both Scotland and the rest of Britain stability, but which should not be regarded as unchangeable. 'If, through experience and consent, we want to adjust the settlement, the machinery is in place,' he said.

What Dewar's settlement did do, however, was change fundamentally the relationship between Scotland and Westminster. It took a long time for politicians, and voters, on both sides of the border, to realise that the ground had shifted. It affected everything from the influence of the Prime Minister over Scottish domestic policy to the way many English people viewed the Scots and Scotland. One of the first to feel the change was Gordon Brown. He had been the senior figure in Scottish Labour politics for such a long time that there was an immediate tension when Dewar was elected as First Minister.

When he was drawing up his devolution plans, Dewar had a blueprint to work from: the work done by the Scottish Constitutional Convention, which had come up with a series of detailed proposals setting out how the parliament would work. It was with this background and with a desire for a break from the Westminster traditions driving Labour forward, that Dewar designed a parliament deliberately not in Westminster's image.

Sir Russell Hillhouse, then the permanent secretary at the Scottish Office, explained to the Holyrood inquiry in 2003 how Dewar saw it as his duty to provide not just an institution but a new building for it too:

> I said: 'Wouldn't it be better to go for a temporary solution and let the parliament decide?'
>
> He [Dewar] said: 'That, of course, is correct in principle, but my fear is that unless we get ahead and do something now the parliament will find it extremely difficult to get round to it. I think it's my duty to endow them with a really good building which will fit the purpose and enable them to work effectively.'

The debating chamber would be more European than British,

with representatives sitting in a semi-circle, rather than challenging each other on opposite sides of the despatch box. The sitting hours, too, were set up to be more family friendly. Out went the archaic rules, still then operating at Westminster, which meant that Parliament only really started sitting after lunch, allowing MPs to work in the morning, in the law courts and elsewhere, and represent their constituents in the afternoons. The relationship with the press was also changed. Westminster's secretive lobby system was ditched, with briefings held on the record wherever possible.

But the two most important changes were the adoption of a proportional electoral system, the additional member or list system, and Labour's decision to deliberately select as many women as men for winnable seats.

The adoption of PR was a bit of a fudge. The Liberal Democrats had been pushing for the single transferable vote system and Dewar did not have to change anything from the Westminster first-past-the-post system if he didn't want to. But he decided that the new spirit of consensual politics, which Scotland seemed to want to embrace, meant that the old ways of Westminster had to be dropped. The list system still allowed for the election of one MSP from each of Scotland's seventy-three constituencies, to appease Labour traditionalists, but another fifty-six were to be elected, seven from each of the eight regions, by a proportional system.

Part of the reason for the change was to construct a system which made it virtually impossible for any one party to gain an overall majority. This was done more to scupper the SNP's attempts to drive forward an independence agenda than to help the smaller parties. But there was also a recognition that the Westminster way of doing things was outdated and a new model of democracy was needed for a new parliament.

Labour's decision to twin constituencies together, selecting one woman and one man for every two seats, proved hugely controversial within the party but it did succeed in guaranteeing the election of a large number of women to the first parliament. Of Labour's fifty-seven MSPs, twenty-nine (51 per cent) were women. In the parliament as a whole, 37 per cent of MSPs were women, the third most balanced ratio in the world.

What all this meant was that the Scottish Parliament was set up almost as a direct counter to Westminster, challenging the traditional ways of running politics from the start. This helped create an atmosphere of independence as far as the institution was concerned, pushing the two bodies apart just as the Scottish Parliament was starting out. To help formalise the new relationship, concordats were drawn up between the UK government and the devolved administrations in Edinburgh, Cardiff and Belfast. The presumption was that there would be disputes and some sort of procedure would be needed to find a way through.

Much to the SNP's dismay but perhaps understandably, a powerful new ministerial committee, the Joint Ministerial Council, headed by the Prime Minister, was given the ultimate role of sorting out any disputes and four, more minor, joint ministerial committees (JMCs) were created below it. The JMCs were due to meet regularly, involving ministers from the devolved administrations and the UK government. But with Labour in charge in London, Edinburgh and Cardiff and the administration in Northern Ireland seemingly not even sure of its stature, let alone its make-up, for much of the period after 1999, the JMCs fell into abeyance.

Labour politicians in each of the capitals found it easy to talk to each other through normal, informal channels. If a Scottish First Minister – Dewar, or Henry McLeish, or Jack McConnell – or even a Welsh First Minister such as Rhodri Morgan wanted to sort out a problem with Westminster, he would just pick up the phone to the relevant minister in Whitehall, who, more often than not, was an old friend. With Dewar, McLeish and Morgan all with long Westminster experience, this proved an easy route to take, if not actually constitutionally the right one.

The JMCs did meet occasionally but it wasn't long before nobody really bothered with them. It was only when Alex Salmond became First Minister in 2007 that he not only demanded the resumption of the JMCs but enlisted the support of Ian Paisley, the First Minister of Northern Ireland, and the Nationalists in Wales, who were in a coalition government with Labour in Cardiff by that time, to push for their reintroduction.

As the Scottish Parliament settled into its role and as the Scottish Executive started to experiment with policies, so it became apparent to politicians in Westminster that the extreme control which New

Labour had exercised over ministers and MPs could simply not be extended beyond Hadrian's Wall. The decision to abolish tuition fees was the first real break in policy terms and it reverberated through Whitehall, not just because Scotland would now be following a completely different path on a key policy area to London, but because of the effect the Scottish decision would have on English students in Scotland and Scottish students in the rest of the United Kingdom.

Suddenly, the old assumptions about the primacy of Westminster in policy terms throughout the UK were blown away. It took something concrete like tuition fees to make many London politicians wake up to the realities of devolution. They had passed the Scotland Act, watched as Dewar had been elected as First Minister and noted, with a passing electoral interest, the inclusion of the Liberal Democrats in government. But it was not until they saw a clear policy divergence on tuition fees that many of them actually realised what it all meant. What made it doubly difficult for Labour MPs in London was that they were dealing with a Labour-led administration in Edinburgh so the scope for criticism was limited.

As devolution started to operate in practice and the Scottish Parliament bedded in, so it diverged from the UK parliament on policy terms, the two institutions gradually growing apart. The process was subtle, hardly noticeable on a year-to-year basis, but clear over time, nonetheless. At the same time, the relationships between the leaders in Westminster and Edinburgh cooled. Scotland's first two First Ministers, Dewar and McLeish, were Westminster MPs with existing relationships with Tony Blair and Gordon Brown. But, two years into the devolution project, they were both gone and with them went their more deferential approach to Westminster.

This was the context for the first ten years of the Scottish Parliament's existence: dominant Labour figures in a powerful government in Westminster and a nascent Scottish parliament determined to find its own way. The relationship between the controlling New Labour government and its infant junior in Edinburgh was always going to be unusual. What no-one really realised in 1999, however – not even Blair or Brown – was quite how different that new institution, and its administrations, were going to be.

4

Two First Ministers and a funeral

JUST after midday on a bright cold day in October 2000, Donald Dewar tripped on the pavement outside his official Edinburgh residence and fell to the ground. He quickly picked himself up and got into his ministerial car, assuring his aides that he had simply grazed his wrist as he landed on the stone steps. Insisting he was fine, he went straightaway to a working lunch at St Andrew's House, the Scottish Executive building at the other end of Princes Street. Seven hours later, Dewar was in the intensive care unit of Edinburgh's Western General Hospital and within twenty-four hours of his fall, he was dead.

Scotland's first First Minister had been in office for just seventeen months. Even though he was sixty-three and had been expected to stand down in favour of someone younger before the next election, his death represented a major blow for both his party and the parliament.

Dewar's health had been an issue before. In April that year, doctors at Glasgow's Stobhill Hospital had detected a 'minor irregularity' in his heart during a routine check. There was no real concern at that stage; indeed, the First Minister was allowed to travel to Japan on an official visit and to address the Scottish Trades Union Congress before further tests were carried out. These later tests uncovered a leaking aortic valve and Dewar was admitted for surgery in early May 2000 at Glasgow Royal Infirmary. The surgery was a success although the First Minister was put on warfarin, a drug which thins the blood but makes blood vessel bursts more likely. It was such a burst following his pavement fall five months later that put Dewar into the coma from which he never recovered.

Dewar's heart operation and his subsequent three-month convalescence through the summer had given his lieutenants in the Scottish Labour Party the chance to jockey for position behind his back. Jim Wallace, the Liberal Democrat Deputy First Minister, stepped in for Dewar in an official capacity, chairing Cabinet and answering for the Executive in First Minister's Questions, but Henry McLeish, the enterprise minister, wielded the power as far as the Scottish Labour Party was concerned.

McLeish was the senior Labour minister; he had been a Scottish Office minister before devolution and it was natural for him to be given the chance, by Dewar, of covering for the First Minister in his absence. But Dewar's precautions, despite his clear instructions that McLeish was to take over his Labour Party role if he was incapacitated, did not provide the calm sort of leadership that he had hoped for. The period of the First Minister's absence, over the summer of 2000, was marked by increasingly rancorous back-biting and manoeuvring by Labour Cabinet ministers.

It culminated when Jack McConnell, the finance minister, published what he thought would be a fairly uncontroversial move to reallocate unspent money around Executive departments at the end of the financial year. With the parliament still in its temporary home of the General Assembly Hall, press briefings were held in a small meeting room, upstairs from the chamber. On 28 June 2000, shortly before the parliament broke for its summer recess, McConnell held a briefing in that tight little room, with the press sitting round the same table just a few feet away. He explained what he thought was a good news story, that £435 million had not been spent in the Executive's budget for the year and this would now be given to departments in particular need.

McConnell was convinced that the story was a positive one because, before devolution, that money would have gone back to the Treasury. But the journalists present soon realised that the £435 million underspend included £135 million from the crucial and sensitive health budget, only £101 million of which was going back to health, with the rest going to other budgets including forestry and historic houses. Within minutes McConnell was having to answer questions such as: 'So this money is being taken from the NHS and will be spent on tree planting and old houses. Is that the Executive's priority?' A good story was suddenly a bad story and Susan Deacon, the health minister, came under fire from the press too for allowing McConnell to take the money from health. This put Deacon and

McConnell on a collision course, an internal battle which was as much about a fight for seniority while Dewar was away as it was about money.

With McConnell and Deacon grappling for power and increasing back-biting in Labour ranks at the leadership of McLeish and Wallace, Dewar came back to his desk in mid-August, earlier than expected and almost certainly to try and sort out the internal problems which had been mounting in his absence. There is no evidence that the timing of Dewar's return contributed to his death but it is clear that the First Minister had little respite from the pressures of office and was back and working his traditionally demanding hours just three months after his operation.

Dewar's recovery was not helped by the death of Enric Miralles, the lead architect for the Holyrood building. The controversial Spanish architect had been Dewar's choice for a building which, even by mid-2000, was heading for serious financial and scheduling problems. A key parliamentary vote in April of that year to press ahead with the project, despite its rising costs, was overshadowed by the news that Miralles was seriously ill in the United States.

At that stage, no-one outside a small number of people closely connected with the project knew how ill he was. So his death on 3 July 2000 at his home in Barcelona, following unsuccessful surgery on a brain tumour, came as a shock to most in the parliament. Bewilderment turned to frustration when it emerged that the extent of Miralles's illness had been known, but not publicised, by the Holyrood project team. Dewar was already under intense pressure over a project which he had shepherded through, and which he was largely responsible for, pressure which only grew with the death of the lead architect.

Dewar was also having to deal with a new opposition leader following the decision of Alex Salmond to leave Holyrood for Westminster. On 17 July, Salmond surprised all but his closest SNP allies when he called a snap press conference in Aberdeen to announce he was standing down as SNP leader after ten years in the job. He said he would concentrate on Westminster, and would be quitting as an MSP at the next Scottish election.

Salmond had sent every SNP MSP a letter that morning, explaining that he was standing down, and his press conference was conducted with the sort of theatrical timing that had become the SNP leader's hallmark. 'This will knock Gordon Brown's spending review off the front pages,' was his opening line at the press conference.

Salmond dismissed suggestions that he was leaving because of the SNP's financial problems, caused by the 1999 election – despite his sacking earlier in the year of the party treasurer, Ian Blackford – instead arguing that it was time to 'pass the torch' to someone else. But it was clear that Salmond didn't enjoy being leader of the opposition at Holyrood. He wanted to be First Minister and his failure to achieve that in the first elections to the Scottish Parliament had started a process which led to his decision to stand down. He was also suffering from a severe back complaint and, as one aide put it at the time, 'he is just knackered'.

There was definitely a part of Salmond that loved Westminster, even though he spent his whole political life trying to extract Scotland from it; he revelled in the sort of guerrilla war which he mounted from the back benches during his time there and he cherished the spark of intellectual debate. Holyrood, at that time, did not carry that weight in any sense and Salmond really believed it was time for somebody else.

Two candidates emerged in the battle for Salmond's place. One was Alex Neil, then a firebrand left-winger from the so-called 'fundamentalist' faction in the SNP – who believed that all efforts should be concentrated on independence and that the 'gradualists', who wanted to work with devolution, were weakening the party's approach. The other was John Swinney, a more reserved and less charismatic politician but one who was much more in tune with the Salmond brand of SNP modernism than Neil. On 23 September, after a short and only mildly bruising leadership battle, Swinney was elected SNP leader at the party's conference in Inverness. However, his moderate and conciliatory attempts to modernise and reform the SNP ahead of the 2001 Westminster elections were, like everything else in Scottish politics, knocked sideways by the death of Dewar just two weeks later.

Like the demise of John Smith six years before, Dewar's death brought the Labour movement in Scotland to a shocked standstill. David Whitton, Dewar's press spokesman, his voice cracking, announced the First Minister's passing at a short press conference at 2.10 p.m. on Wednesday 11 October, less than two hours after the event.

Parliament was suspended. The Scottish Executive convened in shock and then adjourned while friends and parliamentary colleagues gathered in small groups in an attempt to take the news in.

The following morning, Cabinet colleagues, some in tears, gathered in St Andrew's House, both to try to stop an undignified scramble for Dewar's job and to plan for the next difficult few days. An early move emerged for the coronation of McLeish but that was quickly stamped out by McConnell's aides, who insisted there would have to be a leadership contest. With that decision taken, the contest was put on hold for the next few days while the Labour Party, the parliament and the country tried to come to terms with the loss of its first First Minister.

On 18 October, Dewar's funeral took place at a packed Glasgow Cathedral. It was, in many ways, a defiantly 'old Labour' affair. A single red rose was placed on the coffin and although both Tony Blair and Gordon Brown addressed the congregation, neither carried the power or the emotional effect of the 'Internationale', the socialist anthem, which was sung, quietly and unaccompanied by the congregation, as the coffin was carried down the aisle and away. The affection in which Dewar was held, particularly in Glasgow, was reflected by the hundreds who packed into the open spaces outside the cathedral, with more lining the route of the hearse to and from the church.

The wake was held at the Kelvingrove Art Gallery in Glasgow. Everybody of note from the Labour Party, north and south of the border, gathered in the cavernous Victorian atrium to drink tea and talk about Dewar. But, with the Scottish party leaderless for more than a week, it was inevitable that the gathering would be used for political purposes too. By that time it had become clear that McConnell would be McLeish's only real challenger for the Scottish Labour leadership and even then it wasn't definite that the finance minister would actually contest the position. McConnell worked the room as subtly as he could, in the circumstances, as did McLeish.

Blair did not stay for long but the short time he was there was hugely significant. Word reached McLeish that the Prime Minister wanted to speak to him, and his wife Julie Fulton, before he left.

McLeish was ushered forward, with Fulton just behind. Blair shook him by the right hand, put the other hand on his shoulder and spoke a few words before shaking Fulton's hand then disappearing.

McLeish's aides beamed. McConnell was at the other end of the room and Blair was gone. It was clear that, in that moment, the Prime Minister had anointed his choice for Scottish Labour leader and the man he favoured as Scotland's second First Minister. McLeish, though, did not have to wait long to find out that his succession to the First Minister's job would be anything but seamless.

At 7 a.m. on 19 October, less than twenty-four hours after Dewar's funeral, McConnell launched his campaign to become leader of the Labour group in the Scottish Parliament and First Minister from an office in his Lanarkshire constituency. Such haste would have appeared unseemly had it not been for the extraordinary pressure of time which the Labour Party had imposed on any leadership contest. The party had a set procedure for leadership elections which involved a complicated electoral college of unions, party members and MSPs but party managers were forced to work to a much more restricted timetable because of the parliamentary rules. Although Labour would normally have taken a couple of months to elect a new leader, the parliamentary regulations were much more specific – a new First Minister had to be elected within a month or there would be another, full-scale, Scottish election.

Because the new Labour leader would also be the First Minister, Labour managers decided to short-cut their own election process. But even with the parliamentary restrictions, no-one expected it to be so quick. The party decided on a timetable of just forty-eight hours to elect an interim leader of the Scottish party. This was supposed to ensure continuity before a formal leadership election contest could take place but everyone knew that whoever was elected interim leader on 21 October would remain in that position for the foreseeable future.

The system and the timetable were weighted in McLeish's favour. Blair wanted a coronation, as did Brown, but McConnell and his small band of allies in the Scottish Parliament decided to challenge McLeish and, in doing so, challenge the London leadership.

McConnell's audacious and extraordinary start to a furiously quick campaign which no-one really expected caught the party, and

McLeish, by surprise. Within minutes of his launch, McConnell was on the phone to allies and colleagues in the party and was planning a lightning tour round Scotland to meet as many of the constituency representatives as possible. He was up and running almost before the cups and saucers from Dewar's wake had been cleared away.

McConnell had thought hard about the potential disaster that an overwhelming defeat could inflict on his political career but he reckoned, not unreasonably, that any sort of sizeable vote would make him both the clear number two to McLeish in the Scottish Labour Party and his logical successor. He also believed, with some justification, that McLeish could not leave him out of the Cabinet after the election, even if he lost by some distance.

Within that context, and realising he was fighting a difficult cause, McConnell entered the contest. The election was due to be decided by just eighty-one people: the fifty-four Labour MSPs, representatives of the Westminster and European parliamentary parties and the Scottish party's national executive committee, which included constituency representatives. The unions were heavily represented on the executive committee and, with McLeish quick in getting the public backing of most of the MSPs, McConnell had to get the support of at least some of these union barons and constituency representatives to stand any chance of making a good fight of the contest. His blitz campaign was organised by Tricia Ferguson, the deputy Presiding Officer, Karen Whitefield, the MSP for Airdrie & Shotts, and Frank Roy, the MP for Motherwell & Wishaw and a close ally of John Reid, the Scottish secretary.

With no time to set out policy agendas, the contest came down to a choice between Dewar's trusted, if uncharismatic, ally in McLeish and the ambitious young McConnell. At fifty-two, McLeish was seen as the 'safe pair of hands' after the unsettled first year of the parliament's life and in contrast to McConnell, the forty-year-old MSP who promised to change the atmosphere of the parliament by ditching the Westminster feel of both McLeish and Dewar.

The battle between experience and ambition was clear to anyone who met the candidates. There was McConnell, sharp suited, amiable, with a wicked smile and a reputation for briefing destructively behind the backs of his colleagues. Then there was McLeish, sporting greying curly hair and big glasses and with a hesitant, almost reticent style of speaking which was hardly inspiring. Yet McLeish was solidity and ministerial expertise personified; he had always managed to avoid political fallout and stayed on the right side of everybody who mattered.

When the party's Scottish executive gathered for the vote at the offices of Stirling Council, most assumed McLeish would win an easy and convincing victory. After all, his aides had been briefing the night before that he had the support of every single minister and seven trade union representatives. But when the result came, there were gasps all around the small hall, where McLeish and McConnell stood on a small platform. McLeish had won, but only by forty-four votes to thirty-six - the margin of just eight a clear indication of a split within the parliamentary party, with the ministers backing McLeish and many backbenchers supporting McConnell. It was not the overwhelming endorsement McLeish had wanted or expected and it left his administration damaged before it had even started.

Although he had lost, McConnell's gamble had paid off. He was now the clear heir and challenger to McLeish, he had a large group of supporters on the back benches and he could not be ignored by McLeish in his new Cabinet.

One of McLeish's first moves was to try to establish a new style of message for the First Minister's office, sacking David Whitton, Dewar's spin doctor, and Brian Fitzpatrick, the Blairite advocate who had been in charge of the Executive's policy unit. He kept McConnell within the Cabinet and gave him the tricky job of education minister. This was difficult because the department was already faced with two gathering storms: one over teachers' pay and the other caused by a series of extraordinary problems with exam marking by the Scottish Qualifications Authority (SQA). As a former teacher, McConnell was seen by many as the right person for the education brief but it was also acknowledged as the toughest job in the Scottish Executive and one which could easily lead to failure.

McLeish loyalists took most of the other Cabinet positions. Angus MacKay was promoted from the junior ranks to become the powerful minister for finance and local government. Wendy Alexander, another of McLeish's allies, took over his former role as minister for enterprise and lifelong learning while Jackie Baillie was given the role of minister for social justice. In one move to placate some back-benchers, McLeish brought in two left-wingers – Malcolm Chisholm and Margaret Curran – as deputy ministers.

At his election as Scotland's First Minister on 26 October 2000 – just eight days after his predecessor's funeral – McLeish told MSPs, his voice close to breaking point, that he 'would not let them down'. He was, however, to find that a hard statement to live up to.

As for McConnell, he threw himself into sorting out the mess that Scottish education was in. The roots of the biggest and most immediate problem came from reforms to the Scottish Higher exam (the rough equivalent of English A-levels) known as Higher Still and the subsequent disastrous failure of the exams system following its introduction. The SQA had to admit, on 9 August 2000, that 1,400 pupils would not receive their exam results as expected the following day. That was bad enough but it soon got worse when, next day, more than 2,200 pupils failed to get their results, results which they needed urgently to chase university and college places.

Sam Galbraith, McConnell's predecessor as education minister, came under pressure to sort out the problem as further computer glitches led to delays in sending results to schools and then errors in results sent to higher education institutions. It also emerged that problems with the computers had been identified as early as April and that the SQA had been criticised by the teaching unions through the year for failing to get adequate information to schools about the new exam.

By 11 August the exam system was in meltdown, with the SQA admitting that it would have to check the integrity of the results of all 140,000 pupils. Students all over Scotland had no idea whether they had the grades to get them to university. Galbraith met SQA officials for crisis talks while facing increasingly strident calls for his resignation.

However, one interesting part of how this debacle developed was the skilful way in which McLeish kept himself out of the firing line. As the enterprise and lifelong learning minister, the management and competence of the SQA came into McLeish's portfolio but he dodged all the criticism for the exams fiasco, leaving Galbraith to soak it all up. McLeish displayed an uncanny ability to do this right through his political career and he intervened in the SQA debacle only later – and then he managed to appear as if he was riding to Galbraith's rescue.

The problems with the SQA eased as pupils eventually got their results but the political pressure remained intense on the education minister, particularly because the number of appeals against the final exam results topped 120,000. In September, when he reported to the parliament on the issue, Galbraith apologised to pupils and blamed others, insisting that the assurances he had received from the SQA before the crisis had turned out to be worthless.

Galbraith instigated an inquiry to push the issue out and away from the immediate political agenda, at least for a while. But by the time McConnell took over the education brief, at the start of November, his first job was to reassure pupils and parents that the SQA crisis would never happen again and then to make sure it never did.

McConnell made clear to his officials that he wanted the 2001 exams to run smoothly and they, together with the SQA, ensured that happened. It must have been just a little bit tempting, however, for McConnell not to work too hard to sort out the SQA mess, because McLeish had given his word publicly that he would quit if there was a repeat of the 2000 shambles. But there is no indication that McConnell let that affect his approach, driving his officials and the SQA on to make sure the problems were rectified. And indeed in 2001 only a tiny minority had to wait for their results (0.3 per cent), a major success given the failure the year before.

Having completed that part, McConnell went on to reform the SQA. He slimmed down the board, added an advisory board of stakeholders, increased the remuneration package for a new chief executive and simplified its procedures, allowing it to concentrate on exam results. It was a competent and efficient end to what had been a disastrous time for Scottish education.

McConnell also had to sort out one more issue in education, something that had been hanging over Scottish schools for years: teachers' pay. This had been in contention for years, with teachers demanding more money and ministers asking for more in return from teachers. In an attempt to break the stalemate, a committee under Professor Gavin McCrone was set up to recommend a way through. It reported in the summer of 2000, suggesting substantial pay rises for teachers – 14 per cent over two years – but also the introduction of so-called superteachers and more classroom assistants.

In what was seen as a clear bid to get teachers on side after years of grumbles with the government, McConnell gave them the pay rise they wanted: a massive 21.5 per cent over three years, even more than suggested by McCrone. Not only that, but McConnell announced the pay rise in isolation, without any conditions attached in the form of more out-of-classroom work. It may have been that, as a former teacher, McConnell was sympathetic to their needs; it may have been that he decided it was best to acquiesce on this central part of the bargaining with teachers and work the rest out over time. Either way, teachers got an extremely good deal and although early retirement was tightened up and later reforms did introduce superteachers and more classroom assistants, there was a feeling outside the profession that teachers had secured an extraordinarily good deal with McConnell, and they were never really asked to make good on the other, reforming, parts of it.

The pay deal cost £800 million, which had to be wrung out of budgets elsewhere, and put pressure on ministers in London, who were trying to get their teachers to accept an annual deal of just 3.75 per cent at the same time.

In February 2001, Scottish teachers voted to accept the pay package and halt any attempt at industrial action. In the wake of the pay deal, McConnell announced plans to target bad teachers and to reform other parts of the school sector but, however well intentioned, many of these plans ran up against the usual calcifying bureaucracy of local government and progressed only at a snail's pace, if at all.

McConnell had succeeded yet again. He had sorted out the SQA crisis and then resolved a long-running dispute with teachers over pay – even though it had cost the Scottish Executive and the taxpayer hundreds of millions of pounds to do so. But at least education no longer appeared to be the worst of all departments. Scottish education looked better and so did McConnell's chances of political advancement.

While McConnell was concentrating on the mess in education, McLeish was moving closer to a policy shift which would result in the biggest split with Westminster in devolution's short history. The new First Minister made the decision, just two months into his time

in office, to introduce free care for the elderly, not only diverging
from Westminster on fundamental policy terms but also adopting
a scheme which would lead to resentment in England and the
possibility of elderly English people coming over the border to take
advantage of the Scottish Executive's largesse.

McLeish infuriated his Westminster colleagues and members of
his own Cabinet with his decision, driving through the policy
against the advice of many of his Labour colleagues.

Free care for the elderly had been bubbling as an issue across the
UK for several years, principally because of the growing middle-class
backlash against high nursing care fees, which meant that many
elderly people were being forced to sell their homes to pay for care.
In 1997, when Labour came to power, Sir Stewart Sutherland,
principal of Edinburgh University, was asked to set up a royal
commission into the costs of caring for the elderly. The Sutherland
Commission reported in February 1999 and recommended free care
for all, regardless of income.

In October that year, the Scottish Parliament's health committee
started its own investigation into the issue while the Westminster
government continued to mull over Sutherland's expensive proposals.
When he became First Minister in November 2000, McLeish
hinted that he would like to see the Sutherland recommendations
implemented in full, going further in a BBC *Newsnight* interview
than anyone, including his advisers, expected him to. Then, on
6 January 2001, he announced his conversion to free care for the
elderly and said he was determined to see it happen in Scotland.

For the next month, McLeish came under increasing pressure
from Westminster to back down, or at least to dilute his free care
plans. David Hinchliffe, then the Labour chairman of the Commons
Health Select Committee, came north in an attempt to get McLeish
to change his mind. Lord Lipsey, a Labour peer and an ally of the
Prime Minister, was more vocal, appearing on television to warn of
the Highlands being turned into a big nursing home for the ageing
English middle classes.

With these public warnings came many private ones from
Labour Cabinet ministers north and south of the border. Susan
Deacon, McLeish's health minister, was the most consistent critic of
the plans inside the Cabinet. In July 2000, she circulated a minute to

the Cabinet on the Sutherland recommendations warning that the plans would do nothing, either to improve the quality of care or to 'rebalance provision' towards the home. 'These recommendations have assumed a symbolic significance out of all proportion to the benefits they would bring,' she warned. McConnell added his own support to this minute, stating: 'I am content with the approach Susan Deacon proposes.'

Angus MacKay, the influential finance minister and a close ally of McLeish, also cautioned against the policy. In a memo sent in November 2000, he said it would be hard to find the money – then estimated at £60 million a year – for the policy. 'It is hard to see where we could take such a large sum from, without doing more damage than the positive reaction that we might get from a personal care package,' he said. Sam Galbraith was blunter: 'Just because a large body of opinion supported it, does not make it right. There was a time when most people supported the proposition that the world was flat.'

Yet, despite all this, McLeish did not budge. He wanted to do something to set Scotland apart, to allow people to see the advantage of devolution in Scotland and to give the Labour-led Executive something concrete to champion at the next election. He was supported by the Liberal Democrats, although they did warn him at the same time not to back down or risk splitting the coalition.

No. 10 was getting increasingly concerned with the direction being taken in Scotland, and Alasdair McGowan, the Downing Street special adviser with responsibility for Scotland, was on the phone repeatedly to Jonathan Pryce, McLeish's private secretary, demanding to know what was going on. Tony Blair and Alan Milburn, his UK health secretary, had overcome considerable pressure to resist the Sutherland recommendations. They did not need one part of the United Kingdom showing that it could be done and driving ahead with it.

On several occasions it appeared as if McLeish would buckle under the pressure and compromise on the deal, but he never did and it was Deacon, someone who had more misgivings than most about the plan, who announced the Scottish Executive's commitment to universal free care for the elderly.

Deacon had first announced an extension of the existing

arrangements, which would have seen more elderly people given free care but, crucially, not all of them. Faced with a humiliating parliamentary defeat, McLeish then ordered his ministers to go further. Taking the opportunity of First Minister's Questions, which came after the debate but before the vote, he made it clear that he would not ignore the will of the parliament – a signal of his willingness to embrace full free care for all. Tom McCabe, the minister for parliament, then clarified the situation by making an emergency statement just before the vote, announcing that the Scottish Executive would embrace 'free personal care for all'. The parliamentary debate and vote did not end the controversy completely, because McLeish then farmed out the issue to yet another expert group, the Care Development Group, headed by Malcolm Chisholm, the deputy health minister, but this group was at least looking at how the policy could be implemented and financed, not whether it would be pursued at all.

At the heart of the problem over elderly care was the distinction between personal care, which the elderly had to pay for, and nursing care, which they did not. Often the distinctions between the two appeared arbitrary, with some elderly people with specific conditions given free help which others, in a similar plight but with different conditions, were not.

A few days later, it became clear that there was no way Westminster was going to go down the same route for England, with Blair stating categorically that he felt there were better ways of spending NHS money. At this point, McLeish was faced with a bill of at least £110 million a year, with warnings that this would rise dramatically, an angry backlash from within his own Scottish party and from London and the implementation of a complicated policy with limited electoral reward. When the Care Development Group finally reported, it warned that the cost would double in ten years but it recommended that all personal care should be free.

To make matters worse, the UK government then withdrew £40 million in attendance allowance payments, money which had come to Scotland in benefits to help pensioners pay for their care. The Department of Work and Pensions argued that, as care was now going to be free, there was no need for a benefit to help with payments. The Scottish Executive argued that the money should continue to come north to help fund elderly care, but without success. This increased the Executive's financial liability and represented the first real refusal of the UK government to help its fledgling Scottish counterpart.

Free care for the elderly was introduced in July 2002 and it caused possibly more problems than even the harshest critics had predicted. There was confusion among councils as to what was to be paid for and what wasn't; some spent their budgets quickly and ran out of money, leaving elderly people on waiting lists; and some ended up being taken to court for not paying for services provided free by others. The cost rose dramatically from the first estimate of £110 million a year in 2001 to £147 million in 2007 and an estimate of at least £227 million a year by 2022, but as a policy it did set Scotland apart from England, it saved many elderly people a lot of money and it was popular, at least with pensioners. Above all, free care for the elderly was defiantly populist, starting a theme which was to become one of the hallmarks of McLeish's short tenure in charge of the Scottish Executive.

McLeish was not the best parliamentary performer; indeed he was often ridiculed for his 'McClichés', verbal gobbledegook that made little sense, or statements with so many sub-clauses that they ended up all over the place. The McClichés included 'I am saying this in words purely because it is factual', 'There is only one party in this coalition' and 'My best wishes go out to those who were killed'. One of his best was made during the height of the foot and mouth crisis of 2001, when he said in parliament: 'Nobody, Mr Presiding Officer, likes travelling with carcasses, infected or otherwise,' while other gems included 'The future always starts today' and 'I am like a stock, Scottish to the rock' when he had meant to say: 'I am like a stick of rock, Scottish to the core.'

Yet, despite these presentational problems, McLeish had the sort of populist touch which Donald Dewar never had. McLeish understood what it took to be popular and what sort of policies would endear him to the voters.

He had been a professional footballer in youth, for East Fife, although even that led to some ribbing from his opponents later on because, of eleven youth footballers taken on by the great Don Revie to trial for Leeds United in the 1960s, the other ten made it while McLeish went home to East Fife. Nevertheless, he did get an under-18 cap for Scotland and football remained a passion of his, despite his limited professional career.

It was with both his populist eye and his footballing background that McLeish seized on the opportunity for Scotland to bid for the European football championships of 2008. The deadline for applications to host the Euro 2008 tournament was November 2001 but McLeish gave his backing early, making it clear in May of that year that he wanted Scotland not only to bid for it, but to put in a solo bid, rather than trying to get the Irish or the Welsh on board as well.

It was a hugely ambitious decision, not least because Scotland had only four stadiums which met the tough criteria set down by UEFA, European football's governing body, and three of those (Ibrox, Celtic Park and Hampden) were in Glasgow, with the fourth, Murrayfield, just 45 miles away in Edinburgh. UEFA stipulated that applicant countries had to have at least six and preferably eight stadiums with a capacity of at least 30,000. Ideally, these stadiums would be spread fairly evenly across the country, so new grounds would be needed in Aberdeen and Dundee and possibly even Inverness, if the bid was to stand any chance of success. But McLeish was confident that Scotland could and should do it, aware just what a fillip it would give the country if something like the European championships could be secured.

He combined the Euro 2008 bid with a major push to host the 2009 Ryder Cup golf tournament, contested biennially between Europe and the United States. In the event, the 2009 event was moved back a year to 2010, a consequence of all the Ryder Cups being shifted by a year after the postponement of the 2001 tournament because of 9/11.

Golf and football were, and remain, Scotland's two sporting staples and McLeish recognised that. His campaign for the Ryder Cup was linked to a policy of spreading golf throughout Scotland's schools and a pledge that all nine-year-olds would at least have the opportunity to try golf. The campaign for the Euro championships went as well as it could have done through the summer of 2001 but, until the deadline for applications was up and the other bidders had declared their hands, there was no way of knowing its potential for success.

The Ryder Cup campaign came to an end in September and was a mixed blessing for McLeish. The 2010 tournament went to the Celtic Manor resort in Wales, a slightly contentious decision because European Golf Design, the company which won a lucrative contract to redesign the Welsh course, was part owned by the PGA European Tour, whose directors play a key role in selecting the Ryder Cup venue. But, as a consolation, Scotland was given the 2014 tournament and while this was a considerable success, McLeish realised it was thirteen years away, so the beneficial effects would be a long time in coming.

McLeish adopted a slogan for his administration of 'progressive pragmatism', taken from the former mayor of New York Mario Cuomo. He developed this into 'confident, competitive and compassionate' and insisted that his guiding principle would be 'what worked', not ideology. It was a reflection of the New Labour way, which was the dominant force in the government in London, but was also an attempt by McLeish to move his administration away from the Dewar era and to give his Executive a more down-to-earth and populist feel and impression of its own.

McLeish's attempt to court popularity was, in part, a strategy designed to deflect attention from the serious issues which were grabbing the headlines and affecting the Executive's standing. Fears over the combined measles, mumps and rubella (MMR) vaccine for children and its possible links to autism had caused huge controversy. MMR take-up rates were declining and the Scottish Parliament became the forum for heated debate on both sides. Hospital waiting lists continued to lengthen, despite the Executive's attempt to change the emphasis to the more accurate waiting times figures.

All this, however, was overshadowed by rural issues – some manufactured and some unexpected – which dominated Scottish politics after McLeish came to office.

5

Foot and mouth, foxes and fish

ON 13 February 2002, as the final speech on the bill to ban fox hunting was being made, one voice from the SNP benches broke through the heated atmosphere inside the Assembly Hall to decry those who hunted as 'the same people who gave us the poll tax'. A few minutes later the bill was passed, to triumphant cheers from animal rights activists in the galleries and to angry cries of 'Shame!' from tweed-clad gamekeepers sitting alongside, but that one intervention from that SNP MSP summed up the irreconcilable differences at the heart of the legislation.

It was seen – by some on both sides – as a class issue: that somehow hunting was the preserve of the landed aristocracy so an attack on their interests was a victory for the working class. The fact that hunting in Scotland was largely a geographic rather than a class issue, and that doctors, farmers and lawyers were as likely to hunt as landowners, seemed to get lost in the heat of the argument. But what the legislation did was help fuel a grievance in rural Scotland that the urban-dominated, Central Belt-led Scottish Parliament was riding over the interests of rural Scotland – rather as a 16-hand hunter would trample a small hedgerow in pursuit of a fox.

When Henry McLeish came to office in late 2000, there were already signs that the interests of rural Scotland might start to rise up the political agenda. The hunting bill had already been unveiled, as had plans to redraw centuries of land access laws, but no-one predicted quite what was in store for the countryside and those who made their living from it. There had been rumblings for some time about genetically modified crop trials and a demand from environmentalists that Scotland ban GM crops, leaving England to pursue the trials if the Westminster government wished it. One farmer, Jamie Grant, started a GM crop trial at his Roskill Farm near Munlochy, north of

Inverness, and was targeted by protesters, demonstrators and vandals as a result. Farm incomes were plummeting across the country and it was within this context that the foot and mouth epidemic erupted.

On 21 February 2001, the first case of foot and mouth disease was confirmed in pigs at a slaughterhouse in Essex. The crisis was immediate and hit the whole of the country, mainly because the slaughterhouse handled animals from all over the country, including Scotland. It was the first such outbreak for twenty-five years but, because of the way in which animals were now transported all over Britain for sale and slaughter, the effects were much more dramatic than ever before.

People were told not to walk in the countryside and all livestock movements were banned across Britain. Rural events were called off; even the Scotland–Ireland rugby international was postponed as the number of farms hit by the disease grew by the day. The sight of officials in one-piece scientific overalls and buckets of disinfectant at the farm gate became commonplace, as did pyres of burning animals as confirmed cases of the disease continued to mount.

By the end of February, a week into the outbreak, the farm sector was in crisis. It was the first real test for Ross Finnie, the former accountant turned Liberal Democrat MSP and Scottish rural affairs minister, and he did very well. He managed to give the impression that he was in control and that the authorities in Scotland were reacting quicker and with more effect than their counterparts in London, and he appeared to be working every hour to try to head off the worst effects of the crisis. Finnie succeeded, to a large extent, in keeping the farming sector on his side, which boosted his, and the Executive's, reputation enormously.

In London, Tony Blair decided on the slaughter of one million farm animals rather than universal vaccination as the best way to combat the epidemic. He also put off the date of the UK general election until 7 June. The image of troops moving in to help burn and bury hundreds of thousands of apparently healthy animals, with thick smoke rising up from farmland all over Britain, became the abiding one from the spring of 2001.

Finnie and McLeish had come out of the disaster fairly well, with the Scottish Executive being praised for its firm and effective response. However, the foot and mouth crisis marked only one part of the

Scottish Parliament's complex relationship with rural Scotland during this time, a relationship which reached rock bottom over plans to ban hunting and change the whole basis of land ownership in Scotland.

Hunting was a perfect class battle, allowing urban MSPs the chance to change something with their new institution, something which would never have been given the necessary time at Westminster. But, far from being a simple victory for the MSPs over a few aristocrats, the hunting battle came to represent much more than that. For many people in rural Scotland, people who didn't hunt, the drive to abolish hunting came to be seen as a challenge to a way of life from spiteful and vindictive urban MSPs who didn't know and who didn't want to care about what went on outside their own world.

Lord Watson of Invergowrie, the Labour MSP for Glasgow Cathcart, announced his plans to introduce a private member's bill to ban hunting on 21 July 1999, two years before the foot and mouth outbreak, but the slow progress of the parliamentary bill meant that it came to its first real test, in committee, in the spring of 2001 – just when the foot and mouth crisis was at its height.

Watson's hunting bill was the first private member's bill to progress through the parliament. For that reason alone it was hugely symbolic, galvanising anti-hunt campaigners who believed that the Scottish Parliament would herald a new start for the countryside. But it also managed to unite disparate countryside groups in opposition. The Countryside Alliance used the Scottish hunting bill as a trial run for tactics it would use later throughout England and Wales. There were furious legal challenges and arguments, inside and outside the parliament, before the Protection of Wild Mammals Bill was finally passed on 13 February 2002, by eighty-three votes to thirty-six with five abstentions.

The legislation made it illegal for anyone to use dogs to hunt wild mammals, effectively ruling out mounted fox hunting, hare coursing and fox baiting. But the new law allowed the use of dogs to flush out foxes, as long as they were then dispatched with a gun.

The confusion over what the act actually said and what it meant led to intense criticism of the Scottish Parliament's law-making procedures. The entire bill was passed, with amendments, in a single day. The session was extended for a short time but, because of the family-friendly nature of the sitting hours, the Scottish Parliament could not sit on and on through the night to thrash out the sections of the bill properly, as was the case at Westminster. Also, because there was no revising chamber for the Scottish Parliament, any flaws in a piece of legislation – and there were several in the hunting bill – could not be ironed out at a later date.

The political focus on the countryside was then reinforced by one other piece of rural legislation, the Land Reform Bill. This was started by Donald Dewar in 2000, but it took until early 2003 to get it on to the statute book. It was far-reaching and radical, effectively overturning hundreds of years of Scottish land law and countryside access rights. There had never been a law of trespass in Scotland but the Land Reform Bill codified the opposite, giving a presumption of access to anyone over land owned by someone else, the so-called 'right to roam'. It allowed the public to walk, cycle or ride over almost any part of Scotland. Landowners could only keep people out from the land surrounding their homes or if they had very good reasons (such as safety or animal welfare) from other parts.

The other two main provisions of the bill dealt with land owner-ship: one gave communities first refusal on land if a landowner decided to sell – a pre-emptive right to buy the land (including the fishing rights), and the other gave crofting communities an absolute right to buy, forcing landowners to sell to crofters if the community proved it was in its interests to take control of the land. At the same time, ministers set up a fund – the Scottish Land Fund – to finance community buyouts.

The bill was opposed, understandably, by landowners, who were joined in their fight by the Conservatives, some hoteliers and a loose collection of others, many of whom lived in the countryside. However, they didn't come close to defeating the alliance of Labour, the Liberal Democrats, the SNP, ramblers and crofters, who had more than enough support to drive the legislation through.

Another bill, the Agricultural Holdings Bill, was much more minor in scope, simply changing the law on farm tenancies, giving tenant farmers first refusal on their farms if they came up for sale. But together, these two pieces of legislation changed the nature of rural Scotland, undermining the traditional power of landowners and giving much more power to members of the public and small farmers.

Fishermen also felt themselves to be on the fringes of the Central

Belt-dominated parliament and their sector was also in a state of crisis at this time. Home to the vast majority of the UK fishing fleet, Scotland was suffering more than any other part of the country from the swingeing cuts which the European Union was demanding to safeguard fish stocks. Fishermen were restricted in the days they could fish and the amounts they could catch, forcing many out of business. They appealed to the Scottish Executive for help, specifically a 'tie-up' scheme which would compensate them for leaving their boats tied up on shore.

Ministers proposed a more drastic decommissioning scheme which would result in the scrapping of boats, not just a temporary layover. The Scottish Executive promised £27 million for the scheme but a rebellion by four Liberal Democrat MSPs and thirteen Labour MSPs on 9 March 2001 handed the McLeish administration the first defeat of an Executive since the parliament was created two years previously. On top of that, Tavish Scott, the Liberal Democrat deputy minister for parliament and the MSP for Shetland, quit his post after failing to back the Executive in the vote.

The defeat and the ministerial resignation were doubly embarrassing for Henry McLeish as they came on the eve of the Scottish Labour conference in Inverness, which Tony Blair wanted to use to kick off the 2001 general election campaign in Scotland. The Prime Minister's visit went ahead as planned, despite the presence of fishing demonstrators outside the conference hall, and ministers pressed on with their decommissioning scheme.

With the Scottish Parliament sitting and passing legislation throughout, the 2001 general election campaign was the quietest and least important for Scotland in living memory. The UK national picture hardly made for a tense campaign, with Blair comfortable and going for his second election victory and the Tories in all sorts of trouble.

The campaign came and went in Scotland, dominated by both the Iraq War and the foot and mouth crisis, and ended in a continuation of Labour's traditional dominance. Labour won fifty-six of Scotland's seventy-two seats, with the Liberal Democrats getting ten, the SNP five and the Conservatives one – which was at least better than their wipe-out in 1997. Only one seat changed hands in Scotland, Galloway & Upper Nithsdale going from the SNP to the Conservatives while, in the share of the vote, the 2001 election recorded a barely noticeable 0.2 per cent swing from the SNP to Labour. With much the same sort of story across the UK – with Labour on 412 seats, six seats down from 1997, and the Tories up just one (with 166 seats), the election changed very little.

It was more noted for mistakes and gaffes than anything else. The Tory launch was the worst in living memory. The Conservatives had arranged for a mobile poster van bearing the message that Tony Blair had failed to keep his promises on tax. With the media gathered outside the national galleries on The Mound in Edinburgh, the poster van turned up but instead of a Tory campaign poster, there was an advertising hoarding proclaiming the merits of the Tesco at Broadwater Retail Park in Stevenage – now open 24 hours. The driver hurriedly tried to staple the Tory poster over the top but by then it was too late. The damage had been done. Just to add to the surreal nature of the launch, a small Army tank then rolled off a low-loader nearby, at which time Sir Malcolm Rifkind, the former defence secretary, who was leading the Conservative campaign in Scotland, scarpered as quickly as he could.

Then, just as the campaign finished, McLeish became the victim of his own carelessness as the final results were coming through. At 11 a.m. on 8 June, he and Helen Liddell held their final press conference to champion Labour's success. As they waited in an upstairs room for the start of the conference, the two politicians were fitted with radio microphones. They were then left alone for a few minutes before the start time and, forgetting that they could be heard through the microphones, the Scottish secretary and the First Minister started chatting about Liddell's chances of retaining a Cabinet post in Blair's new administration.

Their conversation turned to John Reid, the Scottish MP and Northern Ireland secretary, and together they both exclaimed: 'He's such a patronising bastard,' and then laughed loudly. The conversation was picked up by the radio station ScotFM and later relayed to journalists all over Scotland.

The episode proved deeply embarrassing for both Liddell and McLeish. McLeish's relationship with Reid never really recovered, with Reid refusing to return phone calls from the First Minister for weeks afterwards. But it also shed light on the machinations within the Labour Party, undermining in one short sentence the sense of unity which Labour had managed to maintain right the way through the election campaign.

For the SNP, the 2001 election was a disappointment. The party had hoped to make progress, particularly given the higher profile it had enjoyed since the advent of the Scottish Parliament two years before. It was the first test for John Swinney, the party's new leader, and although the Nationalists always insisted that they expected to do worse at UK general elections, the loss of support to Labour and the loss of a seat to the Tories were not good news.

Alex Salmond had decided the year before not just to stand down as leader, but to return to Westminster and give up his seat at the Scottish Parliament. In some ways this was good for Swinney – he would not have his former boss sitting on the back benches reminding his colleagues of better times – but the loss of the charismatic and well-known Salmond did not help the SNP in the election, nor did the party finances, which had still not recovered from the mauling they received in 1999.

The Tories in Scotland were still trying to forge a clear identity. Many in the party were still finding it hard to come to terms with the reversal in policy which had brought it from being opposed to devolution in 1997 to supporting it, albeit not entirely enthusiastically, a couple of years later. The 2001 election result lifted the Conservatives off the canvas in UK election terms, with Peter Duncan claiming their only Westminster seat since 1992, but the reluctance of many in the Scottish party to embrace devolution as keenly as their Scottish leader, David McLetchie, led to problems. McLetchie managed to prevent his critics from destabilising his leadership but reports of serious problems within the Tory group in the Scottish Parliament refused to go away.

That sense of discontent was blown into the open in August 2001 when the Conservative MSP Nick Johnston announced he was standing down, partly blaming a poisonous atmosphere within the group for his decision. By that time another four Tory MSPs (John Young, Ben Wallace, Phil Gallie and Murray Tosh) had said they would not stand again in 2003 – although Tosh did change his mind later – and this only added to the feeling that all was not well within the Conservatives in Scotland.

At the heart of their problem was the issue of devolution – the resentment over that would only fade with time – but there were other policy differences too, not least the decision of some of the more radical MSPs to favour more powers for the Scottish Parliament, powers which would give the institution the ability to make tax cuts for the Scottish people over and above the 3p variable income tax rate set out in the Scotland Act. This dispute over so-called 'fiscal autonomy' remained at the heart of ideological Conservative debates for the next eight years.

By October 2001, McLeish was able to celebrate his first year in office, having weathered the storm of foot and mouth and established his own voice by driving through his own, populist, agenda against the wishes of Westminster. But already the clouds of another scandal were looming which would provide Scottish Labour with its biggest crisis since devolution and give Jack McConnell the chance he had been waiting for.

6

A muddle, not a fiddle

TONY Blair was enjoying the first course of a formal dinner in the White House on the evening of 7 November 2001, given in his honour by President George W. Bush, when a call came through from Peter MacMahon, Henry McLeish's press spokesman. Alastair Campbell, Blair's press spokesman, excused himself to his hosts and left the room to take the call. Campbell was furious to be called out of a gala White House dinner to take a call on Scottish politics, and he made his views known, but nevertheless, he listened to what MacMahon had to say.

MacMahon was brief and to the point. McLeish would have to resign as Scotland's First Minister the following morning. Campbell said McLeish should sleep on it and decide in the morning, before going back into the dinner and quietly informing the Prime Minister.

The following morning, Thursday 8 November, Blair was in his official car on his way back to Downing Street from Heathrow when he took the call from McLeish that he had been told to expect. McLeish gave his apologies to the Prime Minister and told him he would be resigning later that day.

'I'm so sorry, Henry,' Blair replied, accepting the loss of a second Scottish First Minister in just over a year, but doing little to persuade McLeish to change his mind.[*]

At this time, early on that Thursday morning, rumours were just starting to circulate around a small number of MSPs. McLeish's closest allies had been told of his intention to resign but that circle was growing larger with every minute as the word spread. By 10.30 a.m., unconfirmed reports of McLeish's pending resignation were sweeping

---

[*] See Peter MacMahon, 'Fall of a First Minister, parts 1a & 1b: "So, are you corrupt or just incompetent?"', *Scotsman*, 25 January 2002.

the corridors of the old Assembly Hall on The Mound and up through the press building a short way down the Royal Mile.

The announcement, when it came, was not made by McLeish himself, but by Tom McCabe, the minister for parliament and McLeish's ally and confidant. At 11 a.m. McCabe stood up in the now packed and silent chamber to make a point of order. He told MSPs: 'I inform the chamber that the First Minister has this morning written to Her Majesty the Queen and to the Presiding Officer indicating that he intends to tender his resignation. The First Minister intends to come to parliament later today to make a personal statement.'

The so-called 'Officegate' saga, which brought about McLeish's downfall, had been a slow burner in media terms. It had taken eight months for controversy to mushroom from a single story about the sub-let of a small office in Glenrothes, Fife into a scandal which consumed the media in Scotland and forced the country's second First Minister from his job.

The first that anybody in the First Minister's entourage knew about a problem was at the end of March 2001, when Matthew Knowles, a reporter on the Scottish *Mail on Sunday*, rang MacMahon to ask about McLeish's Westminster constituency office in Glenrothes. Knowles knew that Digby Brown, a law firm with strong links to the Scottish Labour Party, had been renting part of McLeish's office. The whole office was being rented by McLeish and then part of it sub-let to Digby Brown, which had been paying £4,000 a year since 1998.

The First Minister's office acknowledged that the money had been paid into an account in McLeish's name but insisted that McLeish had not benefited personally from the sub-let and refused to say whether McLeish was claiming the full cost of the office rent from the House of Commons. This detail was crucial. There was nothing to stop McLeish renting only part of an office, or renting a whole one and getting some of the rent back from a tenant and the remainder from the House of Commons authorities. However, the real issue was whether he was claiming the full rent from the taxpayer and then getting extra funds from Digby Brown which he was not declaring to the Commons authorities – effectively double-claiming at least part of his office rent from the taxpayer and using this for Labour constituency funds. On 8 April it emerged that McLeish was indeed double-claiming part of his rent, claiming the whole amount from the taxpayer and getting another £4,000 from Digby Brown without informing the Commons. At this point the affair was handed over to the House of Commons standards commissioner, Elizabeth Filkin.

Even though it was against parliamentary rules to double-claim office costs, because McLeish was not benefiting personally from the sub-let – the money was going to local Labour Party funds – opinion was divided among politicians and political journalists as to how damaging this arrangement actually would be for the First Minister. Indeed, once the affair became the property of the House of Commons authorities, the story went cold for quite a while, not least because McLeish left Westminster at the 2001 election and, as a result, Filkin stopped investigating his financial affairs.

The Officegate affair rumbled along in the background through the summer and early autumn without any major revelations until, on 23 October, McLeish announced that he had reached a settlement with the House of Commons Fees Office and had offered to pay back £9,000 to end the controversy. Unfortunately for him, this move did the reverse. Suddenly, every newspaper and news organisation in Scotland focused on a story on which many had been keeping only a watching brief until that point.

McLeish's decision to reimburse the House of Commons Fees Office opened up a range of new questions about his office arrangements. David McLetchie, the Scottish Tory leader, led attacks in the Scottish Parliament, demanding details of McLeish's payment and all his office rental arrangements. McLeish kept insisting he had not benefited personally but came under increasing pressure to reveal how much money he had claimed in rent and from how many organisations, going back much further than 1998.

At this stage, the first unconfirmed suggestions started circulating that McLeish might have claimed up to £40,000 in extra rent for his office over the years he was an MP; a story which had barely registered in the public eye over the summer had now generated more than 100 articles, editorials and commentaries in the course of just one week including one in the *Daily Mail*, the first, calling on McLeish to stand down as First Minister. But in the days after

23 October, despite the intense media coverage and the unanswered questions, the Officegate affair did not appear to be career-threatening for the First Minister.

The weekend of 27 and 28 October was supposed to be one of celebration for McLeish as he marked a year in office, but instead he awoke on the Sunday to two new damaging revelations. First, the police had been called in to investigate his office rents, having had a formal complaint from a member of the public, Alistair Watson, who had been a fraud squad officer. It also emerged that McLeish's parliamentary office had been used as a contact point for the local Labour Party in elections, which was against the rules.

McLeish was under mounting pressure from his political opponents inside the Scottish Parliament and from the media on the outside. It really had become a feeding frenzy, with every little detail devoured and analysed in the press. McLetchie was devastating in his criticism, particularly his mischievous line that McLeish was using a defence of 'I didnae ken, it wisnae me, a big boy did it and ran away'. The Tory leader was both scoring points and inspiring scornful laughter and the First Minister had to do something to rectify the situation.

The crunch came on Thursday 1 November, when David Dimbleby's *Question Time* programme was due to be broadcast from Glasgow with McLeish as a panel guest. McLeish could not duck out, because that would have suggested he had something to hide, so the only alternative was to put in a commanding performance. That was the only way he could take the initiative against the drip-drip of information about his office affairs. McLeish's advisers prepared and prepared and prepared, feeding the First Minister with lines and arguments, pleading with him to stick to the agreed position and not to allow his opponents anything new.

Question Time has been responsible for helping make a few political careers but, on that Thursday evening, it went a long way to breaking one. McLeish appeared both stressed and shifty. He had a nervous cough which he had suppressed for a while but which came back that night on television. He ran his forefinger round his collar, making him look guilty: rather than appearing commanding, he actually managed to make the whole situation worse before he even started speaking.

One question from Dimbleby started a downward slide for

McLeish which he found himself unable to rectify. 'Are you any different from someone who is on benefit and then lets a room for cash without declaring it?' the BBC presenter asked, cutting right through all the parliamentary talk to put the Officegate issue on to a footing anybody could understand.

The First Minister, wisely, refused to answer the question, leaving it hanging in the air. Instead he replied that the concern over his office expenses had been raised with the Westminster standards commissioner and she had passed it on to the Fees Office; they had investigated and reached an agreement with him on the money to be paid back.

Up until that point, McLeish was doing exactly as his advisers had suggested but then came the second question from Dimbleby. Was that the end of the matter, he asked, apparently quite innocently, or was there any other money from any other rents which McLeish had received during his time in the parliament?

'Yes, there was, David, and what we did with the Fees Office—' the First Minister said. Then with members of the audience shouting out 'How much?', he added: 'I don't know what the sum involved was, but let me say this, the Fees Office—'

Dimbleby interrupted, this time with more of an edge: 'You say you don't know how much it was, but there was other money that you received, despite the taxpayer paying for your office, by sub-letting part of it?'

McLeish replied: 'There were other sub-lets which have been in the media, so that's not new.' He stressed that the money had been spent on his parliamentary office and added: 'Not a penny of that was for my own personal benefit. There is a situation of trust here.' McLeish insisted, as he had been advised to do, that he had not benefited personally from the money, but the damage was done. His admission, not just that there had been further sub-lets but that he had no idea how much money had been paid, took the controversy to a whole new level.

It was then compounded when Alex Salmond, who was also on the *Question Time* panel, saw that the First Minister was down and struggling. Instead of pushing him down further, Salmond, wily political operator that he was, rallied to McLeish's aid, gently insisting that nobody thought he was dishonest but advising him in the friendliest possible way to publish all the details of his office expenses. It was a masterful move; it looked gracious and magnanimous and made it seem as if McLeish was in such a bad way that even his political opponents were having to ride to his rescue. By this time McLeish was too battered to fight back against Salmond, appearing to accept his thoughtful intervention with thanks.

McLeish had spent an hour the day before with advisers John McTernan, John McLaren and Peter MacMahon and a further hour on the day of the broadcast preparing his answers. It had all been wasted, something McLeish was well aware of as he travelled back to Edinburgh in silence with those same advisers.

The *Edinburgh Evening News* set the scene the following day with pictures of the First Minister squirming under the *Question Time* lights, and the morning papers followed the day after with a series of highly critical pieces about his performance and demands for answers about the other sub-lets and the money paid by the tenants.

On the afternoon of Friday 2 November, McLeish held a crisis meeting at Meridian Court, the Executive's city centre office block in Glasgow. Lesley Quinn, the Labour general secretary in Scotland, was there, as were McLaren, McTernan, MacMahon and Tom Little, another special adviser.

It was remarkable that, before that point, McLeish had not told even his closest advisers of all the details of his office expenses. But it was at this meeting that he finally brought the bundles of papers in plastic bags containing details of previous sub-lets. He told his aides there had been five sub-lets between 1988 and 2001, worth between £32,000 and £34,000, including the £9,000 from Digby Brown. The universal decision of the meeting was full disclosure, so the preparations were made to put everything in the public domain, in the hope that the controversy could be brought to an end at last.

That night McLeish went to a fund-raising dinner in honour of Sam Galbraith, his former ministerial colleague. He kept up the appearance of good humour, despite the turmoil he was in, telling guests he couldn't make a contribution to Galbraith's gift as he was 'a bit strapped for cash at the moment'.

The weekend of 3 and 4 November saw Team McLeish locked away inside Bute House. McLaren, McTernan, MacMahon and Little started preparing a media strategy while McLeish took a call from the Chancellor. Gordon Brown, McLeish's biggest supporter at Westminster, said the issue had been got up by the media and should be crushed. He suggested a senior accountant to help. The accountant arrived and McLeish retreated to the downstairs drawing room to work through the finances.

On the Saturday afternoon, McLeish's closest political allies, Jackie Baillie, Tom McCabe, Angus MacKay and Iain Gray, arrived for a political strategy meeting. By the time McLeish and his advisers broke for fish suppers on the Sunday night, they were convinced they had devised a strategy to see the First Minister through the crisis. McLeish would make a full statement to the press, through the broadcasters and then – on Alastair Campbell's advice from Downing Street – a full press conference, allowing journalists to ask everything they wanted about the affair. The plan was to publish all the details of all the five previous sub-lets, almost submerging the press in information in the hope that there would be no more questions to ask.*

Tuesday 6 November was chosen for the public disclosure and it was in his first interview, with the BBC's Brian Taylor, that McLeish came up with the soundbite which would define the scandal. 'There certainly was muddle, but there has been no fiddle,' he said. At the subsequent press conference, every member of the press was handed a bright yellow plastic folder containing details of all the sub-lets, and although McLeish faced questions for forty minutes on every aspect of his office arrangements and his approach, he managed to get through it relatively unscathed.

It started to look as if McLeish might survive the saga, but there was to be one final twist.

Tommy Sheridan, the leader of the Scottish Socialist Party, had been told that there had been a sixth sub-let of the office, one that McLeish had failed to mention in his 'full disclosure' press conference. Sheridan was due to ask questions about the sub-let, from Third Age, a charity working with elderly people, in the chamber the following day, but word leaked out to McLeish's aides, who then knew that the First Minister's career was virtually over. There was no way that he could hold such a public press conference, promising to reveal all the

---

* See MacMahon, 'Fall of a First Minister, parts 1a & 1b'.

details of the sub-lets, only for that promise to turn out to be untrue just hours later.

It was at that point, late on the night of Wednesday 7 November, that MacMahon rang Campbell to inform him that McLeish would almost certainly be resigning the following day. McLeish attended a formal Scottish rugby dinner that night, aware that his political career was all but over but insisting to aides that he still had not made up his mind about resigning.

The following morning found McLeish in Bute House. He had finally admitted to himself that he could not continue as First Minister and would have to resign ahead of a parliamentary debate on the Officegate saga. His lack of support on the Labour benches, which had been clear from the number of MSPs who had backed Jack McConnell in the leadership contest the year before, helped push him over the edge. Just when he needed the absolute, total and unequivocal backing of his MSPs, he didn't get it.

No-one from the Labour group forced him to go but the absence of a united parliamentary party backing his every move helped isolate the First Minister still further.

MacMahon rang Julie Fulton, McLeish's wife, who was at home in St Andrews, and she set off for Edinburgh to be with her husband. McLeish made his brief phone call to Tony Blair and then a longer one to Brown, who was more supportive and told the First Minister his loss was a 'tragedy'. A letter of resignation was drafted for the Queen and another for Sir David Steel, the Presiding Officer of the parliament. While this was going on, McLeish's Cabinet colleagues started arriving at Bute House, Wendy Alexander in tears and McConnell standing more aloof, receiving icy looks from McLeish's allies.

At 11 a.m., McCabe made his statement to the parliament, and shortly afterwards McLeish made his final statement as First Minister. He told MSPs:

> What is important is that I take full responsibility. Others who worked with and for me have been criticised, but the ultimate responsibility is mine and mine alone. I recognise the mistakes that I made. I came to parliament, and eventually to the office of First Minister, to serve my constituents and all the people of Scotland. If I

have let them down in this matter, I hope I have served them very well in many others.

He then left his desk at the front of the chamber and walked out of the door on the Presiding Officer's left, passing the Conservative benches. As the MSPs stood to applaud McLeish, David McLetchie held out his hand to the departing First Minister, but he was brushed away by an angry McCabe, who had positioned himself deliberately in front of the Tory benches to make sure that none of them could shake hands with McLeish.

Holding Julie's hand and his eyes red with tears, McLeish walked down the stone steps into the rear courtyard, past the imposing statue of John Knox, and into a waiting ministerial car. With that he was gone.

McLeish's claim that he was brought down by a 'muddle' and not a 'fiddle' was true, but only right at the end of the saga. The First Minister resigned because he had promised full disclosure and then was found not to have done that. He did not reveal the Third Age sub-let, not because he had anything to hide, but because he did not have the records to make it public. It was, in that sense, a simple mistake that ultimately cost him his job.

But if that had been all there was to the case, McLeish would have survived. His problem was the original decision to sub-let his constituency office, after claiming the whole rent from the taxpayer, without telling the Commons authorities. This was against the rules and McLeish ended up paying back £36,000 to the House of Commons Fees Office as a result of this dubious accounting practice. It hardly mattered that he did not benefit personally because the impression given to the public was that he was cheating the system.

McLeish's allies may claim that he was doing much the same as other MPs at the time in Westminster, and that may be true. Certainly Nigel Griffiths, the Labour MP for Edinburgh South, was caught doing something similar, if not much worse, just a month later, and he survived as an MP and went on to become a minister. Griffiths owned his Edinburgh office outright yet he was charging the Commons authorities £10,000 a year in rent for it and then channelling the money into a fund to help care for his autistic sister. He did not declare his ownership of the property in the register of members' interests, as he should have done, yet he escaped censure – despite being found guilty of breaching four Commons rules.

McLeish's problem was that he was held to a much higher standard of accountability by the Scottish Parliament press corps than his colleagues were at Westminster. At the time of McLeish's resignation, there were probably between thirty-five and forty-five journalists working in the Scottish Parliament, covering the business of 129 MSPs. At Westminster, there were more than 650 MPs, reported on by maybe 100 or so regular journalists. Also, the Scottish Parliament's day-to-day business was not nearly as sweeping or as important as Westminster's, leaving the journalists there with the time to chase down expense claims which would not have even been bothered with in London. Added to this was the sense that the Scottish Parliament should be held to a higher standard of public service than its counter-part on the Thames, particularly as the days of so-called 'Tory sleaze' in the final years of the Major government were still fresh in the memory of the press and the public. McLeish could count himself unlucky that all these factors combined to place intolerable pressure on him over this one issue, but he did break the Commons rules and it was ultimately that which brought an end to his career.

It can sometimes seem insensitive to those outside politics how the waters can close over a political casualty so quickly after a resignation and business goes on as normal almost immediately. This was certainly the case with McLeish. Even as his ministerial car was being driven slowly out of the courtyard of the Assembly Hall, his colleagues were moving towards a replacement. But this, as with almost everything in Scottish Labour politics, would prove to be far from straightforward.

7

Strangers on a train

THE regular shuttle trains between Edinburgh and Glasgow are always full at rush hour, as was the case one evening in late September 1997 when John Clement was travelling through to the west.

Clement was a surveyor and a property fixer. His job was to know the commercial property market intimately so he could match clients to suitable accommodation. That warm and muggy evening, Clement had to stand and found himself squeezed in next to a couple of men in suits he didn't know. As the train pushed on towards Glasgow, it became clear that one of them was a senior civil servant in the Scottish Office who had been tasked with finding a suitable site for the prestige new building to house the Scottish Parliament.

'They were bleating on about all the problems they were having,' Clement said later, so he intervened, introducing himself and asking the civil servant, Anthony Andrew, whether he had considered the old Holyrood brewery site, opposite the Palace of Holyroodhouse, as a potential location for the new parliament building.

Clement had the brewers Scottish and Newcastle as a client. He knew the company was privately considering moving its headquarters away from the old Holyrood brewery but would do so only if the site could be put to good use. 'In my mind, the site got a tick in every box,' he said.

Andrew took the suggestion seriously and put Holyrood into the mix with the other potential capital sites already under discussion. However, what neither of them knew was that Clement's chance meeting with Andrew had started a process which would end in the most controversial and expensive public building project in Scottish history, an eight-month public inquiry and a saga so damaging it eroded public faith in devolution itself.

In many ways, it was a typically Scottish establishment tale. Almost everyone in the Central Belt is so familiar with the Edinburgh–Glasgow shuttle trains that they have probably met someone they know or been introduced to a new acquaintance on those frequent 45-minute journeys. So it seems somehow appropriate that Scotland's most infamous building project should start in such a way.

At this stage, Labour had been in power at Westminster for only a matter of months, Donald Dewar was Scottish secretary and there were no new Scottish parliamentarians whose views he had to consider. Anyway, Dewar believed it was his job to take such an important decision as the site for the new parliament, and, as far as he was concerned, there were problems with each of the other potential venues, Calton Hill, Haymarket and Leith.* So, when presented with the option of Holyrood, after Clement's chance intervention in September 1997, Dewar leapt at it. Symbolically, it was just what he wanted. It was a brownfield site, so it could be developed into something new and unique; it was positioned between the royal palace and the law courts, which appealed to Dewar's sense of place and constitution; and it was at the end of the Royal Mile, right in the heart of historic Edinburgh.

As Clement had observed, it did indeed 'tick all the boxes'. The then Scottish secretary thought he was simply choosing a site but, as later events would demonstrate, the choice of a venue for the new parliament would prove to be absolutely crucial to the way that the problems and costs spiralled.

Henry McLeish, then a Scottish Office minister, appeared to be the only one in the Dewar entourage to urge caution. He wrote a memo suggesting the renovation of the old Royal High School building on Calton Hill as a temporary site, spending as little as possible but allowing the new parliamentarians to move in there first and then make a decision on a permanent building at a later date. This rather prescient advice was ignored by Dewar, who was determined to do all he could to bequeath a parliament to the new MSPs when they were elected.

---

* Calton Hill was seen by some in Labour as a 'Nationalist icon' and was favoured by the SNP; the Haymarket site was too small; Leith was considered too far away from the centre of Edinburgh.

Secret negotiations with Scottish and Newcastle went well enough for Holyrood to be unveiled as the home of the new parliament in January 1998. Holyrood had not been tested as the other sites had been – there had not been enough time – but, as far as Dewar was concerned, there was no contest: it was a done deal.

At this point, Dewar was still sticking by the cost estimates which had appeared in the devolution white paper the previous summer, that a new-build parliament would cost between £10 million and £40 million. This was more than slightly misleading, even then. The £10 million bottom line had been included on the advice of Wendy Alexander, then a special adviser to Dewar, as the initial public cost if the building was constructed under the Private Finance Initiative (PFI), a private-build, public-lease system. Alexander later admitted that Dewar had rejected the PFI route fairly early on because he did not want there to be any confusion as to who owned the building, the contractor or the Scottish people. The £40 million figure was also a serious underestimate, but that also was allowed to stand unchanged in all official releases through the back end of 1997 and the early part of 1998, principally because Dewar did not want to scare the electorate with suggestions that the building might cost a substantial amount of public money.

Had Dewar been honest and realistic, he would have put a proper estimate on the building project of at least £100 million. That would have caused a few waves at the time but the country was then still strongly behind Dewar and the devolution project, and such an admission would have been manageable. Instead, Dewar and his officials tried to massage the figures to make the whole endeavour seem as affordable as possible.

There was little, though, that anyone outside the Scottish Office could do about it at this stage. The first key decision, to choose Holyrood as the site, had been taken by Dewar. The cost estimates were already being forced downwards to an unrealistic level and there was a clear demand for speed over cost among those tasked with driving the project forward. Alastair Wyllie, a senior official in the building division of the Scottish Office at the time, said later:

> With the announcement having been made about the Holyrood site, the message was going out fairly clearly that ministers were

determined to get started right away. They felt they wanted to keep
the momentum going. Devolution having been achieved, there was
a feeling that they wanted to see that turned into something tangible.

However, Dewar took two other, crucial, decisions around this
time which set in train the process that was to cause so much
heartache for Scottish ministers for years to come. Both were done
to maximise speed and both were responsible for letting the costs
shoot skywards. The first was to hold a contest to choose a designer,
instead of putting the project out to the usual sort of tender process
normally associated with public buildings, and the second was to opt
for a risky style of construction management which allowed the
building work to begin before the final designs had been agreed.

Dewar had been taken by the idea of having a competition to
choose a designer from the moment he was given control of the
Scottish Office in May 1997. He wanted the world's best architects
to compete to build the new Scottish Parliament, giving him the
chance of picking the one who would do the best job. Experts,
however, urged caution. Dr John Gibbons, the Scottish Office's chief
architect, even used the perfect *Yes, Minister* warning of telling Dewar
he would be taking a 'courageous' decision if he had a competition
for a designer, rather than a design.

The issue was simple as far as Gibbons was concerned: putting the
contract out to tender in the normal way would attract fully formed,
designed and costed options. The best and most economically
advantageous one could then be chosen. Gibbons said later:

> There are many significant examples of projects which have gone
> considerably over budget or have been delayed, projects of all sorts,
> but particularly parliament buildings. The most recent example was
> one that had been completed in the previous year in The Hague,
> where an architectural competition started as a two-to-three-year
> exercise and turned into a twelve-year exercise.
>
> His [Dewar's] reaction to my concerns about controversy was
> that he was used to controversy and it was not necessarily a bad
> thing in the context of a re-emerging country. I was given a little
> bit of a lecture that if that was a reason I was putting forward, 'don't'.

Dewar then went even further, ignoring European Union guide-lines by putting himself on the panel choosing the architect. The guidelines were clear: the panel should be 'independent of the client' (in this case the Scottish Office) but, by the time Dewar had decided on the panel, half of the six members came from the Scottish Office.

The designer-judging panel met for the first time in March 1998 to assess seventy applications from around the world. Designing the new Scottish Parliament would be a prestigious commission for any firm of architects and interest was high.

One of the applications came from Enric Miralles, a maverick, eccentric but also brilliant Spanish architect. Bill Armstrong, an expert architectural adviser who was asked to rank the applications, did not think Miralles merited a place on the shortlist; in fact he put him down in forty-fourth place. Armstrong did not believe he had the resources for the job and would not commit enough time to it. But he found himself overruled by Dewar, who was taken by Miralles and raised him up to a position on the final shortlist.

The shortlisted applicants were Miralles, the respected New York architect Rafael Viñoly, the London-based Michael Wilford and Partners, the American Richard Meier and the Australian firm Denton Corker Marshall. However, if the rules had been adhered to, Miralles should never have even got that far.

Treasury rules stipulated that every firm entering the competition had to show it possessed professional indemnity insurance cover of £5 million. It only emerged later that Miralles had no cover what-soever, that his indemnity insurance had expired, but no-one appeared to notice this at the Scottish Office. It is not known whether Dewar approved such bending of the rules but he was clearly enthused by Miralles when he came to make a presentation to the panel, as the idiosyncratic Spanish architect scattered twigs and leaf stems across a board to show how he wanted his design to blend in with the landscape of Holyrood Park, before explaining his concept of upturned boats. Miralles had seen fishing boats turned upside down and used as fishermen's huts on Lindisfarne, an island off the north-east coast of England, some years previously and believed them to be quintessentially Scottish. He wanted the parliament to carry that character and shape throughout, as well as spreading out into the park.

Having bent the rules over Miralles's insurance, the panel then ignored clear guidelines again when they appointed the Spanish architect without checking his demand for fees.

When deciding from a shortlist, a designer panel should open all the sealed envelopes from the bidders containing their fee requirements, so a cost evaluation can be done of all of them. Dewar's panel failed to do this. Miralles's sealed envelope was opened, revealing a demand for a percentage of the final cost of the parliament as his fee. His request came within the range agreed by the panel beforehand so Miralles was confirmed as the winner without any consideration of the other fee requests. Under EU rules, the Scottish Office had to choose the 'economically most advantageous' tender but, by failing to look at the other fee requests, the panel had no way of knowing how the costs of the different bids would compare.

Rules had been bent and clear guidelines had been ignored but Dewar had the site he wanted, Holyrood, he had the architect he wanted, Miralles, and all he wanted now was for the building to be completed as soon as possible, to capitalise on the goodwill of the people towards the devolution settlement. There was only one piece of the jigsaw left to find before work could start on preparing the ground at Holyrood for the new parliament: the main building contract had to be awarded. That was where the problems really started.

By the start of December 1998, the applicants had been whittled down to a shortlist of four, including Bovis and Sir Robert McAlpine. When the formal selection panel of civil servants and architects opened the four sealed bids on 2 December, it found that the Bovis tender was the second most expensive, at nearly £1 million more than the McAlpine bid. Furthermore, Bovis demanded 1¼ per cent of the budget in fees, compared to McAlpine's 1 per cent. Bovis also demanded another 1 per cent of the budget to provide a 'parent company guarantee', a document which would guarantee the company's ability to finish the project.

Bovis was then dropped from the contest, as Armstrong, now the project manager, believed it should have been. But then something happened behind the scenes and it was mysteriously reinstated by Barbara Doig, the civil servant in charge of the tendering process, on 15 December.

Armstrong was worried about the decision. 'I believed it was entirely wrong,' he said later, adding: 'Under the procurement laws as I understand it, and the Scottish Office's own building directive, once you get the four tenders and you are agreed that they are all able to do the job and you open the tenders, then you are duty bound to take the lowest tender.'

Armstrong was under severe strain at this stage because of problems with Miralles. The project had been delayed by a month in its first seven weeks, it had slipped eight weeks in its first twenty-two and by April 1999, nine months from its inception, it would already be three months late. Much of this was down to delays in Barcelona, where Miralles was working on the design. Armstrong was sending his superiors, including Doig, monthly warnings of increasing delays, particularly as everyone was aware of Dewar's demand for speed.

Miralles had promised to base himself in Edinburgh to design the building, but he stayed in Spain. He failed to provide design drawings on time and everything was held up as a result. 'We were two months into the architect's appointment and, at that point, there was virtually no information coming forward so we were in the dark,' Armstrong said later.

Armstrong's monthly reports were becoming depressingly monotonous. 'It became a situation where I was continually reporting bad news. When you continually report bad news, you become associated with it. There was a feeling in the Scottish Office, among some of the hierarchy, that maybe if I went, the bad news would go as well,' he said. The problems with Miralles pushed him to the edge and the extraordinary decision to bring Bovis back into the tender process for the building project took him over it. Armstrong resigned as Holyrood's first project manager at the end of 1998.

In one of his final memos to his managers, Armstrong warned of a looming disaster with remarkable foresight: 'A stand must be taken to either bring Miralles to heel or to accept his inadequacies – he doesn't believe he has any. The programme will drift, the costs will increase, the design team will make claims, the contractors will make claims and the project will become a disaster.'

Doig, a long-term civil servant who had spent most of her career as a researcher with little building or contract-managing experience, was by now the 'project sponsor', the official in charge of the building.

Relations between her and Armstrong had deteriorated to such an extent by the time he quit that he simply pinned a note on her door saying 'Bye' before walking out. Doig was in the midst of the final stages of the main building contract tender at this stage and neglected for another month to tell ministers that the project manager had gone. 'I didn't think it was necessary to do so,' she said later.

There was clearly now a breach in communication between the people in the mounting chaos on the ground and ministers in their offices, shown by a parliamentary answer published by Henry McLeish in January 1999 in which he claimed the project was 'still on cost and on schedule', at £50 million. That month also saw new negotiations with Bovis over the building contract, something that appeared to be clearly against the rules. A Scottish Office directorate from 1993 stated clearly that post-tender negotiations were permitted only if they did not discriminate against other tenders. Officials could have brought all the shortlisted firms in and asked them to lower their tenders, but not just one.

The late discussions with Bovis resulted in the company dropping its insistence on a parent company guarantee. So, in mid-January 1999, Bovis was awarded the contract to build the Holyrood parliament. Doig announced the decision in a memo to colleagues saying, in a curious remark which raised more questions than it answered, that she had recently become aware of Bovis's 'commitment to the Scottish Office as a client'. McAlpine, which had tendered the lowest bid, bided its time and then, after the Holyrood parliament was finally completed in 2004, announced it was suing the Scottish Parliament for breaching EU tendering laws.

That though, was a long way away when the delighted first batch of eager MSPs were elected in May 1999. One month later the Scottish Office formally handed over the Scottish Parliament building project at Holyrood to the parliamentarians. They were keen to get their hands on it and sculpt it for their needs. But, in retrospect, it is difficult to see how it could possibly have been in a worse state at this time.

The site was not universally popular and was already proving to be too small, constraining the demands placed on it. Guidelines had been ignored and rules broken in the appointment of the designer, EU regulations had been flouted in the award of the main building contract, a legal suit was pending and the lead architect was not keeping to anything like the agreed schedule for drawings and designs. On top of that, the project manager had resigned, the project sponsor was failing to pass on information, particularly on cost over-runs, to ministers, and the lead politician, the secretary of state, was demanding speed at the expense of everything else, including cost.

The public pronouncements, however, were still glowing, packed with claims that the project was proceeding smoothly, on budget and on schedule when it was anything but. The parliamentarians, still coming to terms with new jobs and a new democratic system, had no idea what they were about to take on.

By this time, the official cost estimate had risen to £109 million, substantially more than the figure of £50 million or so which ministers had still been quoting earlier that year, but not so high as to spark any sort of proper public backlash. However, the project still needed parliamentary backing and so, as soon as the parliament was given control over the project, MSPs were asked to give their formal support to it.

The debate and vote on 17 June 1999 were fraught and tight. The SNP objected to the scheme, believing it to be a foolish waste of money. The Conservatives also objected to it, as did some Liberal Democrats, but the weight of the Scottish Executive coalition proved strong enough, just, to give the project the official green light – by three votes.

Dewar told MSPs that both he and the parliamentary authorities would hold to that figure of £109 million 'to the best of our ability' and that it included everything from VAT to fit-out costs. What nobody inside the chamber knew at the time was that they were being misled. The official cost estimates had already smashed past the £109 million mark and were at £130 million, and maybe more, at that time, but the MSPs had not been told. Dewar, who led the debate in favour of the project, was castigated later by opposition politicians for withholding vital information from the parliament, but even he did not know. His civil servants had not kept him informed.

The three civil servants responsible were Robert Gordon, who was head of the Scottish Office Secretariat at the time, Doig, the project sponsor and the closest public official to the project, and

Sir Muir Russell, then the permanent secretary at the Scottish Executive. Gordon later tried to defend his decision not to pass on the full cost estimates to Dewar, telling the subsequent inquiry: 'They were not costs that had to be met but risks that had to be dealt with.' Doig said she and her team had taken a 'management decision' not to pass on the cost estimates to ministers. Meanwhile Russell said that, although the cost estimates had been 'calculated to a high degree of accuracy', he did not believe them so he did not pass them on. He added that it would have been a 'distraction' to give them to ministers. John Campbell QC, counsel to the 2003 Holyrood inquiry, which was set up to investigate the mess that the project had become, was so concerned by Russell's failure to justify the decision that he described the permanent secretary's explanation as 'contradictory' and 'anomalous'.

The new estimate of £130 million had been prepared by professional cost consultants brought in to do exactly what they were supposed to do, provide accurate cost projections for the work. They had set aside £15.86 million to cover potential risks associated with the ongoing work, but this was simply erased from the report before it went to ministers. Fergus Ewing, an SNP MSP and a persistent critic of the project, told the inquiry that he blamed the 'secrecy and also the incompetence and chicanery of the top mandarins'. And he added: 'If MSPs had known the truth, then perhaps even a handful of Labour MSPs might have had the backbone to say "no".'

When the first evidence that civil servants had withheld crucial information from Dewar ahead of the vote was revealed in 2000, in a report into the project by architect John Spencely, Dewar stood by all his officials and refused to sack or discipline any of them. But the withholding of such important information was to prove crucial in the development of the building. Had just two MSPs switched sides for that vote, or three abstained, then the project would have been halted at that early stage, at least for a rethink.

With the Spencely report coming out in early 2000, MSPs were then given a second chance to vote on the project. By this time, the cost estimates had risen to £195 million. But, if anything, the MSPs were in an even more difficult position this time round. They could support a project which was already way over budget and behind schedule and accept assurances that the costs would not rise much further, or they could heed the warnings of experts who claimed the project would cost more and more and pull the plug, costing the taxpayer about £100 million. Once again most MSPs decided to have faith in the assurances made by Dewar, this time voting to push ahead with the building by a majority of nine, but this time making their support conditional on a cost cap of £195 million on the building. 'The firm budget of £195 million and the completion date of the end of 2002 will, I expect, be adhered to,' Dewar declared during the debate.

During this second debate, there was more of a feeling that it would be almost as much folly to stop as to go on, simply because so much work had already gone into the site and the design. But again, real and important information was being withheld from MSPs. Hugh Fisher, from cost consultants Davis Langdon and Everest, was in charge of producing cost estimates for the project right through the building period. At the time of the 2000 debate, he had prepared an estimate which forecast a construction cost of £118 million and an overall cost of £230 million – well above the £195 million cap which the MSPs were voting on. Fisher revealed to the Holyrood inquiry later that the figures given to MSPs, in both 1999 and 2000, had been massaged for 'political reasons'.

The Holyrood project had many trenchant critics because for many outside the parliament, the troubled building site had come to symbolise all that was wrong with devolution. The Scottish Parliament had been set up on a wave of public enthusiasm but many of the social and political aspirations were simply unachievable.

There were bound to be disappointments as the MSPs struggled to come to terms with their new roles and this disillusionment found an outlet in the Holyrood project. It became the most controversial, talked-about and criticised building project in Scottish history and the MSPs – as well as devolution itself – were blamed. There were others, though, who were far more supportive and who backed Dewar's vision of a modern, architectural icon for the new Scotland – but their number was decreasing by the week.

The costs were rising inexorably. At every revised estimate, politicians and officials would announce themselves appalled and all would vow to keep the latest cost rise as the last. This went on until, in the run-up to the election campaign of 2003, the cost hit

£400 million. At that point, Jack McConnell, then the First Minister, decided he had to distance himself, the parliament and the Scottish Executive from the furore so he commissioned a public inquiry to investigate the whole project.

So what had gone wrong?

James Simpson, one of the UK's leading conservationist architects, summed it up as 'a self-indulgent folly driven by short-term political interests and the stubbornness of a small number of individuals'. In some ways he was right but there were also clear and interrelated reasons why the cost kept going up. The first problem was a lack of communication.

A clear example of this came in the design for the debating chamber. MSPs wanted a horseshoe shape, similar to the one they were using in their temporary home at the top of the Royal Mile. Instead, Enric Miralles designed a lecture theatre shape, with a podium and benches at the front for ministers, like many European parliament chambers. Sir David Steel, the Presiding Officer of the parliament, was shocked when he saw the Miralles design but by then it was too late to do anything but 'tweak' the design because the footprint of the building had been designed around it. Steel persuaded Miralles to bring the seats round into as much of a horse-shoe shape as possible, bringing it from a slight curve to a curl, but it was impossible to do any more.

Miralles was a brilliant conceptual designer but he was an erratic worker and did not cope well with the constant demands, first for designs and models and also for numerous changes. On one occasion, when faced with a request for better design information, Miralles sent over a letter which contained lines starting in odd places, phrases in all sorts of different orders and a doodle of four hands, two partly closed and two open – it was not hard to see why those at the Edinburgh end had difficulty working with him.

Another key aspect which forced the costs up and led to delays was the demand for extra space. The Holyrood site was constrained on all sides by roads and buildings. Miralles had initially been asked for a building of about 16,000 square metres. By the time the design was complete, that had almost doubled to 30,000 square metres. Miralles was asked to build in more rooms, more office accommo-dation and more facilities. His original design was for a sweeping set of 'upturned boats', convex shapes with ellipses in a series of mounds. But having to build in more space, all he could do was build upwards, so the upturned boats still remained, but they were placed at the top of towers, rather than being close to the ground, as Miralles intended. The Catalan architect had envisaged something iconic and groundbreaking but the compromises he was forced to make to his original design eroded this initial concept. The shapes remained, but the building ended up being much more bitty and disjointed than he had imagined.

Miralles was also determined that the elongated curve, which he took as the signature of the new building, should be a feature of the whole site. Because of this, nothing could be bought 'off the peg' for the parliament. Absolutely everything, from the windows in the MSPs' block to the roof panels in the committee rooms, had to be made to order. This pushed up the cost considerably, particularly when changes were made after initial designs had been agreed and worked on.

Another major problem was the demand for speed; Dewar wanted the parliament finished as soon as possible. Because of the timetable demands, a large number of packages had to be put out to tender and agreed before they had been accurately drawn up by the architects. On site, this meant builders standing around idle, unable to work on the package they had been hired for because of delays further up the system.

For costs, all Bovis had to go on were the estimates from Davis Langdon and Everest, but these often ended up being hopelessly inaccurate because all they could use was rough guesswork from straightforward buildings elsewhere. The cost consultants had priced the steel works in the main chamber at roughly £2,000 per tonne, well above the £600 per tonne it would cost in a simple building, but even this was woefully inadequate for Holyrood, where the final bill was nearer £4,000 per tonne. One package, for the concrete frame for the debating chamber, ended up costing £30 million, almost as much as the original construction cost estimate for the whole building. Alan Mack, the Bovis project director, told the Holyrood inquiry in 2004 how his team had been forced to constantly rescope, review, reassess and remodel the project because of the thousands of changes being demanded by the client and the architect, and each change cost both time and money. One estimate put the total financial impact of contracts commissioned but delayed at £90 million by the time the project was completed.

By the time the building was finished, there had been more than 15,000 design changes, a clear indication of one of the central problems. Compounding these problems was the deteriorating relationship between the two arms of the architectural conglomerate put together to design the building. Miralles was the lead designer but his firm, EMBT, had formed an alliance with the big Edinburgh architectural practice RMJM for the duration of the project. RMJM understood the demands for speed and efficiency and the importance of keeping the client informed. But, almost as soon as the partnership formed, it started to go wrong with RMJM putting pressure on EMBT for designs, which then failed to materialise or turned up late or not as envisaged.

Then both sides had to cope with the unexpected death of Miralles in May 2000, after unsuccessful treatment for a brain tumour in the United States. Despite assurances that the death of the lead architect would not affect the project unduly, because most of the designs had been done by that stage, there was no disguising the sense of crisis that Miralles's death caused. His widow, Benedetta Tagliabue, also an architect and his partner in EMBT, took over in his stead and the project continued. But when Miralles's death was followed just three months later by that of Dewar, the politician who had done more than anyone to drive the Holyrood option forward, the building project had lost its two greatest proponents and appeared to be rudderless, at the very least, and possibly even about to implode.

Brian Stewart, the lead architect from RMJM, told the Holyrood inquiry how bad the situation had become. 'To ask a body of this nature [the parliament] to procure a building is a nightmare. It is truly a nightmare,' he said. 'I would never do a parliament building again even if I was ever asked. I think it's an impossible thing to deliver.'

Stewart described the ways in which he had to deal with various parliamentary groups as 'Byzantine' and said this was the primary reason for 'delays, conflicts, excuses and, importantly, cost increases'. He also suggested that the politicians were equally keen to avoid the blame when things went wrong: 'With so many masters, many with different axes to grind, it has been at times difficult indeed for the design team to work out a way ahead. "It wisnae me" has become something of a catchphrase.'

Slowly, primarily through the work of George Reid after he became Presiding Officer in 2003, the delays and the cost overruns eased and the project neared completion. Reid did his best to force better and more efficient work from the contractors and he achieved a considerable coup when he persuaded the consultants to cap their fees. But he was helped by the stage the project had then reached. As it neared completion, there were fewer variables. It was simply easier to keep work on time and on budget. There were still hiccups, such as when it emerged in early 2003 that £88,000 was going to be spent on a desk for the reception area, but the parliamentarians eventually moved in over the summer of 2004 with the official royal opening by the Queen on 9 October.

Reid sensibly kept the costs of the royal opening down to the minimum, spending just £210,000 rather than the £1 million spent on the royal opening in 1999, which had included a flypast by the Red Arrows and free concerts.

So, six years after it was unveiled as the site, the Holyrood building was complete, inhabited and working as a parliament. It had cost £413 million to build, ten times the original estimates, and was delivered three years late. It was the subject of two investigations by the auditor general and one by the EU, and was the subject of an eight-month public inquiry, led by Lord Fraser of Carmyllie. That inquiry cost another £1 million but at last the MSPs felt they could start to put the damaging controversy behind them. But it wasn't over quite yet.

On the morning of 2 March 2006, one of the mighty oak beams supporting the complicated roof of the debating chamber swung loose from one end. The strut was left hanging, suspended over the Conservative benches as the chamber was evacuated. The problem was traced to a broken bolt and shoddy workmanship but Reid and his staff realised they could not risk any similar problems. Had the beam actually fallen down, there is no doubt it would have caused serious injuries so every beam, metal support and fastening in the roof had to be checked. The temporary repairs took three weeks, forcing MSPs to spend £400,000 moving to a short-term home at the Hub, a brightly painted former church at the top end of the Royal Mile, and repairing the damage. It was embarrassing for the parliamentary authorities, the builders and the MSPs but eventually the repair work was done and the MSPs moved back in, even if there was more than the odd nervous glance at the roof above them.

At that point, there was only one outstanding issue to be resolved, the legal suit by McAlpine, the building firm which had tendered the lowest bid for the main contract but which had mysteriously been passed over in favour of Bovis. On 5 January 2006 it emerged that McAlpine had dropped the suit after coming to an arrangement with the parliamentary authorities, leaving the parliament and, more pertinently, the civil servants, in the clear.

The Holyrood building still had the capacity to divide. It won the prestigious Stirling Prize in 2005 as the building making the biggest contribution to British architecture that year, but many ordinary Scots felt it was not as breathtaking as it should have been, particularly given the price they paid for it. Architects marvelled at the difficult structures, the lack of straight lines and the way curves and ellipses were built into every facet. Indeed, by 2009 and the tenth anniversary of devolution, it was certainly growing into the landscape but there were few who regarded it as emblematic in the same way as the Sydney Opera House or the Guggenheim Museum in Bilbao.

Miralles started with a vision but it wasn't long before that was corroded by demands from the politicians for changes and more space. Fraser concluded his inquiry by blaming everybody and blaming nobody. He criticised politicians, the architects, civil servants and project managers in general but refused to single out anybody in particular to take responsibility. John Campbell, the counsel for the inquiry, summed this up when he said of the blame game: 'This is like a game of pass the parcel: no-one wants to be holding it when the music stops.' As a result, a few individuals have had their careers dented, but nobody has ended up being ruined by the fiasco.

Sir Muir Russell, the head of the Scottish Office and the Scottish Executive when key decisions were taken, went on to become principal of Glasgow University. Robert Gordon, who was the next closest to the project, moved to other, senior jobs in the civil service and although Barbara Doig retired early from the civil service, she did not appear to suffer unduly despite the serious problems that arose on her watch. Also, the MSPs on the two bodies tasked with supervising the project, the Holyrood Project Group and the Scottish Parliament Corporate Body, who did such a bad job of keeping control over it, mostly remained in politics and in the Scottish Parliament.

The project did take its toll on the architects. John Gibbons retired and came back only to act as an occasional adviser for the parliament. The strain and stress eventually took their toll on Brian Stewart, who quit RMJM and took early retirement. Enric Miralles was dead, as was Donald Dewar, but, ten years on, Benedetta Tagliabue was still thriving. The fees from the Holyrood project had helped her grow her business, in the same way that other consultants – however bruised they may have been during the building process – found at least some compensation in the percentage cuts they took from such a massively expensive project.

Slowly, the building started losing the epithet 'controversial' and headline writers stopped using the terms 'fiasco' and 'scandal' when describing it. By 2009, it had become what Miralles and Dewar hoped it would be, a new, modern, state-of-the-art home for Scotland's nascent democratic institution. What everyone involved in the project was agreed on, though, was the profound regret that it should have had such a painful, expensive and time-consuming birth.

8

Lucky Jack?

NO-ONE would expect a politician to launch a leadership bid by confessing to an extra-marital affair, but that is exactly what Jack McConnell did. On 13 November 2001, just five days after the resignation of Henry McLeish, McConnell insisted to a packed press conference in Edinburgh's Macdonald Holyrood Hotel that he was the right person to take charge of the battered Scottish Labour Party. He also admitted he had cheated on his wife Bridget seven years before.

McConnell had challenged McLeish for the leadership of the Labour group in the Scottish Parliament in 2000, following the death of Donald Dewar. He had come much closer than anyone expected to beating McLeish at that time so was the clear frontrunner to lead both the Scottish Labour parliamentary group and the Scottish Executive after McLeish's resignation. The 41-year-old McConnell had also done well as education minister in McLeish's brief administration.

A former general secretary of the Scottish Labour Party, McConnell was relatively small in stature with dark, swept-back hair and a sharp sense of dress. He was known as a charmer, a fixer and a devious politician with a reputation for briefing behind the backs of his colleagues. He had acquired this reputation while he was general secretary in the early 1990s and it was at this time that he met Maureen Smith, then a party press officer. McConnell and Smith had had an on–off affair in 1993 and 1994 but it finished when McConnell refused to leave his wife Bridget.

Bridget McConnell, a high-powered official at Glasgow City Council, had known about the affair since 1994 and while there were persistent rumours in the press and around the Labour Party, the affair had never been made public. Jack McConnell had thought about confessing all when he stood against McLeish in 2000 but decided against it. When he stood in 2001, and when it became clear that he would be all but guaranteed the job of First Minister, whispers about the affair became louder and more intense.

The crunch came when the *Daily Record* sent a thinly veiled message to McConnell in a leader which warned that candidates for the Scottish Labour leadership would be examined 'in minute detail'. 'If there are skeletons, we will find them,' said the paper. McConnell knew what that meant so, to spike the *Record*'s attempts to intimidate him, he decided to go public with his affair at a press conference. But, in what appeared to be a deliberate ploy to get at the *Record*, his aides let the *Sun* (the *Record*'s bitter rival) know beforehand what the press conference would be about.

So, on 13 November 2001, Jack and Bridget McConnell sat at the press conference in the Macdonald Hotel, side by side, each of them stony faced and grim, to announce details of Jack McConnell's infidelity. By that time, word had spread throughout the political village and the story was not just in the *Sun*. The broad theme of the affair – if not the details – had appeared in almost every newspaper that morning. The press conference was a tough event for both of them but tougher still were the tabloid stories the following day, which dubbed the affair 'Trousergate' and revealed as many lurid details as possible. But the disclosure tactic seemed to work, at least as far as the leadership campaign was concerned. McConnell's relations with the Labour-supporting *Daily Record* did take longer to mend, though.

The media frenzy over the affair itself blew itself out over a couple of days and McConnell was soon confirmed, both as leader of the Labour group in the Scottish Parliament and as Scotland's third First Minister. His election had been uncontested – but only just.

When McLeish resigned on 8 November, it looked as though Labour would have a proper, contested election between McConnell and Wendy Alexander, the 38-year-old Brownite rising star of the Scottish party. Alexander spent the first few days after McLeish's departure bringing a campaign team together and putting out as many feelers as possible to test the views of the party. She had the support of Gordon Brown, the Chancellor, but crucially, she lacked the backing of the unions, most of which made clear to her they were supporting McConnell.

After days of allowing speculation about a leadership challenge to gather pace, Alexander retreated and decided not to stand, leaving behind considerable resentment among her colleagues, particularly those who had gone public on her behalf and who were left stranded when she decided not to contest an election against McConnell. A possible left-wing challenge, from either Cathy Jamieson or John McAllion with the support of the Campaign for Socialism, also petered out, leaving McConnell as the sole candidate. He took the Scottish party leadership on Saturday 17 November and was sworn in as First Minister ten days later, on 27 November.

When he took control of the Scottish Labour Party, McConnell announced that he would not indulge in a 'night of the long knives' and insisted that there had to be an end to factionalism. But those who had backed Alexander's candidacy and feared retribution were right. McConnell's first move was to remove as many Alexander allies as possible from the Cabinet, replacing them with his own supporters. In one ruthless act, which became known in the press as either the Night of the Long Dirks* or The Day of the Jackolites, McConnell purged a third of the McLeish Cabinet on the day he officially took power as the head of the Scottish Executive.

On the morning of Tuesday 27 November, before he had even been sworn in as First Minister, McConnell summoned a succession of Cabinet ministers to his office on the top floor of the MSPs' block on the Royal Mile. Angus MacKay, McLeish's finance minister, was the first to arrive. He was told, abruptly, that his services would no longer be needed. MacKay told McConnell he wanted it to be known that he had been sacked and not resigned. McConnell agreed and ordered his letter of dismissal to be drawn up by officials. Jackie Baillie, the social justice minister, was next, followed by Tom McCabe, the parliament minister, and Sarah Boyack, the transport minister. All suffered the same fate as MacKay. Susan Deacon, the health minister, went after she refused to accept 'demotion' to the role of social justice minister. Scotland's solicitor general, Neil

---

* A dirk is a long traditional Scottish dagger.

Davidson, also resigned, claiming in public that it was because his role was being changed but making it clear in private that he felt he could not continue under the new regime.

McConnell replaced these McLeish appointees with his own allies, bringing in his leadership campaign organiser, Andy Kerr, as the new finance and public services minister, Jamieson as education minister and Lord Watson of Invergowrie, who had piloted the hunting bill through the parliament, was brought in to the tourism, sport and arts brief. Tricia Ferguson, who had organised McConnell's first leadership challenge, in 2000, was rewarded with the influential position of minister for parliamentary business, a role which meant she had to act as the First Minister's link with the parliament and the Labour MSPs. As one Labour MSP said afterwards: 'He promised not to have a Night of the Long Knives and he kept his word – this was done in broad daylight.'

The only Labour minister to remain in post through the change from McLeish to McConnell was Alexander. However, she was 'rewarded' by being given such a large and formidable brief that no-one really expected her to be able to handle it. Alexander was put in charge of enterprise, lifelong learning, transport and planning.

McConnell's final task that day was to address Labour MSPs at the Quaker Meeting House right at the top of the Royal Mile. The atmosphere was tense, with the former Cabinet ministers all present and sitting in silence as McConnell said: 'I want to tell both sides of the party.' Then he stopped and started again: 'I don't want to talk about sides. I want to end the factionalism and lead a united party.' One MSP said that Alexander had sat so still and silent throughout McConnell's address that 'she hardly breathed'.

McConnell had set out to do two things – assert his authority on the administration and reduce Brown's influence in Scottish politics. He achieved both with a ruthlessness few saw coming.

Political parties are, by their very nature, never uniform; they include various shades of political opinion and, more destructively, volatile mixtures of personality, some of whom get on and some of whom don't. This inevitably leads to some form of factionalism and leaders have a choice of trying to be inclusive, choosing a 'ministry of all the talents', or just rewarding their allies and exiling their opponents. McConnell chose the latter route and while that would make his time in government easier to manage on a day-to-day basis, it would also leave a disgruntled set of former ministers on the Labour back benches – the real shadow Cabinet, as one Labour MSP described them – but that was something that McConnell had clearly decided he could live with.

The first manifestation of this new, divided, Labour group came just two days later when McConnell tried to control the election of the deputy Presiding Officer to the Scottish Parliament, attempting to get Labour MSP Cathy Peattie the job. But this was one contest he could not control because the election of all three Presiding Officers is done by secret ballot. This meant angry Labour MSPs could vote against McConnell's chosen candidate with impunity, which is what they did. The depth of resentment among some Labour MSPs at McConnell's efforts to control the election was shown by the fact that they were prepared to vote for a Tory, Murray Tosh, rather than back McConnell's chosen candidate. Tosh was elected and although it was a tiny defeat in the scale of the Scottish Executive, it represented a clear reminder to McConnell that he would have to watch his own backbenchers even closer than the opposition.

McConnell promised to bring some stability to government in Scotland after the turmoil of the Dewar and McLeish years and this became the hallmark of his administration. He was often accused of managing the government rather than leading it but that was actually what the Scottish business and civic establishment was demanding after two years of upheaval, change and scandal.

Public perceptions of politicians in general, and of MSPs in particular, had never been so low. The wave of enthusiasm which had greeted the arrival of the parliament had dissipated into cynicism with the McLeish resignation and the Holyrood building scandal. This overall sense of disappointment was tackled by the Queen in her Golden Jubilee address to the parliament in 2002, when it had moved temporarily to the studious surroundings of Aberdeen University – because the General Assembly of the Church of Scotland needed its assembly hall for the two weeks of its annual gathering in May. The Queen told the parliamentarians that Donald Dewar had recognised that a 'new parliamentary culture' would not be built 'overnight'. And she added: 'After what might be considered a parliamentary adjournment of almost 300 years, that process will inevitably take time. In an age which often demands instant judgements, this is something we would all do well to remember.'

One of the McLeish initiatives which McConnell inherited was the commitment for Scotland to bid for the Euro 2008 football championships. McConnell was not enthusiastic about the costs and the chances of success of entering such a bidding process. Part of his opposition undoubtedly stemmed from the fact that this was such a definite McLeish project, but McConnell was also much more cautious about making such an ambitious bid. So he started to look for partners, anyone who could share the load for such a bid, and the Irish looked the best option.

McConnell made it clear he really wanted to table a bid for the football tournament only if it was a Scottish–Irish collaboration, which then led to considerable delays while the Irish political and footballing authorities thrashed the idea around. The Irish were in, then they were out, and then, right on the deadline, they were in again, just. But even then it was unclear how many stadiums they would provide – possibly only one, which left Scotland having to provide the other five or six.

It was an unconvincing fudge and while McConnell gave his belated commitment to the project, as the Scottish–Irish proposal was submitted formally to UEFA, it never seemed the most committed or organised of bids. That was confirmed in December 2002 when it didn't even come close to winning the contest. It eventually took an ignominious fourth place, behind the winners, Austria and Switzerland, a joint Greek and Turkish bid and a Hungarian submission. It was a dismal failure for what had been talked up, under the McLeish administration, as a real possibility for Scotland. McConnell's lack of will was clearly instrumental in the failure to enter a Scottish-only bid but, after the Irish got involved, the Celtic bid was nowhere near professional or coherent enough to come close to securing the tournament.

Another huge break with the past, and one which led to a massive rift with a significant section of his own party, was McConnell's decision to embrace proportional representation for local government. Labour remained the dominant force in local government in Scotland, especially in west and central Scotland, where the party's hegemony in town halls was virtually unchallenged.

This had led to complacency and was poor democracy, at the very least.

McConnell was instinctively in favour of a fairer way of electing councillors than the traditional first-past-the-post system, which had allowed Labour, in some areas, to get most of the councillors on a minority of the votes cast. But he would never have adopted such a move had it not been for the Liberal Democrats. Labour's junior coalition partners were adamant that PR had to be delivered for local government.

The 1999 deal between the two parties committed the Scottish Executive only to 'make progress' on PR and McConnell's adoption of the policy in December 2001 was an admission that both parties were already working towards a similar partnership agreement for the 2003 election. The Liberal Democrats had made it clear there would be no coalition deal in 2003 without PR for council elections and, by starting the process, McConnell was making the first steps at tying them in to a deal ahead of time. But also, if the Liberal Democrats failed to join a coalition, then there was plenty of time for the policy to be dropped.

What McConnell did was agree in principle to PR for council elections in December 2001, with a view to publishing a white paper in March 2002 and legislative plans in September 2002, with the bill starting its progress through the parliament in the middle of 2003 – after the Scottish Parliament elections. This was another example of McConnell's expedient approach to politics. Although he was not nearly as opposed to PR as some of his parliamentary colleagues, he was more concerned with retaining strong and stable government than he was with appeasing the ranks of Labour councillors who were facing the axe.

But the main bust-up in the Cabinet came in May 2002, when Wendy Alexander refused to take any more of the monster brief she had been given and walked out of the McConnell administration. At 10.30 p.m. on 2 May, she telephoned McConnell at his home in Wishaw asking for a face-to-face meeting the following day. At midnight she went to see her friend and parliamentary colleague Pauline McNeill, telling her of her intention to quit and ringing round a few friends.

At 7.30 the following morning, Alexander arrived on the First

Minister's doorstep. She didn't stay long, just long enough to tell him she was leaving the country for a few days and to hand in her letter of resignation. She had simply decided she could work neither with McConnell nor with the massive portfolio he had burdened her with. Officially, her remit stretched over the economy, transport, business and industry (including Scottish Enterprise and Highlands and Islands Enterprise), trade, inward investment, energy, further and higher education, public transport, roads, lifeline air and ferry services, lifelong learning, training and science.

Publicly, Alexander said she was leaving the Cabinet to concentrate on policy formulation of her own but, fundamentally, she regretted not leaving at the same time as her colleagues, in the McConnell purge the previous November, and she wanted out. She was the only McLeish appointee left in the Cabinet and she was isolated. She was an outsider and she knew it. Added to this was the cool way in which some of her colleagues treated her, allies who had been burned by publicly backing her leadership bid which never happened.

Alexander's resignation presented McConnell with his first real crisis and he moved quickly, replacing her with Iain Gray, a competent performer and someone who McConnell desperately hoped would not follow Alexander's lead and quit. Alexander's departure did not lead to any more resignations, principally because there was no-one else from the McLeish era to leave – they had all either been sacked or resigned.

As the Scottish Parliament neared the end of its first term, heading towards the elections of 2003, so the parties moved to select their candidates. The additional member system used by the Scottish Parliament was a hybrid, a mix of the traditional first-past-the-post system used for Westminster elections and proportional representation.

A total of seventy-three MSPs were elected for constituencies on a straightforward most-votes-wins count, while fifty-six were elected by a proportional system, with seven MSPs taken from each of the eight regions of Scotland. For the Conservatives and the SNP in particular, these lists returned most of their MSPs. If a candidate could secure a high enough place on a regional list, he or she could be virtually guaranteed election to the Scottish Parliament because of the weight of party votes in each region. The Tories could be pretty sure of getting, say, three in North East Scotland and three in

Mid Scotland & Fife, so the candidates in the top places of these lists owed more to their party than they did to their local electorate. Each of the regional list MSPs was acutely aware of the vital importance of gaining a high ranking on their party slates.

Three years on from the first election of 1999, activists and MSPs in the SNP and the Conservatives knew that a high placing on a list could make or break a political career and both parties suffered as a result. The Tories decided to use selection meetings to decide the rankings on their lists, inviting local activists to hustings featuring the candidates, allowing each to make a pitch to the meeting and then giving the activists who turned up a vote on who to select.

The result of the hustings system, which gave disproportionate power to those who turned up at the meetings, was relatively good for most of the existing MSPs but two, Keith Harding and Lyndsay McIntosh, found themselves so far down their lists that they stood virtually no chance of getting elected. Their response was to defect, just before the 2003 election, to the newly formed Scottish People's Alliance (SPA), an odd, right-of-centre party bankrolled by millionaire industrialist Bob Durward. The SPA created a brief flurry of publicity just before the election and then sank with hardly an electoral ripple, achieving the rather dubious distinction of spending more per vote in a Scottish election campaign than anybody else in history (£188,889 spent for only 7,718 votes, the equivalent of £24.47 per vote) with absolutely nothing tangible to show for it.

The controversy in the SNP was actually worse and the party ended up much more severely damaged than the Tories. The Nationalists started 2002 by selecting their constituency candidates. This was important because once candidates had the power base of a local association behind them, they found it easier to secure a high position on the regional lists. Colin Campbell, the party's defence spokesman, became one of the first to suffer as he was deselected for the West Renfrewshire seat in April that year, effectively ending his career as a parliamentarian. But this was only the precursor of the storm which was generated when the regional lists were selected.

The party was split between the moderates or gradualists, who wanted to make the parliament work and move on to independence in an incremental basis, winning supporters along the way before having a referendum, and the fundamentalists. These activists were more left wing, more dogmatic and wanted everything to be done to further the cause of independence, with no distractions and, if possible, no referendum.

The SNP used a delegated voting system to rank candidates on the regional lists. Constituency branches chose which candidates to support and the representatives were then delegated to vote for them. This allowed factions within the party to push a slate of candidates if they could control the local associations.

Andrew Wilson was one of the young stars of the 1999 intake to the Scottish Parliament. A former banker, the 28-year-old was seen as one of the brightest and sharpest MSPs in the SNP parliamentary group when he arrived in the parliament. Unfortunately for him, he was also seen as too moderate, too close to the leadership and too consensual for the left-wingers and the fundamentalists who had taken control of some branches. He had also achieved notoriety within the party for calling on Scots to support the English football team in the 2002 World Cup – one of the most serious crimes possible in the eyes of some Scottish nationalists. Wilson was ambushed by left-wingers when the rankings for the Central Scotland regional list were decided, knocking him out of a top four spot, which was necessary to even stand a chance of getting re-elected. At the same time Duncan Hamilton, another of the young SNP MSPs who had made a mark on the parliament in its first session, had decided to leave politics, for at least four years, to train as a lawyer. John Swinney, the party leader, was suddenly deprived of two of his best young performers.

That same selection process saw Mike Russell, a charismatic, moderate leadership ally, dropped so far down the South of Scotland list that he stood virtually no chance of election. Margo MacDonald, the well-known former MP and outspoken MSP, was also bumped down the Lothians list. She said she would consider standing as an independent, against the SNP, in retribution, something only someone of her stature and political presence could do. MacDonald soon left the SNP and stood on the Lothians list on her own, delivering a powerful snub to her former activists by being returned as an independent MSP in the 2003 election. Two other MSPs, without the sort of power base which MacDonald enjoyed, Irene McGugan and Fiona Macleod, were also effectively deselected in the same process, leaving the way clear for a new batch of left-wingers and fundamentalists to move forward.

Even senior party figures were targeted in the ambush. Roseanna Cunningham, the deputy leader of the party and former MP, was dumped down in fourth place on her list and Nicola Sturgeon, another rising star and leadership loyalist, came second on the Glasgow list, behind the left-winger Sandra White.

The loss of so many allies came at probably the worst time for Swinney. The SNP leader had endured a bumpy ride since taking over from Alex Salmond in 2000. He had not performed well at First Minister's Questions against Henry McLeish or Jack McConnell, and he was fighting to keep his party from lurching to the left.

The parliament's temporary excursion to Aberdeen, in May 2002, had encapsulated quite what a torrid time Swinney was having. Salmond, now the MP for Banff & Buchan and the leader of the SNP group at Westminster, had come to Aberdeen, ostensibly to watch from the visitors' gallery as McConnell announced his legislative programme and to highlight a campaign to save Peterhead prison from closure. But his presence in and around the parliament only seemed to add to the pressure on Swinney, showing the SNP – and its political opponents – what the party was missing.

McConnell's legislative agenda was fairly weak. With only a year to go before the election, there was little that wasn't tidying up or uncontentious yet, despite the absence of any real meat, Swinney failed to score any real debating points against McConnell. He stumbled over his lines and had the support of only sixteen of his thirty-four MSPs in the chamber. Some of the others had gone with Salmond to campaign about Peterhead prison.

Labour MSPs, aware of Salmond's presence in the wings and of his stated desire to return to the Scottish Parliament at some stage, goaded Swinney with taunts that he was nothing more than a 'caretaker leader'. One Labour MSP suggested that the Scottish Executive introduce the Preservation of Swinney (Scotland) Bill as soon as possible. And, as he left the Aberdeen chamber, Swinney was further embarrassed by Liberal Democrat MSPs who handed out petitions, calling on other MSPs to sign up to save the SNP leader from certain extinction.

Swinney tried to assert his authority over the party by taking a more tempered and moderate approach to nationalist politics. This came out clearly in the party's 2002 conference in Inverness. Gone were the harsh yellows and blacks of the past. Instead Swinney's conference backdrop was made up of shades of purple and lilac, designed to appeal to a television audience outside the hall.

Swinney had dropped the disastrous penny-for-Scotland policy of raising income tax by 1p in the pound just before the conference. He needed to do this to prevent the conference from being dominated by the issue but it was still a considerable U-turn for the politician who helped to introduce it back in 1999.

Swinney's speech to the conference was also moderation personified, its message deliberately pitched at wavering Labour voters by insisting there would be no 'land of milk and honey' if Scotland became independent. 'We cannot say that we will all prosper because of oil. We cannot say there will be money for everything simply by becoming independent. Our new approach will be to present independence not as a land of milk and honey but as a land of opportunity,' he told his activists. It was a risky strategy because Swinney knew that he would be under pressure if the SNP's return from the 2003 election dropped below the thirty-five MSPs it secured in 1999 and he would almost certainly face a leadership challenge if he failed to return more than thirty seats.

The lead-up to the 2003 election campaign was dominated by the Iraq War. It crowded out domestic political coverage and coloured the campaign. The SNP and the Liberal Democrats were opposed to the war, Labour was ostensibly in favour, but many activists and MSPs felt they were being forced to back the controversial decision of the Prime Minister to follow the United States into Iraq, even though they disagreed with it.

There were many in the Labour Party, including senior candidates, who found this hard to do, particularly when faced on the doorsteps with strong opposition to the war. One in this difficult position was Malcolm Chisholm, McConnell's health minister. Chisholm had been forced by ministerial collective responsibility to vote for the war in an SNP-inspired debate in mid-March 2003 and then, three days later, he could not restrain himself any longer. Grabbing a megaphone from anti-war campaigners protesting outside his Edinburgh office, an anguished Chisholm apologised in public for supporting the war in the parliamentary vote.

The health minister was not the only member of McConnell's administration to have serious misgivings about the war; there were at least three others, including Cathy Jamieson, the education minister, Margaret Curran, the social justice minister, and Elaine Murray, the deputy sports minister, who shared the same concerns. Murray offered her resignation to McConnell before abstaining in the vote and Chisholm said afterwards he would have resigned if he had voted against the Labour position. It all made for an uncomfortable campaign for the Labour Party but, with the SNP struggling to make any real headway on domestic issues, and Labour still enjoying sustained popularity throughout the United Kingdom, the war made little difference to the outcome in the end.

McConnell had viewed the eighteen months between his accession to the First Minister's job and the 2003 election as an attempt to re-establish stability. That period was heavy on management and control and light on legislative enterprise. It was clearly what was needed after the turbulence of the first two and a half years of devolution. McConnell had issues to deal with but he was so determined to get through to the election, to try to establish his own mandate to govern, that he tried little of any real substance. He was faced with continuing problems over hospital waiting lists and a related funding crisis at care homes, with elderly people taking up space in hospitals because there were no places in homes for them to go to.

The Scottish Executive suffered only its second parliamentary defeat during this time, but only because one Labour MSP pushed the wrong button, abstaining on a vote on fire service reforms instead of voting in favour. Other than that, McConnell managed to run a tight, controlled, if somewhat unexciting Executive. He did lose a minister in November 2002, when Richard Simpson, the deputy justice minister, was reported as having described striking firefighters as 'fascists' and 'bastards' during a private conversation at a business dinner, but that was hardly McConnell's fault.

McConnell's biggest problem, however, was local, when an internal party audit found that some £11,000 was missing from the accounts of his own constituency party, prompting an investigation. The affair would have been difficult for McConnell at any time but its effect was heightened because it came in October 2002, just a year after Henry McLeish had had to resign over what had started as a local constituency matter. McConnell was quick to distance himself from the missing money, putting everything into the hands of the investigators and waiting for the results. He told the parliament he would do 'nothing, absolutely nothing' to bring it into disrepute. It was a brave statement, given the trouble his predecessor had got into, but McConnell was confident he had nothing to do with the missing money.

The murky world of Lanarkshire Labour politics was briefly exposed as a mole-hunt started for the person who had leaked news of the missing cash to the press. McConnell shouldn't really have been surprised that it leaked so quickly; after all, he had spent his entire political career fixing deals, he had made enemies along the way and it was inevitable that some would use any means possible to embarrass him.

The controversy deepened when further investigations revealed that McConnell had paid out of his own pocket for Christina Marshall, his former personal assistant – who had been at the centre of the 'Lobbygate' row two years before – to stay at the Caledonian Hotel in Edinburgh during a conference and had then claimed the money back from a constituency development account. It also emerged that donations from the Iron and Steel Trades Council and from a Labour fund-raising event, the Red Rose dinner, had not been declared to the Electoral Commission.

None of these issues could be linked directly to McConnell but the effect was cumulative and gave the impression that there were serious problems with McConnell's constituency accounts. Critics started asking: if he couldn't run his own party accounts properly, how could he look after the nation?

McConnell fought back, promising full disclosure and insisting he had been absolutely open about everything. At the start of November, the Labour Party called in the police to investigate the missing money, confident that this would isolate the culprit and exonerate the First Minister. This succeeded both in putting an end to the damaging round of daily stories about the affair and in clearing the First Minister. McConnell was exonerated by an internal inquiry and a former local party treasurer, Elizabeth Wilson, was later charged with embezzlement and then fined.

It was with this behind him that McConnell approached the 2003 election with the key message of stability and continuity. He was reeling from the Wishaw accounts scandal, battered by the fall-out from the Iraq War and facing the rocketing costs and delays of the Holyrood building project but he nevertheless insisted that he would stabilise and sort out Scottish politics. Under pressure from Margo MacDonald, the former SNP MSP who was now running as an independent, McConnell wisely announced that he would set up a full public inquiry into the Holyrood debacle, neatly isolating it as a damaging issue until the inquiry could meet.

Luckily for McConnell, his opponents were in an even poorer state than Labour. John Swinney was trying to moderate his party to appeal to a broader base, but was losing internal battles against left-wingers and disruptive fundamentalists. The Tories had their own selection problems, particularly in Glasgow, and were split at the top between those who wanted a more radical, tax-cutting agenda and those who wanted to remain conservative in policy, at least until the party had found its way again in Scotland. The Liberal Democrats went into the election aware that they had to differentiate themselves from Labour, their coalition partners for the past four years, if they were to make any electoral headway, but knowing this would be difficult. But with the agreement on proportional representation for local government almost a done deal, a second coalition between Labour and the Liberal Democrats looked the likeliest outcome as the campaign got underway in April 2003.

What nobody could envisage, however, was how radically different the parliament was going to be after the 2003 election. The political make-up of the chamber was about to change, and in the most unexpected of ways.

9

Free radicals and stalking horses

IT was just after lunchtime on Friday 2 May 2003, the day after polling day. Jack McConnell woke in his Glasgow hotel room, having managed to snatch a couple of hours' sleep while the final results were coming through. He put a call through to Jim Wallace, the Scottish Liberal Democrat leader, who was on his way to his post-election press conference. The call was not unexpected and neither was McConnell's offer of immediate talks to try to sort out a second coalition deal. Labour's total of fifty MSPs was down on the fifty-six the party secured in 1999 but, with the Liberal Democrats' seventeen, the two parties had sixty-seven seats in the Scottish Parliament, two more than the threshold for forming a majority government.

The two leaders congratulated each other on getting elected and it appeared as if Scotland's second Lab–Lib Dem coalition deal was all but done. The basics of an agreement were there but the details still had to be thrashed out and this was not nearly as straightforward as the leaders had expected. Although both parties had been through the process before and knew what to expect, each leader held out for more this time, aware he would be castigated by his own party if he failed to come out with a good deal.

Tentative negotiations started almost immediately, on the weekend after the election. But ten days on from polling day, on Sunday 11 May, there still had not been enough progress to close a deal so late night sittings were brought in to make the progress needed. For three nights, negotiators from both parties lived on pizzas, Thai and Chinese takeaways – they would have had curries but a senior official vetoed the idea, warning that the smell of chicken tikka and lamb Madras would never leave St Andrew's House, the Executive's building, if they did.

Every day Labour's Cathy Jamieson and the Liberal Democrats'

Tavish Scott appeared to brief the press, insisting that encouraging progress was being made. Inside, the picture was rather different. Labour wanted tough new penalties for youth crime, crucially the ability to jail parents for failing to keep their children in order. The Liberal Democrats were fiercely opposed to that idea. For their part, they wanted free eye and dental checks and proportional representation for local government, as well as an extra Cabinet minister.

Even though the parties agreed on just about everything else, it took a long time to get agreement on these outstanding issues. In the end, Labour got its youth crime policy but it was drastically watered down: parents would be jailed only as a 'last resort'. The Liberal Democrats did not get their extra Cabinet minister but they got the free eye and dental checks and PR for council elections. Their PR plans were weakened slightly: there would be multi-member wards of three and four, not the five councillors they favoured, but apart from that, they did appear to have got the better of the deal, once again. It certainly seemed so to Wallace when in celebration he cracked open a bottle of Highland Park whisky, from his Orkney constituency, at 1.30 a.m. on Wednesday 14 May while all his Labour colleagues headed off to bed.

Labour tried to claim success, arguing that 240 of its 242 manifesto commitments had been accepted (the two to be dropped were a policy on congestion charging and direct elections to health boards). But most of the others were uncontentious and were never opposed by the Liberal Democrats anyway, which made Labour's claims look rather hollow.

The agreement of PR for local government was by far the most radical change accepted as part of the partnership agreement and it was the one to grab the headlines, giving the appearance of a Liberal Democrat victory simply because it was the highest-profile part of the deal. The Liberal Democrats had also secured a commitment to reduce class sizes in Primary 1 to twenty-five and an end to national testing for schools, replacing it with a system of 'national sampling', and the scrapping of the tolls on the Skye Bridge, a hugely symbolic move for the Highlands and Islands.

The second Labour and Liberal Democrat coalition deal was signed in the sober surroundings of St Andrew's House on 15 May. It was an appropriately low-key ceremony, a distinct change from the Museum of Scotland event in 1999. Wallace and McConnell signed for the cameras in a large, dark ministerial office before McConnell was voted in as First Minister by the parliament later that day. Then on 20 May, less than three weeks after the election, McConnell had an audience with the Queen at Windsor Castle, receiving the royal warrant and confirming his resumption in the office of Scotland's First Minister.

McConnell had replaced Henry McLeish as leader of the Labour group in the Scottish Parliament on a slogan of 'doing less better' and, now that he had the mandate he so cherished from the electorate, he sought to make a Scottish Executive in his image, in both policy and personnel terms.

That electoral mandate gave him a great deal of confidence. He became more relaxed and assertive in his dealings both with his political colleagues and with his opponents. His first move was to reshape the Cabinet. Wallace was moved, with his agreement, from justice to enterprise. This was an astute move for both, given the Liberal Democrats' reluctance to back tough new measures on youth crime. Also, McConnell had staked his future on growing the Scottish economy and, by moving a Liberal Democrat to the key portfolio for that purpose, he could share the blame if that aim was not achieved. Jamieson, one of McConnell's close allies, took Wallace's place at justice but the key Anti-social Behaviour Bill was given to Margaret Curran in the communities department. Andy Kerr, as a former Glasgow council official, was told to stay at local government and finance so that he could drive through electoral reform.

McConnell cut the size of the administration, slightly, by reducing the number of junior ministers from ten to seven. He also increased the size of the Cabinet from ten to eleven, although he did tell two ministers who attended Cabinet – Frank McAveety at sport and culture and Nicol Stephen at transport – that they would have to make do with junior ministerial salaries.

The new deal was not without its headaches for Labour. Even on the day that McConnell was elected as First Minister, Jim McCabe, a veteran Labour council leader from North Lanarkshire and an old-style political bruiser, had 'declared war' on the party leadership, warning of a four-year battle over the introduction of PR, a move he knew would destroy Labour's dominance in Scotland's town halls and end the political careers of hundreds of Labour councillors.

Although the overall result of the election – at least in terms of the winners – looked similar to 1999, there were big changes underneath. The Tories stayed static, securing the same number of seats, eighteen, as in 1999, but it was the SNP which really suffered. If the Nationalists believed they had done badly in 1999, when they came a poor second with thirty-five seats, they were in for a major shock in 2003, when they slipped back to just twenty-seven.

The SNP was being squeezed by the rise of the smaller parties and the independents. The 1999 election had seen the first try-out of the list system of voting in Scotland. In the intervening four years, the Greens and the Scottish Socialist Party (SSP) had honed their messages, concentrating exclusively on the list vote. 'Second Vote Green' was the simple Green election slogan and it worked, spectacularly. With two votes to play with, many people took the opportunity to vote for two parties, supporting their usual, main, party in the constituency vote and giving their regional vote to someone else, which turned out, more often than not, to be the Greens or the SSP. The two parties most likely to be squeezed were the Conservatives and the SNP because they relied on the lists for most of their seats. In the event the Tory vote held up but the Nationalist vote did not.

Instead of just one Green MSP and a sole Scottish Socialist, as had been the case in 1999, by late morning on 2 May 2003, when the results were in, there were seven Greens and six Socialists in the parliament. The SSP's success had been predicted by the polls but the Greens' was unexpected. Even party managers had not prepared for it. A Green press conference, which was due to be held in a small room above a pub in Edinburgh's Grassmarket on the morning after polling day, had to be moved because it was not big enough to hold all the MSPs and the journalists, all of whom had realised that the rise of the Greens was turning into the big story of the election. In delightfully chaotic scenes, the Greens tried to move their press conference to a different venue while trying to keep track of exactly who had got elected and where they were.

But if the Greens provided the story, it was the SSP which provided the colour. The one image of the night which came to embody the rise of the smaller parties was of Colin Fox, an SSP candidate in the Lothians, who had not thought he would even come close to winning a seat, vaulting over the barriers at the edge of the platform of the count at Meadowbank Sports Centre in sheer delight.

Tommy Sheridan, the SSP leader, had been used to being the sole standard bearer for the hard left in the parliament and, at first, he didn't seem sure how to deal with an actual parliamentary party, particularly the more publicity-hungry members of it. It wasn't long before he found himself obscured by the antics of Rosie Kane, a charismatic young single mother from Glasgow who had become politically active by protesting against the extension of the M74.

All MSPs have to declare an oath to the Queen before taking their seats. Some, including Sheridan, had done so before but only after protesting first that they believed in the sovereignty of the Scottish nation. Kane took the oath to the Queen, standing in front of the mace in the Scottish Parliament wearing tatty jeans and an off-the-shoulder top. As she raised her right hand, it became clear that she had written on it, in ballpoint pen, the words 'My oath is to the Scottish people'.

Rosemary Byrne, another SSP MSP, declared: 'We are all Jock Tamson's bairns [we are all the same under the skin], we are all equal and we should not need to be taking oaths.' Not to be outdone, Fox gave an unaccompanied rendition of Robert Burns's egalitarian classic 'A Man's a Man for A' That' when it came to his turn to take the oath. Kane had already announced:

> We are going to bring colour, imagination and all sorts of diversity and attitude to the parliament. We're going to completely change the place. I hope that the parliament is going to become a bit like the *Big Brother* house and that people are going to watch it to see what's happening. They're going to be amazed at all the madness and the craziness that's happening in there.

The seven Greens and the six SSP MSPs were joined in the parliament by four others. Dennis Canavan was back as the independent (formerly Labour) MSP for Falkirk West. Margo MacDonald, the former SNP MSP, made the result even worse for the Nationalists by winning a seat on the Lothians list. John Swinburne was the first elected representative in British political history for the 'grey vote', becoming a Central Scotland list MSP for the Scottish Senior Citizens Unity Party. But probably the biggest shock came with the election of Dr Jean Turner, a single-issue hospital campaigner who defeated Labour's Brian Fitzpatrick in Strathkelvin & Bearsden, protesting at plans to close Stobhill Hospital.

After the excitement of the election campaign, the arrival of the new MSPs, particularly the SSP ones, suddenly made the supposedly modern, inclusive Scottish Parliament look as staid and conservative as the House of Commons. This new 'rainbow parliament' certainly made the job of the incoming Presiding Officer, George Reid, more difficult than it had been for his predecessor, Sir David Steel. Not only did Reid have to keep an eye on the antics of the so-called 'Trots' inside the chamber as they protested and grandstanded their way through the parliamentary sessions but the smaller parties and independents were now represented on the Parliamentary Bureau, the secretive group which decided parliamentary business.

The actual election night, over the course of 1 and 2 May, had proved to be a strangely topsy-turvy affair. The early results were all from constituencies, mainly from the Central Belt, and gave little hint of the turmoil that was to ensue from the regional list results, which did not begin to be declared until after 4 a.m. and continued well into the late morning.

But there was one constituency which became something of a barometer for the rest of the results, Glasgow Govan. This constituency, on the banks of the Clyde, had had a volatile past, often bucking the national trend. Gordon Jackson, the Labour candidate and leading advocate, appeared to have done everything possible to lose the seat. He had gone off on holiday during the campaign and was sunning himself in Spain when the Prime Minister came to the constituency to campaign on his behalf. He had also aroused further anger by booking himself in for a stint in court, for the day following the election.

The Nationalist candidate, Nicola Sturgeon, was one of the SNP's best and had fought the seat before, in 1999. As the polls closed, both parties claimed victory and Govan came to symbolise the contest as a whole. When it was declared, at 3.09 a.m., Jackson had won a comfortable victory, with a 1,200 majority. It really did seem to set the scene for much of what followed.

The SNP did stage a brief rally, taking Aberdeen North, Ochil and, unexpectedly, Dundee East, but they failed to take Dundee West, their top target seat, where Labour was defending a majority of just 121. Opinion formers in the newspapers started wondering over the next couple of days whether George Robertson, the former shadow Scottish secretary, had been right all along and that devolution was indeed going to 'kill nationalism stone dead'.

For John Swinney, the party leader, the result was hard to take but he insisted he would fight on, even though everyone in his party knew that such a bad election would probably pave the way for a leadership challenge. 'I will be leader of the SNP in four years' time,' Swinney declared, but that appeared to be a possibility only because there were no stand-out candidates to replace him. The party had lost a quarter of its seats, Swinney had lost some of his closest allies and best performers in Mike Russell, Andrew Wilson and Duncan Hamilton, and, within days, the sniping started behind Swinney's back.

Having fought the 2001 general election as party leader, and not done too well at that, and now having lost ground in the 2003 Scottish election, Swinney knew he would be unlikely to survive another poor result. With the European elections of 2004 looming, one MSP summed up the feeling of many in the party when he said: 'Three strikes and you're out.'

Swinney's position was looking increasingly perilous through the summer, the only bright spot for the SNP leader being his marriage to the BBC reporter Elizabeth Quigley in July 2003. But that was eclipsed by the news, which emerged just two days before the wedding, that Swinney was to be challenged for the SNP leadership at the party conference that autumn.

The challenger was Bill Wilson, a quiet, bespectacled activist who had no chance of defeating Swinney but who was willing to put his name forward to explore the leadership options and act as a stalking horse candidate. The 39-year-old Wilson was on the fundamentalist side of the party, a left-winger and a senior academic in environmental science. The theory was that if he could put a big enough dent in Swinney's authority through a leadership vote, it would then encourage one of the party heavyweights, such as Alex Neil, to emerge as a much more potent contender – although Neil distanced himself from the Wilson campaign in public and was not among those who pushed Wilson to stand. He insisted he was playing no part in the leadership challenge but, nevertheless, failed to give a full endorsement of Swinney, instead calling for a 'debate' into the direction the party should go.

The loss of leadership loyalists such as Hamilton and Andrew Wilson had allowed left-wingers and fundamentalists to become MSPs, including Campbell Martin, a new SNP MSP for the West of Scotland. Swinney was trying to maintain a united front in his parliamentary party against Bill Wilson's challenge, but he was undermined when Martin publicly backed the challenger, claiming that the vast majority of SNP members shared Wilson's concerns over the direction of the party, including about ten MSPs.

Wilson wanted to stand on a ticket of open debate in the party over the best way to achieve independence. This was clearly a coded message that Swinney was not driving that core agenda fast enough. However, despite the now concrete threat to his leadership, Swinney continued to try to reform his party, first demanding that MSPs donate £3,000 a year from their salaries to build an election fighting fund and then pressing ahead with internal reforms designed to limit the influence of factions within the party.

Swinney was determined to bring in one-member one-vote elections for candidates on the regional lists. For the 2003 elections, list candidates had been elected by a delegated vote system. Branches voted for favoured candidates. This played into the hands of factions, such as the left-wing fundamentalists, who had gained control of some small branches and wielded extraordinary influence to get their own candidates high up the list at the expense of leadership loyalists. Swinney also wanted centralised membership, taking more control – both of members and of finance – away from branches.

Wilson derided Swinney's reforms as a 'New Labour programme for the SNP' and, in many ways, he was right. However, what he saw as a criticism many others saw as a complement, having seen how effectively the New Labour agenda had worked for the Labour Party.

Swinney arrived in Inverness on the eve of the SNP conference on 23 September 2003, facing a fight for his political future and, as he saw it, for the future of the independence movement itself. The poor 2003 election had crystallised the fight for the SNP's soul between those, like Swinney, who believed the SNP had to stop being a movement and become a modern political party and those who wanted the SNP to be about one issue, independence, bringing together all those who backed the idea. Swinney believed that his party should be able to win power on the back of a proper, coherent set of policies, in the same way as any other political party, and use that to move towards independence. His opponents disagreed.

Roseanna Cunningham, Swinney's deputy, took on the role of his enforcer on the conference's first day, using her address to lambast Wilson and his supporters. She focused on two veteran nationalists, Jim Fairlie and Jim Sillars, both of whom had been deputy leaders, for particular criticism, labelling them the 'long-dormant twin-Jim volcanoes' and adding: 'Give it up, guys, your time has been and gone. Get over it, move on.' Cunningham then mauled Wilson and his backers in the hall, moving the argument about the future state of the party to centre stage. 'I want power – do you?' she asked. 'I want the SNP to win – do you? I want the SNP to form a government in Scotland. This party does not exist to be in permanent opposition and I passionately wish that some members would stop giving the impression that that is what they would prefer.'

Cunningham was backed by Alex Salmond, who used his own broad appeal in the party to offer support to his beleaguered successor. 'When you elect a leadership, then back it,' he told activists, and added: 'Do not undermine it and above all, fight the unionist parties, do not fight each other.'

Wilson retorted that the SNP had already lost 200,000 votes under Swinney's leadership so something new was needed to win back that support. He also called for a party debate on the referendum policy. The leadership advocated a pre-referendum policy – winning power, calling a referendum, winning it and then suing for independence from London. The fundamentalists believed that winning power would be enough to start the process of breaking away from the rest of the United Kingdom.

Friday 26 September 2003 was the key day for Swinney. It was the day of his leader's speech to the conference and the day before members voted on his future. He had to stamp his authority on the party; he needed the strongest performance of his career from the platform – and he delivered it.

In a passionate and highly charged speech, Swinney branded his opponents as 'ninety-minute patriots'. He described the 'independence or nothing' agenda as a dead-end strategy:

> It ends in the language of ninety-minute patriots, of faint hearts and fearties [cowards], in blaming voters for not being as principled and pure as we think we are; and when you end up blaming the voters, you end up with a lifetime on the margins. We will never win independence from the margins of Scottish politics.

And he added: 'I don't want the SNP in government because I want a ministerial Mondeo, I want the SNP in government because I want independence.'

It was a storming performance, brave and committed, and he was cheered to the roof of the Eden Court Theatre by the majority of the activists while the rebels sat in silence.

The speech used the word 'independence' twenty-five times and Swinney was careful to stress his left-wing credentials as a way of winning round some waverers. And it worked: Swinney got his reforms through the party and he won the vote against Wilson comprehensively, as he expected, by 577 votes to 111. He was delighted and believed he was now safe, at least for the foreseeable future. But there were still voices in the party warning that Swinney was on probation and that he had not done enough to convince the party as a whole that it was going in the right direction. As it turned out, that period of probation did not last very long at all.

10

King over the water

A LEX Salmond could not have been clearer. It was 22 June 2004. John Swinney had resigned as SNP leader three days before and Salmond was asked on television whether he would return to lead his party once again.

'I am not going to stand. If nominated, I will decline, if drafted, I will defer and if elected, I will resign,' he declared.

Within three weeks Salmond had, in fact, decided to stand. He accepted the nomination, he did not dodge the draft and, on 3 September 2004, he duly got elected.

If that was one of the most surprising and speedy decisions in Scottish political history, the same could not be said for Swinney's departure. The SNP leader saw off his critics by trouncing leadership rival Bill Wilson at the 2003 party conference in Inverness (see Chapter 9) and that bought him a little time, but not much. The European elections took place just nine months later, on 10 June 2004. Privately, Swinney set himself the minimum goal of retaining the party's two MEPs (out of seven for the whole of Scotland) and staying ahead of the Conservatives. Publicly, he had declared his target as replacing Labour as the most popular party in Scotland.

He came nowhere near that public aim and only just succeeded in meeting his much more modest, private, target. The SNP did return its two MEPs but, with only 19.5 per cent of the vote, the Nationalists recorded their lowest election rating for seventeen years and stayed ahead of the Tories by just a whisker.

Mike Russell, the former SNP chief executive who had lost his Holyrood seat the previous year, had stirred up the case against Swinney in April that year by writing that 'the men in grey kilts' would come for the SNP leader if the party failed to do well in the European elections. That phrase, an allusion to the 'men in grey suits' who were said to have told Margaret Thatcher she was too unpopular to stay in office more than a decade before, wounded Swinney grievously. He brushed it off, at least in public, but it was such a good phrase, and so apposite to the situation which Swinney found himself in, that it resonated round and round the Scottish political village – even if such a body of anonymous party worthies did not actually exist.

The Scottish European election results were announced later than the English ones, on Monday 14 June 2004, from the top of the Mercat Cross, an ancient meeting place and rallying point on the Royal Mile. It was a very old-fashioned sort of announcement, shouted out over the heads of the politicians and members of the public milling around below. It was also somewhat bizarre given that the election was certainly one of the more modern to be contested in Britain, fought as it had been under a full system of proportional representation, with the whole of Scotland acting as one giant constituency returning the seven MEPs together.

With everybody involved gathering around the Mercat Cross in the early summer sunshine, there was no escape for the party leaders. All had to wait and mingle with the press, with no way out and little help available from spin doctors.

First, there was relief for Swinney when it emerged that the SNP would keep its two MEPs but then it became clear that his party's share of the vote had fallen below 20 per cent. As he was surrounded by reporters, Swinney tried to focus on Labour's share of the vote, which was the lowest the party had achieved since 1918 in Scotland, but all that did was draw attention to his own party's result, which was even worse than Labour's.

Campbell Martin, one of the new intake of fundamentalist left-wingers, who had become an MSP in 2003, immediately called on Swinney to go. 'I think he has to be big enough to realise that now is the time for him to go because the party can't take any more of this – he is going to kill the party if he stays,' he declared. Martin's attacks were unsurprising. He had already been suspended from the SNP for his constant attacks on the leadership but his views started to spread deeper and further within the party and some, normally loyal, activists and MSPs started asking whether it was time for a new leader and a new direction.

Exactly a week later Swinney was gone. He endured seven days of worsening headlines, increasingly vocal calls for him to go and polls of constituency branches favouring a new leader. On Monday 21 June, Swinney called his wife, Elizabeth Quigley, from the parliament and told her he had decided to quit. He made the same call to his parents then rang Roseanna Cunningham, his deputy, and asked to visit her at her home in Crieff. He went to see her that evening. She guessed his decision before he told her and said she was sorry. Cunningham was the only MSP to know of his decision that evening although Swinney's policy and press advisers were brought in after his return from Crieff to help polish his resignation speech.

At 8.30 the following morning, Swinney was at the SNP's headquarters in Edinburgh's Macdonald Road with his resignation letter for Peter Murrell, the SNP chief executive, and it was from there that he telephoned Salmond, informing him of his decision. The media were told to be at Macdonald Road for a mysterious press conference later that morning and the SNP MSPs were all texted at 9.30 a.m. with the news – a rather perfunctory way of spreading such an important announcement but one that represented the distrust that Swinney now had for some of his colleagues.

So, at 10.30 a.m. on Tuesday 22 June 2004, Swinney announced to the press he was standing down as SNP leader after four difficult years and three elections in the job.

Just two hours later Duncan McNeil, the Labour MSP for Greenock & Inverclyde, opened the weekly meeting of the Labour group in the Scottish Parliament with the words:'We meet here today to honour the memory of a man who has made a singular contribution to the growth of the Labour Party over the last four years.' This was greeted with applause, laughter and hoots of appreciation. However, neither McNeil nor his Labour colleagues would have been quite so celebratory had they been aware at that time exactly who Swinney's replacement was going to be.

At that time there was no suggestion that Salmond would return from London to lead the party once again. Cunningham was first to declare her intention to stand for the leadership, making an announcement just a couple of hours after Swinney's resignation speech, and it was assumed that she would soon be joined by one or two other ambitious MSPs. This assumption was realised when

Nicola Sturgeon, the 33-year-old high-flier and leadership loyalist, and Russell both joined the race. Cunningham, aged fifty-two, had been Swinney's deputy, so was seen by some as closely allied to the unsuccessful Swinney era but she was more left wing than Swinney. She was known as 'Republican Rose' in the party and in the press because of her vocal anti-monarchism. Sturgeon was close to Salmond and was also seen as a leadership loyalist but she was also younger than the others and represented more of a fresh start for the party. The fifty-year-old Russell was always the outsider for the contest, principally because he was not an MSP and it was difficult to see how anyone could do the job without being there for the day-to-day affairs of the parliament.

That was, of course, until Salmond declared his intention to stand. He had quit the Scottish Parliament in 2003, preferring to stay at Westminster. That decision was applauded by some in the party at the time because it allowed Swinney to place his own stamp on the party without the former leader leaning over his shoulder. But when the three-way contest started to develop, through June and July, some senior figures in the party went quietly back to Salmond and asked him to reconsider his decision not to enter the contest.

Salmond had already been leader for ten years, from 1990 to 2000. He quit after becoming tired and jaded by the job and it was with that sense of weariness that he made his now infamous statement on 22 June 2004, making it clear that nothing and nobody would persuade him to enter the leadership race again. But over the next few days and weeks, a stream of senior figures in the party appealed to him to reconsider. All politicians have egos, some bigger than others, and it must have been gratifying for Salmond to be told – repeatedly – that he was the only person who could rescue the party. At last he became convinced that he could not only save the party but win the 2007 election too.

There was no doubt that Salmond was still the biggest political hitter the SNP possessed; this was clear from the moment he entered the leadership contest on 15 July 2004. The 49-year-old former leader not only managed to brush off his embarrassing declaration that he would not stand for the leadership but eclipsed the other contenders the moment he entered the race.

In a way which was typical of his rumbustious but effective

political style, Salmond managed to lift himself above the leadership battle and into a direct confrontation with Jack McConnell, the Labour First Minister. 'I am not just launching a campaign to be SNP leader. I am launching my candidacy to be First Minister of Scotland,' he announced. From any of the other candidates, that would have seemed overblown and ridiculous, but Salmond got away with it because he was the only figure formidable enough to do so.

And what about that line on not standing, which he had adapted from General William T. Sherman's comment to the Republican National Convention of 1884? Sherman had said: 'I will not accept if nominated and I will not serve if elected.'

Salmond's response was simple. 'When I quoted General Sherman,' he said, 'I intended to quote General MacArthur, who said: "I shall return."' It was cheeky but it worked.

But rather than emulating either American general, there was a feeling in the SNP – which has always had edges of hopeless romanticism to it – that Salmond was more like James Stuart, the Old Pretender, the so-called King over the Water. It suited the misty-eyed view of some Nationalists for Salmond to return from his sort of self-imposed exile in London to lead the party once again.

What it did not do was help the other leadership candidates. Sturgeon immediately withdrew, saying she would not stand against Salmond and would stand for the deputy leadership. But that left Cunningham and Russell. Neither of them really stood much of a chance against Salmond, but they both stayed in the race until the end, although neither was happy at Salmond's sudden and unexpected arrival or at the deal stitched up with Sturgeon. There were immediate rumours that Salmond had only stepped in because it looked as though Cunningham was beating his favoured candidate, Sturgeon, that he was the 'stop Roseanna' candidate.

Sturgeon was rewarded with a joint leadership bid with Salmond. This meant that, if successful, the pair would run the SNP in tandem, with Salmond in overall control but Sturgeon taking charge of affairs in the Scottish Parliament, including the weekly jousts with McConnell at First Minister's Questions. That helped Salmond cope with awkward questions about how he could run the SNP without being an MSP and it effectively killed off the hopes of the other candidates for the deputy leadership as well: Fergus Ewing and Christine Grahame.

The leadership and deputy leadership contests were taken out to SNP activists all round the country through the summer and autumn of 2004. There were many hustings meetings; the various candidates excelled at some and not at others but the result, when it was announced at the SNP conference in September, was predictable. With almost 80 per cent of the party's 8,200 members voting, Salmond was elected leader with 76 per cent of the vote, Cunningham was second with 14 per cent and Russell third with 10 per cent. In the contest for the deputy leadership, Sturgeon won with 54 per cent of the vote, Ewing came second with 25 per cent and Grahame third with 21 per cent.

The speed with which they buried the Swinney years was breathtaking. Sturgeon used her speech to the conference to announce a full review of all party policies, marking a clear break with the previous four years and holding out a conciliatory offer to the fundamentalists who still wanted to see radical change.

Salmond gave his party the task of raising £250,000 to fight the following year's general election from scratch. With the election expected to be only eight months away and for a party in such a poor state, financially and politically, it was a huge challenge. Salmond also told activists the party would not be able to increase its debt. The SNP had run up about £485,000 in debts during the unsuccessful 2003 Holyrood election campaign, taking its overall debt to almost £1 million. Although that had come down a bit by the autumn of 2004, the debt was still in the region of £750,000 when Salmond made his announcement at the 2004 Inverness conference.

If there is one pastime which has always been able to draw Salmond away from politics it is horse racing; indeed the new SNP leader remained a tipster and racing columnist for the *Scotsman* until late in 2005. But his decision to take over the SNP for a second time represented by far his biggest gamble to date.

During his ten years in charge, Salmond had built the SNP up from the fragmented and rather unruly movement it was in 1990 into a parliamentary party of some authority, if not power. He had undoubtedly left it in a better position than he found it again, four

years later, in the wake of the woeful European elections. By that
time, the SNP was vying with the Conservatives for the third place
in Scottish politics, it was riven with division and it was all but broke.

Salmond had little time, not only to get the SNP back to where
it had been when he left it in 2000, but to go further than that and
overtake Labour. He had just two and a half years to lift the SNP to
the top of Scottish politics and inflict the first defeat on the Scottish
Labour Party in fifty years. No-one really knew if he could get
anywhere near it but, at least in public, he continued to maintain
that, not only was his target achievable, but he would do it too.

Over at the Scottish Executive, McConnell was on course to
embrace the most radical and far-reaching policy in its short history.
But this was not put together by strategists in air-conditioned government offices or honed by focus groups over weeks or months; it was
blurted out, almost by accident, in the back room of a pub in
Dublin's Temple Bar.

The Labour First Minister went on a fact-finding trip to Dublin
in August 2004 to see how the Irish smoking ban, which had been in
place since March that year, was working. McConnell had been
flirting with the idea of a ban on smoking in public places and he
was being pushed very hard in that direction by Tom McCabe, who
was then the deputy health minister and in charge of the ongoing
consultation on smoking. But the First Minister was also well aware
of the potential difficulties and was cautious about the impact of an
all-out ban. His trip to Dublin was supposed to be low key, giving
him the chance to assess the Irish experience so he could make an
informed decision. It was not supposed to provide the platform for
an announcement of a major policy change – but that was before the
press got involved.

McConnell was accompanied to Ireland by representatives from
half a dozen of Scotland's newspapers. They were desperate for a
story, at least partly to justify their editors' decision to send them to
Dublin in the first place. Because they were there, McConnell agreed
to hold an impromptu press briefing at lunchtime on 31 August in
the back room of the Porterhouse Bar in Parliament Street with the
Irish health minister, Micheál Martin. McConnell said how
impressed he had been with the way Ireland had adapted to the
ban. That was undoubtedly true. The one message from the Irish

government which had made a profound impact on McConnell was simple: 'It's not going to be nearly as difficult as you think it is.'

Martin was a persuasive advocate of smoking bans. He told McConnell that Irish ministers had travelled to New York, after the ban had been introduced there, and had been told that implementation was much simpler than they feared. They experienced the same and passed on that message to McConnell.

The First Minister wanted to show he was moving towards a smoking ban but was not ready to go the whole way, if only because such a move had not been endorsed by his Cabinet. However, he was pushed again and again and again by the reporters sitting round the small pub table to say whether he was in favour of a total ban. At last McConnell went further than he had ever gone before. He stated: 'I am more convinced now than I was in January that, at the very least, something approaching an all-out ban is enforceable and practical and desirable in Scotland.'

In purely political terms, McConnell had not gone as far as an outright ban, but in journalistic terms, he had done so. As in most situations like this where the message is not immediately clear, the reporters got together after McConnell's departure to go over the quotes and work out what 'the line' was. There was general agreement that the First Minister had given his backing to a ban and the key word was 'desirable'. As far as the press was concerned, McConnell had given a clear signal that he wanted a ban and, as First Minister, if that was what he wanted, that's what he would get.

But even the First Minister, who was well used to the vagaries of the press, would have been surprised by the coverage the following morning. Several newspapers were definite – an all-out smoking ban was on its way for Scotland and all enclosed public places would be smoke free in eighteen months. Magnus Gardham, the political editor of the *Daily Record*, went one step further, working out how long the legislation and the information campaigns would take and predicting – with some certainty – when the ban would be enforced. The paper carried the date of Sunday 26 March 2006 on its front page and told its readers smoking would be banned from that date – a remarkable leap really, given that the Cabinet had not even agreed the issue at that time.

In the end, though, the *Record*'s prediction was extremely prescient.

It had found out when National No Smoking Day was going to fall in 2006 and guessed this would be the first day of the ban, and it was right. Sunday 26 March 2006 marked the start of a new health-conscious era in Scotland as smoking was banned in all enclosed public spaces from that date. It was, without doubt, the most controversial, but ultimately most successful, policy introduced by the McConnell government.

This was one issue on which McConnell did show real leadership. Once he had been persuaded of the arguments – and once he had seen in the newspapers that he was backing a ban, even though he may not have got there all by himself – he led from the front.

There was huge opposition to the policy, from the licensed trade, from tobacco manufacturers, from elements of his own party, including some inside the Cabinet, and from Labour clubs all over the country. There was also opposition from Labour in London, where John Reid, the health secretary and a long-time smoker, was against an all-out ban. Reid did not agree with the state legislating on such matters and made it clear to McConnell that he did not want to see a ban in England or Scotland. McConnell did have the support of the SNP, however, which meant that he would have a clear parliamentary mandate for the move if he could get it through the Labour group. The First Minister asked for his party's support, which he got, although with reservations from some MSPs terrified that they would be torn apart in their local Labour clubs as a result.

But there was also a significant amount of political calculation in McConnell's move. New York already had a smoking ban, the Republic of Ireland had a ban, Northern Ireland was considering one, as was Wales, while England was shifting towards a partial ban. McConnell could see the trend towards bans right across Europe and he calculated, not unreasonably, that every western country would have a smoking ban in place within five to ten years. If it was going to happen anyway, then why not be at the forefront of the campaign?

So, while the smoking ban was radical and showed real leadership from McConnell, it was a practical move – a recognition that such bans were on their way in any case. It was perhaps a shame for the First Minister that his judgement was not quite so finely honed on other matters during this time.

The weekend of 5–6 June 2004 had been marked down in the

diaries of leading politicians and heads of state from around the world for some time beforehand. It was the sixtieth anniversary of the D–Day landings and a weekend of commemoration was planned. George W. Bush, the US President, was due to be in Normandy, as were the Queen and Tony Blair, the Prime Minister.

McConnell, as Scotland's First Minister, had received an invitation to join them. But when it arrived, McConnell's aides realised that he had already accepted an invitation for the evening of Saturday 5 June. A keen golfer, he was due to be at St Andrews with the Duke of York, a fellow enthusiast, to help the Royal and Ancient Golf Club celebrate its 250th anniversary. That was a prestigious event and one McConnell was looking forward to. He was asked whether he wanted to withdraw from the St Andrews dinner to go to Normandy but he decided not to, sending an email round to his Cabinet colleagues asking if any of them wanted to go to Normandy to represent the Scottish Executive on his behalf.

It was a decision of staggering political naivety. If McConnell did not see the danger in snubbing Second World War veterans and the Queen for a golf dinner then his advisers should have done so. When it emerged, on Thursday 3 June, that he would not be going to Normandy to commemorate the casualties of the D–Day landings, the First Minister was pilloried. The outrage and opprobrium which greeted his decision was so widespread it quickly became apparent that this was the biggest crisis he had faced in the three years he had been First Minister and one which had the potential to cause him irreparable harm.

McConnell decided the following morning, on Friday 4 June, that he would go to Normandy after all. Andy Kerr, the finance minister, who had been primed to go in his place, was stood down. It was definitely McConnell's worst weekend as First Minister, which was then capped by a delayed flight from Normandy to London on the Sunday which forced him to miss his return flight to Edinburgh.

If there was one image, however, which came to sum up this rather error-strewn period in McConnell's career, it was the slightly rushed snap of the First Minister standing, hands on hips, on a New York sidewalk, wearing a tight pinstripe kilt and a loose, blouson ghillie shirt. In the picture, the First Minister looks uncomfortable and more than slightly camp, while a pedestrian with a moustache and wearing a heavy raincoat and tartan cap looks on with a bewildered expression on his face. The First Minister endured more ribbing over this picture and suffered more from it than any other in his tenure.

McConnell had helped build up Tartan Week in the United States – the week-long series of events to promote Scotland in North America. One highlight was the Dressed to Kilt fashion show, a catwalk event to promote Scottish designers. McConnell had agreed to wear a kilt by the innovative Scottish designer Howie Nicholsby for the event.

The First Minister had been busy in the run-up to the show and had not had the chance to go to any fitting sessions. Nicholsby turned up at McConnell's hotel before the event with a series of kilts in the hope that one might fit him. But McConnell had been putting on weight as First Minister, grabbing irregular meals, not exercising and travelling everywhere by ministerial car and, as a result, was simply too fat to get into any of the kilts except a modern-looking black pinstripe number. Unfortunately, even though he could wear that kilt, he couldn't get into its matching jacket so opted for a loose ghillie shirt instead. This particular kilt was designed to be worn with a jacket and waistcoat and, without them, it just looked odd.

McConnell thought he had carried it off until his wife Bridget, who was back in Scotland, rang him the following morning with news that every paper in the country was ridiculing him. Commentators condemned the First Minister for wearing the pinstripe kilt but that was never the problem, as STV's Mike Crow showed when he hired the entire outfit for the annual press dinner for the politicians later that summer. Crow showed that, if the ensemble was worn together, it was both modern and smart but, by opting for a blouson shirt, McConnell just looked camp and embarrassed.

McConnell had made a conscious effort when he won the 2003 election to become a little more colourful. He had ditched his drab ties and always tried to be more extravagant in his clothes: the kilt decision was part of that process although, after suffering so much ridicule, he did retreat somewhat. He also started looking after his weight by hiring a personal trainer from the Army to put him through workouts in the basement of Bute House once a week.

However, McConnell was not just having to cope with errors and gaffes from his own team; he was also having to deal with deteriorating relations between Labour and the Liberal Democrats. The coalition partners had been together for five years and the strain was becoming evident.

Tavish Scott, then the junior finance minister, had taken issue with the Executive's fishing policy for the second time in November 2003. As a minister, Scott should have been bound by collective responsibility but he challenged that concept, and the First Minister, by calling for the Common Fisheries Policy to be scrapped, which was clearly counter to Executive policy.

Worse was to come the following year when Jim Wallace, the Liberal Democrat leader, claimed in an interview that his party was responsible for most of the successful policies adopted and pursued by the Scottish Executive. Then fourteen Liberal Democrats abstained during a crucial vote in the Scottish Parliament, inflicting an embarrassing defeat on the Executive. The atmosphere became so poisonous that McConnell had to intervene during a meeting of Labour MSPs, telling them not to get involved in personal squabbles with the Liberal Democrats. The simmering discontent was stoked further by the intervention of Ian McCartney, the Scottish chairman of the UK Labour Party. He accused the Liberal Democrats of 'overegging the pudding' by claiming credit for Executive successes and claimed they were 'on the side of the yob' by not backing Labour's youth crime crackdown.

Much of this was simply posturing ahead of the 2005 general election, with each party wanting to distance itself from the other, but it hardly helped relations at the core of the Scottish Executive. It exposed one of the central difficulties of having two different parliaments with two different electoral timetables. The two parties were in coalition at Holyrood but were preparing to fight each other to a standstill in a Westminster election.

Wallace was generally fairly conciliatory as far as Labour was concerned but he had his own issues to deal with. Since taking over the enterprise and economy brief, he had found it difficult to win over the business community. He just did not have the trust of big business in Scotland and he was hardly helped by his Labour colleagues, who sniped at him behind his back, warning that the

Scottish Liberal Democrat leader was in danger of failing to meet the
Executive's number one priority – growing the economy. Furthermore, Robert Crawford, the former chief executive of Scottish
Enterprise, had warned in February 2004 that Wallace had no 'clear
view' of the way forward for the Scottish economy and was incapable
of achieving 'new and exciting things'.

To a certain extent, Wallace was hamstrung by Scotland's reliance
on the public sector. In 2004, health and education received massive
rises in public spending, of up to 55 per cent, while enterprise and
economic growth got an increase of just 7 per cent, when the average
rise across the board in the Executive was 13 per cent. The public
sector in Scotland employed between 25 and 30 per cent of the
workforce and enjoyed spending levels per head which were well
above England's. The private sector was not nearly as well developed
or as self-reliant as in England and there was more of a culture in
Scotland to rely on the public sector.

McConnell did acknowledge that the public sector was too big,
in June 2004, but he claimed that the best way of redressing the
balance was not to shrink the public sector, but to grow the private
sector. That was a good idea in principle but every economist in
Scotland realised that, at the country's then sluggish growth rates,
that would take years to achieve.

The First Minister was achieving some of his own objectives,
however. He had driven through his young offenders bill and he
had pushed on with his plan to relocate civil service jobs outside
Edinburgh – to let the rest of Scotland share in the dividends of
devolution – even though the proposed move of Scottish Natural
Heritage to Inverness did spark anger and resulted in staff walking
away from their jobs rather than moving north. Meanwhile he was
still fighting a war of attrition with Labour council leaders over the
introduction of PR, but he eventually managed to buy them off by
promising substantial 'golden goodbyes' to long-serving councillors
and a restructured package for those that remained, which meant
proper salaries for councillors for the first time. Additionally,
McConnell had begun a high-profile campaign against sectarianism,
deciding to act on a scourge which had been ignored by most
politicians in Scotland for years in the hope that it would go away,
and he had launched his Fresh Talent initiative, to attract more

qualified foreigners to stay in Scotland, recognising that something had to be done to halt Scotland's falling population.

But just when the First Minister felt he was at last starting to emerge into an era he could control, when he reshuffled his team, put an end to the gaffes and reasserted some sort of authority over the discontented elements in his Executive, he was blown off course once again, this time over his New Year holiday.

McConnell had been friends with Kirsty Wark, the BBC *Newsnight* presenter, for a number of years. Their families were close and McConnell had no hesitation in accepting an invitation from Wark for their families to spend the New Year holiday of 2004–5 together in Wark's Majorcan villa. It was Wark who suffered, though, on their return, with critics warning that it would be hard to view the presenter as independent and non-partisan given the closeness of her friendship with Scotland's Labour First Minister.

For Wark, it was a problem. Her holiday with McConnell gave the Tories and the Nationalists the ammunition they needed to attack her if she put them on the defensive during television interviews. Nor did it help either McConnell or Wark that the controversy surfaced during the traditionally quiet post-Christmas period. This meant the story ran on for a month, rather than for a day or two, and it was given extra impetus when it emerged that McConnell had failed to declare the hospitality in his register of members' interests. It eventually died down in February 2005, but not before several newspapers had investigated, and published, details of all the links between Wark and Labour in Scotland.

The story was another graphic example, not just for McConnell but for all politicians in Scotland, of the extra level of scrutiny they were now under. This was then brought into stark focus by the most lurid allegations directed at a Scottish politician in living memory followed by a sensational legal challenge, culminating in what would become one of the most famous and extraordinary court cases of Scottish political history.

11

Splitters and swingers

ON Sunday 31 October 2004, the *News of the World* published a story under the headline 'Scottish *News of the World* girl Anvar, a married MSP and the wife swappers' club orgy'. In some ways it was typical *News* fare involving sex, drugs and at least one celebrity, although in this case the newspaper did not name the MSP involved. The story formed part of the promotion campaign by Anvar Khan, a Scottish *News of the World* columnist, for her book, which contained further intimate details of her alleged encounters with the politician and trips to a swingers' club in Manchester.

The rumour mill at the Scottish Parliament went berserk and it was not long before one MSP, Tommy Sheridan, leader of the Scottish Socialist Party, felt so pressured by the questions that he issued a flat denial, a denial which was then used as the basis for a follow-up article. Once the phrase 'Tommy Sheridan denies any involvement in. . .' appeared for the first time, the focus was on the forty-year-old 'sunbed socialist', as he had become known.

The SSP's executive committee came together for its November meeting just a few days later. It was to prove a crucial meeting because it became central to both sides in the court battle which followed. Some who were there claimed that Sheridan owned up to visiting Cupids, the swingers' club in Manchester named in Khan's article, but others insisted there was no such confession. There were then some suggestions that Sheridan was voted out of his leadership role by the executive committee and other, counter-claims that that was not the case.

What definitely happened, however, was that within days of the meeting, Sheridan resigned as leader of the SSP. He insisted that he was standing down to be with his wife Gail, who was going through a tough pregnancy. He admitted meeting Khan in 1992 but strongly denied any suggestion that he had been involved in orgies or had visited swingers' clubs.

The following Sunday, 14 November, the *News of the World* published yet more allegations, this time naming Sheridan and claiming he had had a four-year affair with Fiona McGuire, a former SSP candidate. Sheridan issued a writ against the *News of the World* and initiated legal action to sue the newspaper for defamation.

At the same time, his political party was facing meltdown. The party hierarchy was split, with some staying loyal to Sheridan and some turning against their charismatic former leader. The problem for the party was that, to a large extent, the SSP *was* Tommy Sheridan – or it was to large numbers of Scottish voters. Yes, the party had six MSPs but the only one who was well known was Sheridan. Without his driving force, the party was facing the prospect of being trounced at the next election and sinking under the £200,000 debt the party had accrued. The SSP tried to get by on a 'collective leadership' until a proper leader, Colin Fox, another MSP, could be installed but the rifts in the Sheridan case were tearing the party apart.

Rosie Kane, one of the new MSPs and the most publicity hungry after Sheridan, had claimed after the 2003 election that the SSP would turn the Scottish Parliament into a version of *Big Brother*, the reality TV show (see Chapter 9). She could not have known how accurate that would turn out to be as Sheridan's court action against the *News of the World* started on 4 July 2006.

The timing for the Scottish press pack could hardly have been better. The sensational court case started just after the Scottish Parliament had adjourned for its summer recess. There was little other news about and acres of newsprint to fill. It was lurid and sensational and involved one of the best-known figures in Scotland, not just in Scottish politics.

Sheridan was an old-fashioned soap-box orator, with a style of public speaking which left everybody else in Scottish politics trailing. He was the only political figure in Scotland who would elicit cheers and friendly applause just by walking down a street, and not just in Glasgow. The celebrity side of his court case was huge but Sheridan was also a divisive character. He was cheered by left-wingers but treated almost with contempt by the more mainstream political parties, which were wary of his influence and dismissive of his politics. Inside the SSP too he had had his problems, as his ego and his desire to be the 'voice of the left' sometimes appeared to come ahead of the political struggle which the party was engaged in.

Raised in a broken home in the deprived Pollok area of Glasgow, Sheridan excelled at school and went on to Stirling University, where he first met Jack McConnell. He joined the Labour Party and quickly aligned himself with the Militant wing. After graduating with an honours degree in economics, he went back to being a student as part of an unsuccessful attempt by Militant to take over Scottish Labour Students. Purged by Neil Kinnock from the Labour Party along with other Militant members, Sheridan then became instrumental in setting up a new socialist party. But it was the poll tax which really pushed him into the public eye when he led the campaign against it. Jailed for attending a demonstration against warrant sales, in defiance of a court order, he then fought a successful campaign from prison to be elected councillor for Pollok on Glasgow City Council.

The defamation court case against the *News of the World* started with the brief political martyrdom of the SSP's press and policy coordinator, Alan McCombes, who was jailed for twelve days after being held in contempt for refusing to hand over the crucial minutes from that November SSP executive committee meeting. But after that small piece of political theatre, the real fun started. The allegations came thick and fast: Sheridan had been involved in group sex with a prostitute in a Glasgow hotel suite, he had been to other swingers' clubs, he had had affairs with married women.

The first few days appeared awful for Sheridan and fabulous for the press. Witness after witness claimed to have slept with Sheridan or to have seen him taking part, or participated with him, in sex sessions. Three women claimed to have had affairs with him while he was married; two of them said they had visited Cupids with him. Every day the allegations became more and more salacious, with the evidence moving from ice cubes and nipple clamps to spanking and torture.

Then it was Sheridan's turn. He denied everything, he wept in court, he professed his love for his wife Gail, who stood by him throughout, and, at one point, he offered to strip for the jury to show how hairy he was. He claimed that a cabal within the SSP had forged a minute of the crucial meeting in November 2004 at which he was alleged to have confessed to visiting Cupids. The minute, he said, was 'as bent as a ten-bob note'.

However, the most extraordinary move came half way through the trial when Sheridan sacked his legal team, led by Richard Keen, one of the country's leading QCs. Keen was the lawyer who had won an acquittal for one of the men accused of the Lockerbie bombing and was known as 'the Rottweiler' for his tenacious courtroom manner. To the astonishment of the judge, Lord Turnbull, Sheridan decided to represent himself instead, using as a prop a simple wooden lectern which he was used to from his tub-thumping campaigning days. Legal and political opinion was universal – it would prove to be a fatal move; no-one could possibly hope to win a court case of this complexity and magnitude without professional legal representation.

But his trump card was his glamorous wife, who had wowed the features desks on the daily newspapers with her stylish outfits, never appearing in the same one twice, as she turned up to court every morning. Tommy Sheridan put Gail on the witness stand, where she told the jury her husband was a 'boring' man, obsessed with playing Scrabble. She professed her love and pride in him. If he had done the things the newspapers claimed he had, he would have found himself at the bottom of the Clyde, she said, with a look that suggested she meant it. By the end of that particular exchange both the Sheridans were in tears.

Tommy Sheridan then took on the *News of the World* witnesses – Fiona McGuire, Anvar Khan, a self-styled 'sexpert' who claimed she had visited Cupids with him and Katrine Trolle, a former party activist who said she had had a long-running affair with him. Sheridan claimed that most of them had been paid for their stories and continued to deny all their allegations.

McGuire's claims, which had prompted the legal action from Sheridan in the first place, appeared the flakiest. She had a hazy recollection for dates and details and admitted to being under the influence of drink and drugs when she first met Sheridan. Five days after she had signed a £20,000 contract with the *News of the World* for her story she tried to commit suicide. Sheridan claimed that that was her idea of an 'honourable' response to her guilt at lying. Gail Sheridan helped dismantle McGuire's evidence by claiming that she would have mentioned Tommy Sheridan's body hair in her graphic descriptions of sex sessions with him and it was this which prompted Sheridan's offer to remove his shirt for the court.

Khan's evidence also started to look less solid when she admitted that her original news story, about the unnamed MSP, had been a puff for her book, which was itself a jumble of real life and creative writing. Trolle, on the other hand, was slightly different. She was the most believable of the witnesses. The plain-spoken Danish occupational therapist was coherent and described in a matter-of-fact way her relationship with Sheridan.

But Sheridan portrayed the court case not just as a battle for his reputation and political career, but as a political battle against what he claimed were the most sinister forces of capitalism – the Murdoch press empire. Against him were eleven members of the SSP hierarchy, all of whom said that Sheridan had confessed to visiting Cupids at the vital executive committee meeting.

The final act came when Sheridan made his closing statement. Using the sort of rhetoric that had made him famous, Sheridan took eighty-five minutes to ridicule the inconsistencies in the *News of the World* stories, attacking the paper for threatening the life of his unborn child and claiming that, if the jury believed he would go to orgies and swingers' clubs with his public profile, then their verdict must be that he was a 'complete idiot'. Sheridan might not have known about the law, but he knew about public speaking and how to sway an audience.

In response, Mike Jones for the *News of the World* spent six hours on a detailed reprise of the evidence, accusing Sheridan of being reckless, in denial and ready to brand others as perjurers simply to save his skin. Anybody who imagined that so many people would risk their careers just to undermine him politically had a 'truly monstrous ego', Jones claimed.

In the end, the jury took just three hours to decide in Sheridan's favour by seven votes to four and Scotland's most famous socialist was awarded £200,000 in damages from the *News of the World*. Alice Sheridan, Sheridan's mother, who had sat listening to the case for the past month, wept from the public gallery while Sheridan turned to his wife and friends and mouthed the words: 'I'm okay.'

The silence of the courtroom was in marked contrast to the cheers which greeted the Sheridans as they emerged into the August sunshine, Tommy with one fist clenched in the air and the other clutching the beaming Gail by the hand.

Striding to the microphones, Tommy Sheridan compared his court victory to Gretna Football Club taking on Real Madrid in the Bernabéu stadium and winning on penalties. He declared: 'What this verdict proves is that working-class people, when they listen to the arguments, can differentiate the truth from the muck. They [the *News of the World*] are liars and we have proved that they are liars.' Had he lost the case, Sheridan could have been found liable for the *News of the World*'s legal expenses, an estimated £500,000, and would have faced probable bankruptcy. Instead, he was awarded the largest sum of damages in a defamation case in Scottish legal history.

Bob Bird, editor of the Scottish *News of the World*, said:

> I am absolutely astonished by today's verdict. This result suggests that eighteen independent witnesses came to this court and committed monstrous acts of perjury. We simply cannot accept that is what has happened. On that basis, we will be lodging an appeal. The basis of that appeal will be that the verdict was perverse.

So Sheridan's £200,000 windfall was put on hold while the appeal process started, but the most prescient point towards the end of the case came from Lord Turnbull, speaking outside the jury's hearing. 'It seems to me pretty much inevitable that there will have to be a criminal inquiry at the conclusion of this case into the question of whether witnesses have committed perjury. Witnesses who committed perjury would be liable to be sentenced to imprisonment for a lengthy period,' he warned.

Turnbull was right. It took two and a half years but, on Sunday 16 December 2007, the police acted. Sheridan was detained by three plain-clothes police officers as he left the Talk107 radio station in Edinburgh's South Gyle Crescent. He was taken to Gayfield police station, where he was charged with perjury, and his home in Glasgow was searched. The police took the action following an investigation and review of the court transcripts by the Crown Office. Sheridan claimed he was the victim of a 'political witch-hunt' and vowed to clear his name.

At the end of January 2009, the Crown Office confirmed that Tommy Sheridan would face two charges, one of perjury and another of attempting to persuade someone else to commit perjury. Gail was also told she would face one charge of perjury. Both consistently denied the charges but were told that a preliminary hearing would take place at the end of February 2009 with the full case expected to be heard later in the year. However, the perjury charges were not the only damaging ramifications of the Sheridan defamation case.

It has become a tradition for parties on the hard left to fragment, for any number of reasons. For the SSP, the cause was the court case, and Tommy Sheridan, the man who had once united Scottish Militant Labour and the Scottish Socialist Alliance into an effective and successful political party, was instrumental in the fracturing and disintegration of that very organisation. Three MSPs, Colin Fox, Carolyn Leckie and Rosie Kane, had given evidence against Sheridan, while Byrne had backed him publicly in court. They could hardly bear to be in the same room as each other, let alone in the same party.

Sheridan had been estranged from the SSP since November 2004 but it was not until the wake of his successful court case, in August 2006, that he launched his new party of the left, Solidarity. By this time there were two factions in the SSP, United Left, which refused to work with Sheridan, and Majority, which wanted him reinstalled as leader. With Sheridan now turning his back on the party he had helped create, many of the SSP Majority group moved across to join Solidarity. Unlike other splits among the hard left, there was no real policy difference between the two parties, just a difference of opinion over Sheridan's personality.

The problem for both parties was that Sheridan was linked into the SSP in many ways, but particularly because he and Byrne, as MSPs, had paid a portion of their salaries every month into SSP funds, money which the party needed to pay employees and cover the mortgage on its Glasgow headquarters. Those headquarters were the SSP's first casualty, as the party needed to sell them to cover the loss of revenue from Sheridan and Byrne. Fox, the new SSP leader, insisted there was no crisis in the party but it was clear that it was heading downhill, fast. The prospects looked slightly better for Solidarity, because the high-profile Sheridan was at the helm, but even his reputation as a working-class hero had been damaged by the allegations thrown up by the court case.

When it came to their first real electoral test as separate political parties, the 2007 Scottish election, both the SSP and Solidarity failed spectacularly. The SSP received only 13,256 votes throughout the whole of the country, on both the constituencies and the lists, compared to the 245,735 it had secured on both ballots in 2003. Its share of the vote was just 0.6 per cent in 2007 and the party lost all six of its MSPs. Solidarity attracted the support of 31,066 voters in 2007, 1.5 per cent of the vote, but still well short of the 6 per cent or so the party needed to secure the election of one MSP.

The collapse in support was partly due to the way the main parties tightened their campaign messages to squeeze out the smaller ones and partly down to the two-party contest that the election had turned into, but there was more to it than that. The demise of the hard left in the 2007 elections was mostly attributable to the way the SSP had torn itself apart, up to, during and after the Sheridan court case. The party which had announced itself as a force in Scottish politics in 2003 with six MSPs ended that parliamentary session in acrimonious dispute with former colleagues, in debt and not only with no MSPs, but with a paltry share of the vote which left it trailing behind the British National Party and the Christian People's Alliance.

The SSP had achieved some successes in the parliament and had championed causes, sometimes within the rules and sometimes outside, to get publicity for issues which had never featured in the parliament's deliberations before.

The party which had promised to shake up the Scottish Parliament did do that for a short period of time. On the last day of the parliamentary session before the summer recess of 2005, four SSP MSPs, Fox, Leckie, Kane and Frances Curran, held a protest in the parliament chamber, refusing to sit down and then refusing to leave their desks despite demands from the Presiding Officer for them to do so. Their crime was seen as extremely serious by the parliamentary authorities and they were banned from the parliamentary complex for a month, losing a month's salary too. Kane was then jailed for two weeks in 2006 for refusing to pay a fine after she had been one of ten protesters to chain themselves to the Royal Mile in a model nuclear submarine, protesting against nuclear weapons.

As far as more conventional politics was concerned, Sheridan put the issue of free school meals on the agenda in the Scottish Parliament and introduced a bill to abolish poindings and warrant sales (the Scottish system of selling off a debtors' possessions), which was then taken on in a similar form by the Scottish Executive.

In June 2003, when she came to open the new session, the Queen praised the 'rainbow parliament' which that year's election had produced – even though the Socialists refused to turn up to hear the hereditary monarch they so despised. By 2007, that rainbow parliament had been dissolved. The SSP had taken the politics of the street into the parliament. They had protested, they had hectored and they had infuriated the other parties with their tactics. Ultimately though, they were taken down by their own failure to stick together as a party. The SSP achieved its great 2003 success on the back of Sheridan and the party owed its failure in 2007 to Sheridan as well, this time for splitting it over his court case. It was a brief, but colourful, interlude in the short life of the parliament.

12

Grand designs

IN 2005, Malawi was generally seen as a far-off country of which most Scots knew little. Jack McConnell set out to change that in the most dramatic way he could. The First Minister was preparing to help host the G8 summit that summer, which was taking place at the Gleneagles Hotel, but he wanted to make his mark, and Scotland's, on the world stage before that gathering of the world's most powerful leaders took place.

The twin themes of the G8 summit were Africa and poverty so it seemed only natural for McConnell to do something which would promote those causes. But he was restricted. The devolution settlement was clear: neither the Scottish Parliament nor the Scottish Executive had any remit in international affairs, or in development aid: these were strictly reserved to Westminster. McConnell had been in power for four years by this point and he felt hemmed in by the confines of the settlement, so he told his advisers to find a solution.

On 16 March, the First Minister unveiled his answer. He would set up a £9 million Scottish Executive fund to help the Third World. He would get round the restrictions by giving grants just to Scottish charities working abroad, rather than to foreign governments or international aid agencies.

McConnell also announced his intention to help Malawi. With twice the population of Scotland at this time but an economy smaller than Falkirk's, the southern African country was one of the poorest in the world and needed all the help it could get, but the key for McConnell was that Malawi had long and deep Scottish connections. David Livingstone, the Scottish nineteenth-century missionary and explorer, had spent considerable time there and was credited with 'discovering' Lake Nyasa, now known as Lake Malawi. The city of Blantyre in Malawi is named after Livingstone's birthplace, Blantyre in Lanarkshire, and Livingstone had made the first significant western contact with the country. He was followed by many other Scots missionaries who settled in what was then Nyasaland. The Church of Scotland's connections remained strong and its ministers were among many liberals in Scotland to help campaign for Malawian independence through the 1960s.

Aware of the history and recognising that Scotland's role in international aid would be limited, McConnell decided to throw everything he could at Malawi. He decided that it was better to do as much as possible for one small country than to allocate the very limited funds he had made available around a range of needy countries and achieve very little. The First Minister reckoned, rightly, that the effect would be felt in Malawi in a way that it wouldn't if spread too thinly. But he also was determined that the Scottish Parliament should begin to look outwards, after six years of domestic concentration, and that it had the chance to be a force for good – albeit in a small way – on the international stage.

McConnell's decision to branch into foreign affairs caused some resentment among his Labour colleagues at Westminster. The First Minister had been careful to square off everything with the Foreign Office before making his announcement so there was no criticism from there – more a watchful wariness. But, as far as some Labour MPs were concerned, McConnell was reaching far and away above his remit and was playing into the hands of the SNP by promoting the Scottish Executive in an international context. The whispering against McConnell grew louder, particularly as it started to sink in that he had planned a high-profile trip to Malawi for May that year, just ahead of the G8 summit.

Privately, the SNP was delighted. McConnell was showing his credentials as a small-N nationalist and was taking on the Labour establishment in London by raising the profile of the Scottish Executive. Publicly, it was more cautious as it watched to see whether the whole enterprise would come crashing down.

On 22 May 2005, the McConnell expedition left for Lilongwe, the Malawian capital, complete with advisers, television cameras, broadcast journalists and representatives from most of Scotland's newspapers. McConnell had £9 million of development aid cash to spend but even he was unsure how the trip would go.

It came as a shock to him, and to his entourage, when he was greeted at Lilongwe airport by a limousine protected by soldiers in uniform who ran alongside the car in perfect formation as it whisked the First Minister off from the tarmac to the VIP lounge in the airport, where he had the first formal talks with Cassim Chilumpha, Malawi's vice-president. McConnell managed to look both pleased and apprehensive at the same time as he was feted with the sort of courtesy and treatment normally reserved for heads of state.

The Malawi government was delighted to have Scotland's First Minister as a guest but it also wanted action, help and, above all, money. The restrictions placed on the Scottish Executive meant that McConnell could promise aid only to Scottish charities working in Malawi, not to the Malawian government, which was not what Malawian ministers wanted to hear.

The next day saw McConnell, now accompanied by the British high commissioner and travelling round in a consulate-flagged Range Rover, taken to Bottom Maternity Hospital just outside Lilongwe. The hospital had got its name after the whites opened another for their own care at the top of a hill, leaving the blacks and Asians to suffer with whatever they could find at the bottom.

The place had been cleaned up before McConnell's arrival. Some sheets had been found and put on the beds, stinking debris in the corridors had been removed and the hundreds of family members who usually waited in the shade outside the front of the hospital had been moved to the uncovered sun-bleached area round the back. Even the wards, which were usually so full of patients that many had to lie on the floor, had been 'trimmed' to a presentable level. But nothing could hide the gut-wrenching hopelessness of the facilities and conditions.

Graeme Walker, one of the doctors from Edinburgh's Royal Infirmary (ERI) who was in Malawi to help on a short-term basis, made it clear how much needed to be done:

> Here, a mother dies every six days. I have been working at the ERI for eight years and have never had to witness that. They have blunt scissors. They have no clips to do C-sections with and, if they do, they have no swabs. If I want a hundred swabs, I can have them in Edinburgh. They have got none here.

Bottom Hospital had just two midwives for about forty births a day. The hospital stank of urine and sewage and the windows were broken. There was only one working incubator and, if that was in use when a sick baby was born, the unlucky infant was handed back to its mother to die.

There were two clear problems which needed to be resolved before places such as Bottom Hospital could start to recover, both of which McConnell could help with but neither he could solve. One was financial help and McConnell pledged £360,000 from the Executive's development fund to finance the secondment of doctors and midwives from Scotland – like Walker – to Bottom. The other was the exodus of health staff from Malawi to work in Britain. The temptation for health workers to leave Malawi was huge, they could get away from the appalling conditions they had to endure at home and earn as much in a week as they would earn in a year in Africa. McConnell also promised to do what he could on this front, even though his influence on immigration policy was strictly limited. He ended up signing an agreement with Malawian President Bingu wa Mutharika to help persuade expatriate Malawians home and not to entice them to Scotland in the first place.

Over the next two days, McConnell was taken to a school in the bush with classrooms and students but no equipment, not even desks or chairs to sit on. He was also shown a feeding station in Linthipe, in central Malawi, where 1,200 children, most of them AIDS or famine orphans, were given one free nutritious meal every day.

Up until this point, the Scottish media had taken a fairly stand-offish approach to McConnell's trip. Most of the editors in Scotland thought he was simply grandstanding and did not give the visit much coverage. There was nothing on the television news, because the broadcasters did not have the facilities to report back live. The BBC did broadcast daily radio reports, but these did not do enough to generate an enthusiastic response back home.

Then, on the day of the Linthipe feeding station visit, everything went berserk in the sort of chaotic fashion which only the British tabloids can create. Magnus Gardham, political editor of the *Daily Record*, had managed to persuade his desk to carry more than just the usual few paragraphs on the First Minister's visit and to launch a *Record* appeal to raise money for Malawi. At the same time, the *Sun* decided to run its own appeal and its Scottish political editor, Andrew Nicoll, was told not only to write all he could on the plight of the Malawians, but to get McConnell to back the *Sun's* own appeal for Malawi. Through that evening, the demands from each newsdesk became more and more intense with Gardham and Nicoll having to file yet more copy setting out in graphic detail how bad the situation was in Malawi.

Instead of having a restful evening in his Blantyre hotel, McConnell found himself pestered by increasingly insistent editors from the *Sun* and the *Daily Record* to back their individual appeals. He was pleased with the attention but worried that this most bizarre of tabloid wars – as neither had shown much interest in Malawi up to that point – was getting out of hand. It did start to appear as if each paper was more interested in beating its rival to McConnell's support than in actually promoting the interests of Malawi.

The following day, when McConnell's entourage was faxed through copies of that morning's competing and raucous Scottish editions, it was clear that the First Minister had to act. He had been planning to launch a Malawi appeal on his return to Scotland but he was forced to bring it forward, announcing in Malawi that he wanted a Scotland-wide fund-raising appeal when he returned. He backed neither the *Sun's* nor the *Daily Record's* appeal, in a desperate attempt not to court favouritism with either of Scotland's best-selling news-papers.

The *Daily Record* championed its appeal for a few days, resurrected stories about it a couple of times afterwards but eventually forgot about it, even turning on McConnell a year later when it emerged that his trip had cost £34,500 – more than his appeal had raised in its first eight months. The *Sun* did even less; indeed it appeared that its Malawi appeal had been hardly more than a spoiler – an attempt to undermine the *Record* – but with little other intent. The *Record's* appeal ended up raising £30,000, which the newspaper claimed had paid for a doctor to be hired and placed on duty through the night at Bottom Hospital, something it had not had before.

McConnell's official appeal eventually raised £300,000 for Malawi – much, much more than the cost of his trip. This was then matched by the Clinton Hunter Development Initiative, a collaborative venture between the former US President Bill Clinton and the Scottish philanthropist Tom Hunter to generate money for Malawi, and the combined total was enough to start building a new hospital at Bottom. But as far as McConnell's Executive-funded largesse was concerned, the effects were less pronounced. The Scottish Executive spent a total of £6.6 million in Malawi between 2005 and 2007, but only £10,000 went directly to Bottom Hospital, and this for a private area for HIV/AIDS counselling. A further £360,000 went, as planned, to pay for Scottish experts to come over and train Malawian midwives. So although a new hospital was on its way, thanks to the generosity of the Scots and the Clinton Hunter Development Initiative, conditions at the original Bottom Hospital actually went backwards in the immediate few months and years after McConnell's visit.

The situation for the other major project which McConnell promised to help, a school at Minga, a few miles south-east of Lilongwe, was even more mixed. By 2007, £13,000 from the Scottish Executive had provided a new science laboratory and library. But both were empty because there was no money for equipment and books and there were still no desks and chairs for the pupils to use.

McConnell was severely restricted in what he could do for Malawi and he was frustrated because of that. He wanted to help, to use the Executive's development fund more widely, but was constrained by the devolution settlement. He had to endure criticism from Labour colleagues and some newspaper columnists back home for his 'grandstanding' and there was undoubtedly some truth in that. He was made a 'chief' in one town and given an 'authority stick'. He was also feted wherever he went, called 'Your Excellency' and treated with courtesy and deference.

Besides all that, the McConnell trip did two things, one practical and one political. It raised significant sums for Malawi; it is doubtful if a replacement for Bottom Hospital would ever have been built without his visit. On a political level, it gave the Scottish Executive a role – however limited – in the world for the first time. It was, in effect, allowing the Scottish Parliament to flex its muscles abroad in what was a clear sign of the growing maturity of the institution, even though that may have been derided by some MPs at Westminster.

If his Malawi trip had given him a taste of life as a diplomat, an event later that year in Scotland would see McConnell – and the

Scottish Executive – take an even bigger step onto the world stage: the G8 summit. These meetings of the leaders of the eight most powerful and economically wealthy nations on earth had become synonymous with protests and even riots as a mixture of anti-globalisation groups, anarchists and environmental campaigners from all over the world converged to disrupt events.

The 2004 G8 meeting had been held on an island off the Florida coast in an attempt to keep the leaders isolated from the increasingly violent protests. So, when the Gleneagles Hotel was chosen as the venue for the following year's summit, the biggest worry was security. This made it difficult for Scotland's political leaders. They wanted to support the G8 because of the profile it would give Scotland and the boost in terms of tourism, trade and publicity that the event would attract, but they were also worried about the effects of widespread demonstrations and the cost of securing the world's most powerful leaders at Gleneagles.

As the summit drew closer, so relations between the Scottish Executive and Westminster became more and more strained. Indeed, it caused the biggest and most serious bust-up between McConnell and Tony Blair. The summit was a UK event and, as such, was the responsibility of the UK government both to organise and to fund. With security costs rocketing and early estimates suggesting that the final bill just for policing the event could top £150 million, McConnell was adamant that the Treasury should pick up the entire tab.

McConnell raised the issue with the Prime Minister several times in the months before the summit and each time he was told: 'Don't worry about that – it will be taken care of.' But he did worry because by this point he no longer trusted Blair and wanted a proper guarantee that the Scottish Executive would not be left with any partial bill for the policing costs.

After weeks of procrastination from Downing Street, McConnell felt he had to issue an ultimatum. He told Blair that he would go public with the row over the security expenses unless he received a written assurance that the Treasury would pick up the bill. The First Minister told his aides to pencil in a date when he could go to the Scottish Parliament and announce that the Prime Minister had failed to keep his word on security costs. In public, McConnell remained totally supportive of the Prime Minister and the G8; in private he was getting increasingly angry and concerned. He was being pushed hard by the press and the SNP to explain how much the summit was going to cost and how much the Scottish Executive was going to have to pay and he was getting nothing from Downing Street.

McConnell eventually received a categoric assurance from Gordon Brown that Westminster would cover the security costs and in response, he backed down over his threat to go public with his dispute with Blair. But relations between the two failed to get any better. In fact, they sank to a new low at the Scottish Labour conference in the spring of 2005, when Blair used his speech to praise a number of Scottish Labour figures, but not McConnell. His only reference to the First Minister came when he poked fun at McConnell's ability to make gaffes.*

McConnell felt humiliated and angry. 'I would never publicly humiliate a colleague like that and Blair would never do it to anyone else,' he told colleagues afterwards.

The tense political by-play between Brown and Blair started to sway the lead-up to the G8 too. A campaign called Make Poverty History had sprung up with the aim of persuading world leaders to end poverty, backed by Bob Geldof, the musician and anti-poverty campaigner, who called for a million people to come to Edinburgh to protest.

Geldof's million-person march was planned for Edinburgh for the weekend before the summit. Brown, keen to establish his credentials on this issue, called for a huge turnout, urging people to come to the Scottish capital to demonstrate. It was a risky move, particularly as the police expected the march to be hijacked by the more militant and violent elements of the anarchist and anti-globalisation groups.

That march, on Saturday 2 July, which attracted 225,000 protesters, passed off without serious incident. It was only the following week, when anarchists and other, more aggressive, demonstrators appeared, that the first real trouble erupted. Bands of activists from across Europe brought Edinburgh city centre to a standstill on 4 July, the day before the summit opened, clashing with riot police and smashing

---

* See Lorraine Davidson, *Lucky Jack: Scotland's First Minister* (Edinburgh: Black & White, 2005).

offices and shops, particularly those owned by big global corporations. At the end of this day of violence, ninety demonstrators had been arrested and thirty people injured, some of them police officers. It did not bode well for the following few days but, on the scale of previous G8 summits, it was actually relatively minor.

The Gleneagles Hotel was, in many ways, a good site for the G8. It could be ringed by high fences and walls and was relatively easy to defend. One problem, however, was that there was not nearly enough accommodation nearby for the 1,200 members of the world's media who were due to attend, plus all the representatives of other organisations and groups which had a legitimate right to be there. The result was that hotels in Edinburgh were taken over for the summit, with delegates and journalists bussed up to Perthshire each day. The contract for that bus service had been put out to tender and awarded to an English company, which was fine in cost terms but meant that many of the drivers had little idea where they were supposed to be going.

This was then exacerbated as demonstrators went out early on the first morning and blocked key roads around Gleneagles. The bus drivers were given alternative back-road routes but some just got lost and ended up taking their complement of journalists round and round rural Perthshire, sometimes passing convoys of buses going in the opposite direction. The buses carrying Scottish journalists were generally alright because they had local guides to direct them to the venue.

On one occasion a bus was stopped by a group of demonstrators who had lain down in the road to block all transport to the summit. The police did not feel they could move them on physically and there was a standoff which was only resolved when one member of the Scottish press got down from the bus, went over to the demonstrators and told them that the bus was carrying representatives of the world's media, not delegates for the summit. At that point the demonstrators got up and allowed the bus to pass.

As for McConnell, he had managed to secure a high-profile role at the summit. He was at Prestwick airport in Ayrshire to welcome the leaders as they arrived. The first television shots of the summit showed McConnell greeting George W. Bush, the US President, and Gerhard Schroeder, the German Chancellor. McConnell was also

Donald Dewar *right*, First Minister, and his deputy, Jim Wallace, sign the agreement creating Scotland's first government in 300 years at the Royal Museum of Scotland, 14 May 1999. (Jon Savage/*Scotsman*)

Dewar *left* with the Queen and Sir David Steel at the official opening of the Scottish Parliament, 1 July 1999. (Paul Chappells/*Scotsman*)

The Church of Scotland General Assembly Hall,
first home of the Scottish Parliament.
(Paul Chappells/ *Scotsman*)

Enric Miralles, the
lead architect of the
Scottish Parliament
building, discusses
some of the finer
details with Dewar. In
the foreground is a
model of the project.
(Graham Hamilton/
Scotsman)

Two views of the completed Scottish Parliament building.
(Ian Rutherford/*Scotsman*)

An emotional Henry McLeish arrives at the Scottish Parliament
to announce his resignation as First Minister and Labour leader
in the parliament, November 2001. (David Moir/*Scotsman*)

The Scottish Socialist MSP Rosie Kane takes the oath of allegiance to the Queen following her success in the 2003 general election. Written on her hand are the words 'My oath is to the people'.
(David Cheskin/PA)

First Minister Jack McConnell wears his infamous pinstripe kilt to publicise Tartan Week in New York, 2004.
(Lloyd Smith)

McConnell visits the Henry Henderson Institute, Blantyre, as part of his tour of Malawi, May 2005.
(Donald MacLeod/*Scotsman*)

Lord Watson of Invergowrie leaves Edinburgh Sheriff Court after pleading guilty to wilful fire raising, September 2005. (Andrew Milligan/PA)

Tommy Sheridan celebrates victory in his libel case against the *News of the World*, August 2006. (Ian Rutherford/ *Scotsman*)

SNP leader Alex Salmond makes his first speech at the Hub after the announcement that his party has beaten Labour in the 2007 general election. (Jane Barlow/*Scotsman*)

The SNP's John Mason is jubilant after winning the Glasgow East by-election with a 22 per cent swing against Labour, July 2008. (Ian Rutherford/*Scotsman*)

the only non-head of state invited to the royal banquet that night, a move which certainly upset some of his Westminster colleagues again. But he also managed to make more practical progress, arranging a meeting with China's President, Hu Jintao, to help boost Scottish trade with China, and a dinner with Thabo Mbeki, the South African President, and Kofi Annan, the United Nations secretary general. It was a perfect riposte to his critics, who claimed once again that he was 'grandstanding' and that he would be doing nothing but floating round the edges of the summit.

Those first two days were marked by the farcical — President Bush fell off his bicycle while trying to ride and wave to a policeman at the same time — and the chaotic, as demonstrators tried to break in through the 'ring of steel' erected by the police to keep them out. On the evening of 6 July, a group of demonstrators did break through one part of the security fence and fought running battles with the police in the long grass and moorland outside Gleneagles. The media inside were not allowed out and no other journalists were allowed anywhere near the site. All the watching journalists could do was go onto the balcony of the press bar, which afforded the best view, and stand there, clutching gin and tonics and watching the battle going on below as massive Chinook helicopters flew in low with reinforcements and the battle lines moved forward and back. Sometimes all that could be seen was flashing lights and a line of yellow police jackets and it was not long before some members of the press pack realised they could see more if they retreated back into the bar to watch events unfold on television, through the lenses of the news helicopters hovering above.

The scale of the G8 summit was immense. There were 900 writing stations for newspaper journalists in the press centre: that is 900 desks, each with a phone, a computer link, a light and several power points. Geldof, his compatriot and fellow musician Bono and the American actor George Clooney turned up to lobby for more help for Africa and everywhere there were talks, meetings, press conferences and bilateral discussions. It was really possible to believe what the comedian Eddie Izzard had declared at the Live 8 concert at Murrayfield Stadium the weekend before: 'Scotland, you are the centre of the universe.'

Given the massive profile which the G8 brought for Scotland, the attitude of the Nationalists was oddly ambivalent. One senior SNP figure called for the summit to be scrapped and the money invested instead to combat disease in Malawi. Another leading MSP, Alex Neil, provoked groans of ridicule from the entire UK press corps when he sent out a press release at 12.47 p.m. on 5 July, warning that Scotland might lose out financially from the London Olympics. The decision on the Olympics had been announced at 12.46 p.m. that day and to complain about the decision the moment it had been made appeared small minded, churlish and typical of the worst forms of parochialism that the SNP had been trying to avoid.

For McConnell the summit was going very well. He had managed to appear on the world stage and had secured important meetings with key figures. He had represented the Scottish Executive at the biggest and most expensive global summit ever staged in the UK and Scotland had come across well as the sun shone and the Perthshire countryside sparkled.

But events on 7 July disrupted everything. The bombings in London, which took the lives of fifty-two people on three Tube trains and a double-decker bus, brought the G8 to an immediate halt. The world leaders stood united in a show of solidarity before Tony Blair rushed back to London to deal with the aftermath. The summit continued, but under a cloud, and although communiqués were agreed and signed on the main themes of Africa and poverty, it was all overshadowed by events in London.

For McConnell, this turned his triumph into nothing more than a muted success. The publicity that Scotland had received had been enthusiastic up until the terrorist attacks in London. From that point onwards, the G8, and Scotland, were understandably relegated to the inside pages and the later items on broadcast news bulletins. A survey later of almost 5,000 news articles on the summit found that the vast majority, 94 per cent, were neutral about Scotland, 1 per cent were negative and 5 per cent were positive. Scottish ministers claimed that the benefits to Scotland from hosting the summit would be worth millions in years to come but Alan Wilson, professor of marketing at Strathclyde University, claimed that the television pictures of rioters on Princes Street had created a stronger impression than the hours of 'positive' coverage. McConnell insisted that the whole event had been a success, although this was challenged by business leaders, particularly those representing traders in Edinburgh who had seen their shops smashed up by protesters.

The most damaging part for the Scottish Executive was that it did actually end up with a sizeable bill for the security costs, despite Gordon Brown's guarantee that this would not happen. The Executive had to pay out £60.1 million for the police costs, with the UK government paying £30.6 million. The other expenses, amounting to a further £13 million, were picked up by Westminster, including £4 million on media facilities, £1.5 million on transport and £22,000 on a programme of events for the spouses of the world leaders.

What was certain is that the G8 summit was the biggest, most impressive and most expensive event of its type ever held in Britain. McConnell managed to tread the same stage as international leaders for a brief time before the whole event was subsumed by the terrorist attacks in London.

However, the summit did leave the Scottish Executive with that large bill. The whole concept of G8 meetings started to appear unrealistic and expensive and there have since been moves to scrap them. Because of that, and because of the problems between Edinburgh and London, Scotland is unlikely to host one ever again. That will be celebrated by the people of Perthshire and Edinburgh who had to deal with demonstrators and closed roads but probably not by McConnell, who, for a couple of long summer days, got to experience what it would be like to lead one of the biggest countries in the world, not just a small, devolved administration in one part of Britain.

13

The harder they fall

IF the first term of the Scottish Parliament was characterised by the loss of two First Ministers, then the second was defined by political scandal. Tommy Sheridan was not the only politician to see his career disintegrate; three other MSPs achieved notoriety and lost their jobs as a result of their actions and one even ended up in prison. All three scandals surfaced during an intense ten-month period starting in November 2004, the first of which was so extraordinary that it stunned not only the Scottish Parliament but the whole of the country.

Every year, the *Herald* and STV joined forces to put on the Scottish Politician of the Year dinner and awards ceremony. Held in early November, it had become one of the highlights of the parliamentary calendar.

On 11 November 2004, the black-tie event was held at Prestonfield House, the smart seventeenth-century mansion on the south side of Edinburgh which had just been named Scottish Hotel of the Year. The televised awards ceremony and the dinner were held in the Stables, a large circular dinner and events venue in the grounds. Guests were greeted by flaming torches lining the carriage sweep in front of the white gabled entrance to the hotel while a piper welcomed them in for pre-dinner drinks. The ceremony itself was as glitzy and glamorous as Scotland's political establishment could make it. Afterwards some guests went home but others were invited by the hosts to continue the evening inside the main house, where there was plenty to drink for those who wanted it.

Lord Watson of Invergowrie, who had piloted the fox-hunting ban through the parliament, was one of those still in the house at 2 a.m., drinking with Malcolm Dickson, the editor of *Holyrood Magazine*. Shortly afterwards, Dickson left Watson on his own for a few minutes. It was then that the fire alarm went off. All those who remained were ushered outside onto the lawn while staff investigated the incident. A curtain was found to be on fire and it was extinguished before guests were let back in. Senior managers at the hotel immediately checked the closed circuit television pictures from the reception room where the fire broke out. The pictures, which were timed, showed the following:

- 2.12 a.m.: a man is standing at one side of the reception room below a circular mirror hanging on the wall.
- 2.13: the man moves to the right and appears to crouch beside some curtains. One minute later, he walks away. He is wearing a kilt and light-coloured socks. He passes another guest, who is looking the other way.
- 2.16: the same man comes back into camera. He is at the far end of the room. He looks at the curtains. A flame is lapping the border of the heavy drapes. Two minutes later, the flames are reaching the top of one side of the curtains. Smoke begins to billow across the ceiling.

Initially, there were hopes that the fire was nothing but an accident. However, when staff found evidence of a separate attempt to set fire to curtains in a nearby room – which had failed to ignite – it was clear that they were dealing with a case of deliberate fire raising.

As the managers played the footage over and over, one of them commented on a resemblance between the man bending down over the curtains and Watson, who had just left in a taxi. The following day, Watson was confronted by journalists from the *Herald* with frames from the CCTV cameras. When asked whether he had set the curtain on fire, Watson replied: 'Absolutely not . . . I was aware of smoke, I remember smoke, I remember a fire alarm, that's all. I don't remember seeing it [the curtain] on fire, that's for sure. I remember smoke, I don't remember seeing flames, I remember smoke.' And when asked whether he accepted that pictures showed him setting fire to the curtains, he replied: 'I don't accept that, because it's inconclusive. I can't identify for sure. I do remember having a look in some of the other rooms, but that's a fairly normal thing to do.'

What was certainly not a normal thing to do was setting fire to curtains in a packed hotel at 2 a.m., a hotel which was full of

Scotland's senior political figures, any number of whom could have been killed had the fire taken hold in the 300-year-old house.

Watson might not have been able to remember what happened but the CCTV pictures were clear enough for Lothian and Borders Police. Officers from the force interviewed Watson and took away the curtains for detailed analysis. The Labour peer was then charged with fire raising three days after the event, on 14 November. Labour leaders moved quickly to distance themselves from Watson and suspended him from the party, preventing him from acting either as a Labour MSP or as a Labour peer.

If Sheridan's trial had been salacious and sensational, Watson's was simply incredible. Here was a peer of the realm, someone who had been an MP and a Scottish minister and was still an MSP. Yet he was accused of wilful fire raising in one of the country's most prestigious hotels at the end of a grand black-tie awards evening for the country's top politicians, and doing so when many of the guests were still in the building.

The 56-year-old politician had been the MP for Glasgow Central. He had left Westminster politics when his constituency disappeared in boundary changes. He then lost a bitter candidate selection battle with Mohammed Sarwar for the Glasgow Govan seat before the 1997 election. As a consolation, he was made a life peer shortly afterwards and then he stood for election again in 1999, this time for the Scottish Parliament, and was elected as the MSP for Glasgow Cathcart. He was a high-profile figure, having brought forward the hunting bill, and he had been minister for culture, tourism and sport in Jack McConnell's first Executive, in 2001, before being axed from the administration after the 2003 election.

The charges he faced were: setting a curtain alight in the reception area at Prestonfield House and doing so wilfully, and setting fire to a curtain in the Yellow Room at the hotel, again wilfully, endangering the lives of those in the hotel.

When the case was heard at Edinburgh Sheriff Court at the start of September 2005, Adrian Fraser, the procurator fiscal depute, set out the case for the Crown. He told the court that witnesses had seen Watson at a bar where staff were clearing up and the peer was rude to them, asking 'forcibly' for more wine. Watson would not accept that no more alcohol would be served and, to calm the situation down, staff gave him an open bottle of wine from a nearby table. About fifteen minutes later, the fire alarm went off; staff found the fire in the reception room and put it out.

Fraser told the court that CCTV footage showed Watson entering reception and lifting something from a cabinet. He took hold of a lamp and pointed it round the room like a torch. He then bent down at a curtain and left the room. Fraser said:

> At that point, the curtain was smouldering. As the accused left, he placed something in the sporran of the kilt he was wearing. The footage also shows the accused returning to the room shortly there-after and looking at the burning curtain. He then left and made no attempt to report what he had done or the fact that the curtain was burning. Shortly afterwards, flames are seen to travel up the curtain ... and the room then filled with black smoke.
>
> Part of the evidence linking the accused to the fire was that he was later found with matches which he appeared to be attempting to conceal.

A fire officer told the court that the occupants of the hotel had been put in a potentially very dangerous situation.

The case lasted only a day. Watson had decided to plead guilty to the first charge and not guilty to the second. The Crown accepted his pleas. Watson could not come up with an explanation for what he described as his 'inexplicable' actions, merely saying that they were 'totally out of character'. But his guilty plea meant he was immediately convicted of fire raising and was bailed for three weeks, after which he would be sentenced.

The three-week break before sentencing allowed Labour to get ready for the time when they would disown the MSP completely. Watson helped the party by resigning from the Scottish Parliament, cutting his main link to the Scottish Labour Party, and preparations for the by-election went ahead.

Everything seemed to hinge on whether the sheriff felt Watson had endangered life. If that was the case, then it really looked as if Watson would be sent down. That would be an ignominious end to his political career and a severe embarrassment for his party. But there was a feeling among MSPs of all parties that there was no way the court could avoid a prison sentence. Several newspapers had found criminals from modest backgrounds who had been jailed for fire raising and the court could not be seen to be lenient with someone in as privileged a position as Watson.

On 22 September 2005, Watson was back at court to hear his sentence. His lawyer appealed for leniency, claiming that Watson had a drink problem and was struggling to cope with his wife Claire's loss of a baby after IVF treatment. But the sheriff, Kathrine Mackie, told Watson:

> Fire raising is a most serious crime. By pleading guilty to this charge, you have acknowledged that you intended to set on fire property at Prestonfield House Hotel whereby property was damaged and lives were endangered. The potential for serious injury to guests and staff within the hotel and for significant damage to the hotel was considerable. That there was neither injury nor more serious damage was due entirely to the prompt and efficient actings of staff and the standard of safety equipment properly and readily available at the hotel.
>
> No explanation has been offered for your actions. A large amount of alcohol appears to have been consumed but that neither excuses nor fully explains your behaviour.

Mackie said background reports showed that Watson posed a high risk of reoffending, and she added: 'I believe a custodial sentence is the only appropriate disposal. No other disposal would, in my view, address the concern for public safety.'

His wife was in tears as Watson was given sixteen months and led down from the court in handcuffs. He was taken to Edinburgh's Saughton prison and he was there, earning £8 a day for serving in the kitchens, when he heard that his final ties with the Scottish Parliament had been severed just eight days later when a new MSP was elected as his replacement in Glasgow Cathcart.

McConnell had been anxious to get the by-election over as soon as possible, in an attempt to move on from the scandal, but things did not quite go according to plan. Charlie Gordon, the Labour leader of Glasgow City Council, wanted to stand for the seat but he and McConnell had clashed in the past and the First Minister wanted

Charan Gill, a millionaire restaurant entrepreneur, to become the Labour candidate. McConnell pushed Gill's name forward but then it emerged that Gill had only just become a Labour Party member. The party rules were clear that a candidate must be a member for a year before standing for election so Gill was barred from the contest.

This allowed Gordon to come through as the Labour candidate and paved the way for an embarrassing campaign launch for both Gordon and McConnell on 13 September. Everyone present knew that Gordon was not McConnell's first choice and, by the time the press conference started, every member of the press had seen copies of derogatory comments Gordon had made about McConnell in an interview in 2003.

The conference got worse and worse for Labour and better and better for the press. Gordon was asked why he had described New Labour as 'bullshit' – he said it was just an example of his 'exuberant' debating style. He was then asked why he had said about McConnell, in the same 2003 interview: 'I was going to say Jack's a pragmatist – but that's to impute to Jack a degree of sophistication.'

Clearly flustered by this point, Gordon could only reply: 'I was ruminating at that point, wasn't I?'

McConnell, looking equally uncomfortable, was then asked to explain why he was endorsing Gordon as the Labour candidate when everyone knew he really wanted Gill to contest the seat. He fended off the questions then stood up to make a speech on Gordon's behalf and, in an appropriately symbolic gesture, accidentally knocked over a huge 'Vote for Gordon' banner.

Finally, the pair were asked about Watson, the fire raising and the cause of the by-election. 'It was a terrible crime – but it wasn't the Labour Party who set fire to those hotel curtains,' replied Gordon. At that point it really appeared as if McConnell could not wait to get out of Glasgow and back to Bute House.

On 29 September, Gordon held the seat, but Labour saw its majority halved, from 5,112 to 2,405, with a swing to the SNP. Another by-election on the same day, this time for the Westminster seat of Livingston – caused by the death of Robin Cook – was worse for Labour, but again the party still held on to the seat, its majority cut from 13,097 to just 2,680 by the SNP.

Holding both seats was a success for Labour, particularly as the party had been in power at Westminster for eight years and at Holyrood for six years. Experts and election commentators said it had been a bad night for the SNP. Alex Salmond disagreed and claimed, to widespread disbelief, that the 10 per cent swing to his party in Livingston showed that the SNP would go on to win the 2007 election.

Meanwhile, as the Watson scandal was coming to its conclusion, another controversy was just starting to build, this time involving David McLetchie, the Scottish Conservative leader. McLetchie was the longest-serving of the main party leaders at Holyrood, having been in place since before the 1999 election. He had always been a solid performer, experienced and good at using his lawyerly training to mock and dissect his political opponents in the chamber. He had also stopped the freefall which the Scottish Tories found themselves in after their 1997 wipeout.

But the Scottish Tory leader had claimed more for taxis than any other MSP – £11,565.19 over the six years from 1999 to 2005, an average of nearly £2,000 a year or £17 for every sitting day of the parliament. There were other politicians with significant taxi bills, for example Salmond, who managed to run up £9,553.40 in the two years he sat in the parliament, and Brian Monteith, a Tory MSP, who claimed £10,033.06 in the six years from 1999. But McLetchie's bill was the largest and there were then suggestions that he might have used taxis paid for by the parliament to take him to the offices of his law firm, Tods Murray, in Edinburgh's Queen Street.

McLetchie refused to publish details of his taxi journeys and although the parliamentary authorities did do so, the destinations had been blacked out, apparently to protect the Tory leader. But all this did was fuel a sense within the press pack that he was hiding something. McLetchie's problems were heightened by the fact that he had once said of Henry McLeish: 'If McLeish has nothing to hide, then he has nothing to fear.' This was thrown back at him constantly by his Labour opponents, who relished all forms of retribution against the person they blamed for McLeish's downfall.

McLetchie's party rallied behind him but then further allegations emerged, this time that he had allowed his secretary – who also worked part time for Tods Murray – to travel to his law firm in taxis assigned to him, which, if true, was certainly not for parliamentary or constituency business. The crunch came, however, when the information commissioner, Kevin Dunion, ruled that the parliamentary authorities had been wrong to black out the destinations of McLetchie's taxis and ordered the Scottish Parliament to publish the full details of the Tory leader's receipts.

In an attempt to pre-empt that disclosure, McLetchie announced that he had claimed about £900 over five years to go to Queen Street, sometimes to his law firm and sometimes to the BBC Scotland studios nearby. He insisted that his claims were legitimate because he had conducted parliamentary and constituency work at his law offices. His taxi receipts were then published and while this did not immediately lead to any further pressure on the Scottish Tory leader, the receipts did provide leads to other potential controversies. There followed allegations that he had taken a taxi to a party event in Perth, which would be against the rules; to the Edinburgh home of a Tory activist, Sian, Lady Biddulph; and to the home of a private client of Tods Murray.

It then emerged that McLetchie had already paid back more than £250 in travel claims for party events, for which he should not have claimed in the first place – £166 for a flight to Bournemouth to the Tory conference and £90 for a taxi to Selkirk for another party event. This just added to the sense that McLetchie had abused the rules of the parliament. He did really seem to be in a downward spiral which he could not get out of. The criticism from his opponents did not die down; instead it got worse so, on 26 October 2005, McLetchie offered to pay back any money he had wrongly claimed in an attempt to finally bring this damaging series of stories to a halt. 'If an error has been made, I will certainly reimburse the parliament. I will not haggle over a few pounds,' he said. But he added: 'I have no intention of resigning.'

However, in an uncanny echo of McLeish's wavering on *Question Time* when he confessed to not knowing how many sub-lets he had been involved in, McLetchie was asked on *Newsnight Scotland*: 'Did you take a taxi [at the public expense] to see a legal client?'

'I don't know,' he replied.

The affair eventually reached its painful conclusion during the final weekend of October, when McLetchie met the Conservative national council for a private meeting. While the senior party figures gave their leader their full support in public, privately the ground was shifting beneath his feet. McLetchie realised that many Tories had come to the conclusion that the affair was dragging the party down and they felt the only option was for him to quit. A straw poll of constituency chairmen found that a third of them wanted McLetchie to stand down. So, after months of pressure and almost daily sniping, McLetchie reluctantly came to the conclusion that it was time to go.

On 31 October 2005, McLetchie stepped down as Scottish Conservative leader. He said he knew the controversy over his taxi expenses was damaging the party and he quit with immediate effect. He had become the first victim of the Scottish Freedom of Information Act, the legislation which allowed the public and press access to documents previously kept secret and, more importantly, which created the position of information commissioner. Had it not been for Dunion's intervention, there would have been no way anyone could have linked McLetchie's taxi journeys to his law firm. One result of the McLetchie affair was that the Scottish Parliament decided to reform its expenses system, announcing the following day that, in future, all expenses, including all details and receipts, would be published on the web.

For McLetchie, it was a disappointing end to the leadership of the party he had been in since his childhood. He was one of a rare breed of so-called 'tenement Tories', Conservatives who had come from humble backgrounds to success within the party. Raised in Leith, he won a scholarship to George Heriot's, one of Edinburgh's leading private schools, before going into the law. His rise to the top of the party was similar to his political demeanour: solid, steady, successful but slightly unexciting.

The Tories had a swift leadership election to replace McLetchie. Annabel Goldie, who had been McLetchie's deputy, stood as the sole candidate after Murdo Fraser, a young right-winger, decided not to take the risk. She took over just forty-eight hours after McLetchie's resignation, having received the unanimous backing of the parliamentary party. Fraser became her deputy, putting him in the ideal position to take over as leader after Goldie, whenever she stood down. Goldie, from the centre-left of the party, promised stability and no splits with the UK party. There was also a sense of seamless continuity with the McLetchie era as Goldie, a 55-year-old lawyer from Glasgow took over from McLetchie, a 53-year-old lawyer from Edinburgh.

There was one more scandal which rocked the parliament in this period. Given Tommy Sheridan's high-profile court case, Lord Watson's imprisonment and McLetchie's resignation, it was perhaps politically appropriate that the other victim to controversy would be a Liberal Democrat.

Keith Raffan was an eccentric and rather camp Liberal Democrat MSP. He had never been considered for ministerial office and was seen in the parliament as an amusing, if slightly odd, member of the colourful Liberal Democrat parliamentary group.

When the annual report on MSPs' expenses claims and allowances was published in December 2004, Raffan's name stood out. The list MSP for Mid Scotland & Fife had claimed a mighty £41,154.64 in travel expenses for the single year of 2003/4. It only took a few minutes to work out that Raffan had claimed for 84,000 miles, the equivalent of three and a half times round the world – in one year. When this was put into the context of his home, which was just round the corner from the parliament in Edinburgh, and the area he represented, Mid Scotland & Fife, which lay just over the Forth Bridge, the claim started to look ludicrous. Raffan's claim equated to driving a total of 466 miles for every sitting day of the parliament, which would mean, even driving constantly at 60mph, he would have had to spend almost eight hours a day behind the wheel of his car – which turned out to be a small old Skoda. Reporters were sent out to Raffan's constituents and found, unsurprisingly, that no-one knew who he was – which suggested he may not have been touring his patch as extensively as he had claimed.

Raffan insisted he had not claimed mileage in previous years and he had brought all his claims together for this one year, which was why it was so high. But then, on 7 January 2005, Raffan resigned as an MSP. He said he was standing down because of his health, although this was treated by suspicion in the parliament because he quit just two weeks before the full details of his expense claims were due to be published under the Freedom of Information Act.

When the full details were published, it emerged that Raffan had included back-dated claims, going back several years, but the new information also raised some more, potentially devastating, questions about his expenses. First, he claimed round trips to places as far away as Stirling (41 miles) and Dunkeld (61 miles) on days when he was taking part in long and important debates in the parliament. But then it emerged that he had claimed £29.51 in mileage for driving around Scotland on 12 March 2001 – when he had been on a two-day expenses-paid parliamentary trip to the Isle of Man, where he had been the guest speaker at a Commonwealth dinner. He also claimed £72.78 in mileage on 7 December 2001, when he had been in Germany. On 11 March 2002, Raffan claimed £90 for parking in Edinburgh's Crowne Plaza Hotel, a day when he also claimed to have been to Cupar in Fife and back to the parliament.

By the time these details were published, Raffan had disappeared to London. He was no longer in contact with his party – he had quit the Liberal Democrats – or the parliament and refused to talk to members of the press. But four days later, on 26 January 2005, the Scottish Parliament authorities called in auditors Deloitte & Touche to examine every one of Raffan's claims. The auditors reported back to George Reid, the Presiding Officer, with their analysis in September.

The parliamentary authorities were, by now, in a difficult position. They could not let Raffan off without punishment but he had become quite ill – his decision to resign on the grounds of ill health did seem to have some truth in it. Compounding this was the fact that Deloitte & Touche had found irregularities but nothing which they felt warranted a major police investigation.

The parliament wanted a way out, particularly as Raffan was ill, so a deal was done allowing the former Liberal Democrat MSP to pay back a portion of his travel expenses without further action. The Scottish Parliament Corporate Body was shown medical evidence proving that Raffan was ill and, on that basis, allowed him to claim his parliamentary pension early, giving him £15,000 a year and a £25,000 retirement grant – although after a meeting with Raffan in which they questioned the mileage claims from twenty-two separate days, the parliamentary authorities decided to withhold £6,000 from the grant.

The Raffan affair did little damage to the Liberal Democrats, because he had quit the parliament and the party very soon after the controversy first surfaced, but it did much more harm to the parliament itself.

With the Raffan, McLetchie and Watson scandals all happening within a few months of one another, the reputation of the parliament sank, sank and sank again. At each stage, the increasingly incredulous public asked whether it could possibly get any worse, and then it invariably did. In the background was the culmination of the Holyrood building fiasco and the inquiry which revealed just how bad things had got with that project.

Watson's fall was caused by his own hands, literally, and an inexplicable moment of madness. For McLetchie and Raffan, the circumstances were rather different. Both were victims, not just of the microscopic scrutiny which MSPs were under, but also of the Freedom of Information Act. The act came into force on 1 January 2005 and was quickly used by journalists to undermine the careers of both McLetchie and Raffan.

The legislation forced public authorities to release information in almost all cases. There were exemptions but any member of the public could demand information, then appeal to the information commissioner if that material was not produced. The overall assumption was a reverse of the traditional secrecy which public bodies used to hide behind. Many bodies found it difficult to adapt, particularly as some journalists used the early days to set out on 'fishing exercises', sending out numerous catch-all requests in the hope of getting something juicy back.

The McLetchie and Raffan cases seemed likely to presage an era of scandal and chaos within politics and government, but that did not happen, principally because it was simply coincidental that the McLetchie and Raffan cases happened just as the law came into force. Both MSPs were brought down, one from the leadership of his party and the other from the parliament, because they had been lax and free with the rules and perhaps because neither really appreciated the extraordinary level of scrutiny they were under in the Scottish Parliament. Had they been MPs at Westminster, it is doubtful whether either would have been in any sort of trouble, first because the expenses regime in London was much more fluid and not as transparent as it was in Edinburgh and also because lobby journalists in the Commons do not have the time or the concentration of numbers to pursue the sorts of issue that are chased down at Holyrood.

But at least for them, their offences were relatively minor in legal terms and they could go on with their lives without a criminal conviction hanging over them. For Watson, a member at various times of the Commons, the Lords and the Scottish Parliament, the punishment was far more painful. He was by far the biggest political figure to see his entire career collapse around him during this time and, as such, his fall was by far the hardest.

14

The seven-year itch

IT was May 2006, the England football team was preparing for the World Cup in Germany and English nationalism was rising to unprecedented heights. Scotland had not qualified and the contrast was marked between the flags of St George outside pubs and on cars south of the border and the complete indifference in Scotland.

On 24 May, Jack McConnell, Scotland's First Minister, took part in a light-hearted football phone-in on Radio Clyde. Would he be supporting England?

'No, I won't be,' McConnell stated, adding: 'Scotland, my team, is not there, so that's disappointing. There are people who think that, as First Minister, I should be supporting England instead, but football is not about politics so I will not be. I will be supporting other teams in the various games I will manage to watch.'

Asked which teams that might be, McConnell mentioned Angola but also Trinidad & Tobago, one of England's first-round opponents. The First Minister then appeared to add to his snub by stating that he would support the underdog and teams with 'flair' – notably not England. It was a jokey exchange and was greeted without much reaction in Scotland, where that sort of attitude was commonplace. In England, though, McConnell's remarks provoked an extraordinary backlash. Not only was he viewed as treacherous and disloyal but his comments ran completely counter to the line taken by his compatriot Gordon Brown, who had announced he would be backing England.

It was clear that McConnell and Brown were appealing to two distinct markets. Brown needed the support of England if he was to succeed when eventually he became Prime Minister and McConnell's only constituency was Scotland. As if to prove that, John Kaylor, chairman of the Perthshire branch of the Tartan Army, the Scotland supporters' club, responded to McConnell's comments by stating: 'He's really gone up in my estimation and the fans will support him for this.'

McConnell had delivered a major forward-looking and thoughtful speech a couple of days before, looking at where Scotland might be in twenty years' time. He had been attempting to move the debate on regarding devolution and Scotland's place within the Union. Instead, all of that effort was subsumed by something as basic as who Scots would support at the World Cup.

McConnell's comments genuinely shocked many south of the border. They came to crystallise, in the minds of many English people, the distance that Scotland had travelled away from England in the seven years since devolution and the creation of the Scottish Parliament. Newspaper letters pages were full of views on the subject, radio phone-ins were devoted to it and television news bulletins gave over features to the issue. It was almost as if the new, uneasy relationship between Scotland and England was encapsulated by the modern equivalent of the Norman Tebbit cricket test.

For decades, Scotland had defined itself in relation to England and everybody in Scotland knew that, whether they admitted it to themselves or not. Now, England was being forced to define itself in relation to Scotland, something, as the much bigger of the two, it had not had to do before.

But, while many English people had been surprised and angered by McConnell's stance, the whole country was shocked and appalled by what happened next. It started small: first an England-based company publicly pulled out from a planned conference in Scotland, angered by McConnell's remarks, but then it got violent. Two people, one a seven-year-old boy and the other a disabled man, were attacked in Scotland for wearing England football shirts. Tony Blair condemned the attacks in the Commons but then managed to make matters worse by blaming the Tartan Army, claiming that the attacks had 'besmirched its reputation'.

By this time, McConnell was in a difficult position. He could not back down but he did not want to do any more to inflame an already dangerous situation. His relief, when England exited the tournament after defeat to Portugal, was immense. His light-hearted comments on a local radio station had provoked a nationwide debate, which was certainly healthy, but after this debate there had then been at least two violent attacks and, by that time, McConnell was desperate to rein everything in.

The legacy of that national and outspoken discussion, however, was profound, as both the Scots and the English started to reappraise their joint relationship and how they viewed each other. It also came in the middle of a more testing relationship politically between Holyrood and Westminster, a reflection in part of the Scottish Executive's growing confidence but also a recognition, within all the parties in the Scottish Parliament, that after seven years devolution had bedded in and it was now time to become more assertive.

Part of the drive for this came from McConnell's mission to Malawi, where he decided he would tread on the remit of the Foreign Office and the Department for International Development if necessary, and part from his new-found confidence at the G8 summit. But there were other factors too, which had been smouldering for some time.

One was the long-running dispute over free care for the elderly. Henry McLeish's flagship policy had been introduced and was working, with varying degrees of success, across Scotland. An official Scottish Executive report had warned in August 2004 that the cost of care, a major part of which was the Scottish Executive's policy of free care for the elderly, would rise by more than £1 billion over the next fifteen years – an 81 per cent increase on the 2004 price tag. Ministers insisted they would not change, dilute or end the policy, aware that the UK government had refused to hand over millions of pounds in attendance allowance payments that the Scottish Executive believed should rightly be coming to Scotland every year.

Then Stephen Ladyman, a health minister at Westminster, intervened directly in devolved matters by describing the Executive's free care policy as 'not sustainable' and one that 'didn't make sense'. He then went further, warning that McConnell would be forced to do a U-turn and abandon the whole idea. This cooled the relationship between the health departments in Edinburgh and London. It was followed over the next two years by a succession of spats in a variety of different areas which tested relations between the Labour-led administration in Edinburgh and the Labour government in London like never before.

McConnell had already publicly disagreed with the Chancellor when Gordon Brown demanded that whisky companies introduce strip stamps across the tops of all bottles to help counter bootleg Scotch. With the industry warning that the move would cost millions and produce little of benefit, McConnell said he was 'disappointed'. His remark was certainly on the mild side, but it was the first time he had taken issue with the Chancellor on anything, particularly plans set out in the Budget.

On 4 March 2005, Glasgow toddler Andrew Morton was shot and killed by an airgun in the Easterhouse area of the city. The country was appalled and the boy's bereaved parents started a campaign to ban air weapons in Scotland. McConnell, correctly reading the public mood, promised to do all he could to crack down on airguns, but with firearms law reserved to Westminster, he could in fact do little about it. With the SNP promising to ban airguns, McConnell put increasing pressure on Westminster to legislate on the issue. He won some progress from the Home Office – a new licensing system for air weapons – but not everything he wanted.

Later that year the Scottish Executive was at odds with the Home Office again, this time over the treatment of failed asylum seekers. A campaign had been growing over the late summer and autumn in Scotland over so-called 'dawn raids'. These were organised by the Home Office to catch and deport asylum seekers who had had their asylum requests turned down for the last time.

The highest-profile case came about when the Vucaj family, including three children, were taken from their home in Glasgow at dawn and deported to Albania. Malcolm Chisholm, the communities minister, described the Home Office tactics as 'totally unnecessary, heavy handed and over the top' and Kathleen Marshall, the Scottish children's commissioner, warned that these dawn raids were 'traumatising children and families'. McConnell tried to be more conciliatory, insisting that he would work with the Home Office to try to find a better way of handling these sensitive cases but even he made it clear he opposed the UK government's tactics. In response, he got a straight knock back from the Home Office. Tony McNulty, the UK immigration minister, made it clear he would not have reserved policy dictated by the Scottish Executive. 'These are not happy occasions for the families involved and they are full of risks for the immigration service. It is an easy target for people, but I think some of the language and criticism has been over the top and pretty intemperate,' he said.

By the end of 2005, Blair had David Cameron to contend with. The new Conservative leader was the first since Labour came to power to appear sharp and competent enough to do Labour some damage.

Without any sort of regard, or perhaps any care, to the feelings of his colleagues in Westminster, McConnell invited Cameron to meet him at the Scottish Parliament to discuss how a Conservative government at Westminster might work with a Labour-led adminis-tration in Holyrood. It was an incendiary offer and showed that, by now, McConnell had put his own interests and those of his parliamentary party in Scotland ahead of the desires or demands of his supposed masters in London. One Labour MP, John Robertson, who had won the by-election following Donald Dewar's death, demanded to know why McConnell was giving Cameron 'credibility' and said the First Minister should have been 'a bit more sensible' but McConnell did not care.

On 20 December 2005, Cameron held a short private meeting with McConnell. Little of merit was discussed but it was important, symbolically, for both politicians. For McConnell, the meeting was vital to show that he was in charge in Scotland and he would not stand or fall as a result of elections for Westminster. For Cameron, it was about burying once and for all the Tories' reputation as a party opposed to devolution and, perhaps just as importantly, about getting Labour acknowledgment that a Tory election victory was at least possible. It was also noted, to the benefit of both, that Blair had not managed to come to the new parliament building once since it had opened.

But the one issue which caused more problems than any other between England and Scotland was money. Back in 1977, the then chief secretary to the Treasury in James Callaghan's Labour govern-ment, Joel Barnett, devised a formula to allocate money around the constituent parts of the UK. It was based on population, with 85 per cent of all domestic departmental spending going to England, 10 per cent to Scotland and the rest to Wales. Northern Ireland's funding arrangements were a special case, even then.

The formula was adapted slightly over time, with some notice taken of need, and it had been changed to lessen Scotland's advantage gradually – the so-called 'Barnett squeeze'. But it caused enormous resentment in England because of its practical effects. Put simply, the Scots had been getting more money per head of population than the English because the Scottish population only equated to about 8 per cent of the UK total, not 10 per cent. In 2005, when this issue really started to gather pace at Westminster, government spending in Scotland stood at £7,640 per head as against £6,270 for England overall, while in the south-east of England it was just £5,480 per head.

Spending in different parts of the country did not really feature as a political issue until devolution. But then, because the Scottish Executive was given a block grant for all its needs and told to spend it how it liked, the differences became much more pronounced. The Scottish Executive introduced free care for the elderly and the English did not, the Scottish Executive abolished student tuition fees and the English did not, and so on. With each perceived advantage that Scots gained, so more and more people in England – often egged on by their MPs – started to complain. They believed that the Scots were getting a better deal simply because Scotland was getting more money per head.

This was a hugely simplistic argument because it took no account of the decisions that Scottish ministers had to make. They may have introduced free care for the elderly, but they had to find the money for it from somewhere else, and while Scotland did get more per head than England, its needs were much greater, with life expectancy in parts of Glasgow worse than in Gaza or Ghana and a health record that was, without doubt, the worst in Europe.

Despite these complications, a feeling of grievance in England towards Scotland and the Scottish Parliament began to grow. It became political when English MPs started to use that sense of inequality to try to save their own political futures. In May 2005, aware that the Tories were starting to make inroads in Labour areas, Andrew Dismore, the Labour MP for Hendon, told the *Scotsman*: 'Inevitably, the economic powerhouse of the country is always going to be London and the south-east, and we are always going to pay in more than we get out. But the position has now got so far out of kilter that people are starting to get very concerned.' Phyllis Starkey, chairwoman of the South-east group of Labour MPs, then called for a full review of the Barnett formula, a call which was picked up by other Labour MPs from all over the country.

Intertwined with discontent at the Barnett formula was the so-called 'West Lothian question'. This had also been devised by a veteran politician, this time Tam Dalyell, the long-time MP for West Lothian and then Linlithgow and a staunch opponent of devolution. In 1978, as the Scotland Bill, which would have established a Scottish assembly, was making its slow progress through the Commons, Dalyell kept asking the same question about democratic accountability. Why was it, he asked, that, as a Scottish MP, he would be able to continue voting on English domestic matters, but his English colleagues would no longer be able to exercise the same influence over Scottish domestic policy, because this would now be decided in Edinburgh? 'Why can I vote on education matters in West Bromwich but not in West Lothian?' Dalyell recalled asking Labour ministers. After Dalyell had raised this issue for the umpteenth time, Enoch Powell intervened from the opposition benches to say that the question had been asked so often it should be abbreviated to 'the West Lothian question' and the name stuck.

The West Lothian question was back on the political agenda when the Scotland Bill establishing the Scottish Parliament was being debated in 1998 – Dalyell was still there in the Commons, warning that the democratic deficit would lead to the break-up of Britain – and it was still causing friction in 2005 and 2006 as politicians on both sides of the border tried to find ways of appeasing increasing English unrest over devolution.

When Labour came to power in 1997 it was committed to Scottish and Welsh devolution. Aware that this would leave the constitution unbalanced, the party also proposed regional assemblies for England. But, when the first of these was rejected in the north-east, it left England at an unfair disadvantage. Not only could Scottish and Welsh MPs vote on English domestic issues without any reciprocal arrangement for English MPs, but Labour Prime Ministers could – and did – use their block votes of Scottish and Welsh MPs to force English domestic legislation through the Commons. The English felt the system was unfair, with good cause, but the Labour government did absolutely nothing about it, partly because it needed the Celtic block vote.

The Conservatives came up with an 'English votes for English matters' strategy, which would have seen Scottish MPs banned from voting on English domestic issues. This was later watered down to a proposed ban on Scottish MPs voting on amendments to English bills, while allowing them to vote on the principles of an English bill. The Liberal Democrats wanted a fully federal system in the UK, which, while complicated, would at least have provided stability and democratic balance around the country. The Nationalists had the easiest answer, though: just let Scotland go its own way and there would be no need for any Scottish MPs at all.

During this time, in the mid-2000s, the Cabinet appeared to be top heavy with Scots. But that was not really to do with numbers, it was to do with influence. Gordon Brown, as the Chancellor, was seen – rightly – as the most influential figure in the Cabinet, particularly as he had been at the Treasury since 1997 and was heading for No. 10. His closest ally was Alistair Darling, an Edinburgh MP. He had held various Cabinet posts, including Scottish secretary, during this time. Robin Cook had been Foreign Secretary and then leader of the House, from which position he resigned in protest at the Iraq War in 2003, while John Reid caused even more English discontent as he took charge of first the Department of Health and then the Home Office in Whitehall in the 2000s – both of which were English-only departments. This meant he would be presiding over policies which he would never have to answer to his own constituents for.

To any Englishman or -woman of a suspicious or xenophobic bent, it really did look as if the UK was being governed by a 'Scottish McMafia', as it was once described. Taken with discontent over the Barnett formula, the apparent largesse of the Scottish Parliament towards Scots and the democratic deficit of the West Lothian question, it is easy to see why a sense of grievance built up over this period. All this coincided with Jack McConnell and his ministers becoming more assertive, putting more strain on the devolution settlement than ever before.

While the pressures were becoming more evident, on both sides of the border, through this time, something else quite fundamental to the political debate was happening in Scotland.

At the time of the 1997 devolution referendum, there was a clear divide between nationalists and unionists. The nationalists almost exclusively supported the SNP and the unionists the other three parties. The constitutional debate was polarised between these two extremes and there was very little in between. As the Scottish Parliament bedded in over the next five or six years, so the debate became more fluid and, instead of just two opposing positions on the constitution, there was now a spectrum of views between the two sides and activists and elected politicians could lie anywhere along this line.

This was most marked in the Conservative Party, which had struggled to find a coherent identity after its opposition to devolution in 1997. Some senior Conservatives, on the more free-market and libertarian wing of the party, felt that the devolution settlement could be pushed forward and expanded, providing scope for some more radical fiscal policies. What if, they argued, the Scottish Parliament was given the power to raise its own money, not just spend it? Maybe then it could become a tax-cutting institution, attracting business through a more competitive and radical tax regime.

The Tory MSPs Brian Monteith and Murdo Fraser were the high-profile exponents of this agenda but neither really pushed it as hard as he might with the party leadership. In Monteith's case this was because he had been forced to resign as an MSP in November 2005 after admitting he had secretly plotted to remove David McLetchie from the leadership. Without the party's backing he failed to get re-elected in 2007. Fraser was a more moderate version of Monteith and, when he became deputy leader following McLetchie's resignation, he knuckled down and accepted the party line, which was not to push for such free-market policies.

Wendy Alexander, who had quit as McConnell's enterprise minister in 2002, started pushing the boundaries of Labour thinking in this field too. She came very close to endorsing full fiscal autonomy as well, deciding that the Scottish Parliament needed to have more responsibility for the money it raised. Alexander was well aware of the growing English backlash against Scottish devolution and felt that more fiscal responsibility could help appease that anger and give the parliament the chance to make more radical choices – rather than just getting a big bag of money every year to spend. Alexander was a unionist, as were Monteith and Fraser, but they were much further along the spectrum towards nationalism than any of them would have admitted, at least publicly, back in 1997.

The Liberal Democrats undertook a more formal investigation of the devolution settlement. A commission was set up under the chairmanship of Sir David Steel, the former Presiding Officer, in 2004 and reported in March 2006. The Liberal Democrats were already coming at the issue from a federal background: the party had backed a stronger Scottish Parliament for some time but the commission's role was to add more detailed plans to the party's aspirations.

The Steel commission recommended the adoption of reserved powers over firearms, drugs, asylum and immigration, employment law and some welfare policy. But it also called for the handover of significant tax powers to the Holyrood parliament, firmly supporting the idea of 'fiscal federalism'. So now there were 'fiscal autonomy', favoured by some Tories, 'fiscal responsibility', backed by some in the Labour Party, and 'fiscal federalism', supported by the Liberal Democrats – all of which were simply variations of the same theme.

Some politicians thought that Holyrood should be given control of stamp duty; others wanted income tax; others thought excise and customs duties should be devolved, or VAT; and so on. There were problems with each proposition and although many politicians were willing to start the debate, none was prepared to actually hone it down into a coherent policy. But all this did move the debate over the constitution along considerably from where it had been in 1997. All the parties were aware of the growing English backlash and the unsolved issues of the Barnett formula and the West Lothian question, and there were thinkers in each of the main unionist parties willing to try to find solutions.

It was perhaps not surprising, then, that in this context, with the constitutional debate moving along the spectrum towards nationalism in some form in each main party, this period would also coincide with the transformation of the SNP from a disparate pro-independence movement to a sharp and effective potential party of government.

15

The long walk to freedom

EARLY in 2002, two leading Nationalists, Jim Mather and Andrew Wilson, started ringing Scotland's biggest companies. They were not asking for money, they were asking for time; and they got it.

Mather and Wilson spent the next year touring the boardrooms of Scotland giving a simple laptop presentation, explaining the business case for independence. It was modelled on John Smith's 'prawn cocktail' offensive in the early 1990s, when the then Labour leader had gone round the City of London persuading the country's biggest financiers that his party was no longer anti-business. Aware that it suffered from exactly the same image problem, the SNP did likewise. Mather and Wilson formed a perfect double act for this initiative because they knew how to communicate in 'business-speak'.

Mather was then a very rare breed in the SNP – a successful businessman and a self-made millionaire. He was not then an MSP but would become one in 2003. He was relatively short, with close-cropped grey hair and with an extraordinary level of enthusiasm for the economics of independence which was almost evangelical. But, most importantly, he was trusted by Scotland's business leaders because he was so undeniably one of them. Wilson was different and, in many ways the perfect foil for Mather. Elected to Holyrood in 1999 on the Central Scotland regional list, he was one of the SNP's young stars. Wilson was sharp and witty with a boyish sense of humour which often threatened to get him into trouble. But he was an economist who, before he became an MSP, had worked in Edinburgh's financial sector. So although he came from a different background to Mather, he too knew the people, the culture and the climate. Their message was taken on board because it was communicated in terms which the business community could understand. 'Would you run a business', Mather asked them, 'if you had control over spending money but not making it?'

A central part of Mather's case was the gravitational pull of London, taking away Scotland's finest employees, entrepreneurs and company headquarters. Two other, related warnings from the SNP duo concerned low growth and dire productivity, and they produced statistics to show just how small, independent Ireland was doing in comparison to Scotland.

But the main theme was subliminal; it was what they did not say. For years the Nationalists had been portrayed as the party of 'grudge and grievance', a party which blamed everything on England with a 'whit aboot us' whinge. Here, by contrast were two leading nationalists who did not go on and on about 'Scotland's oil' and did not blame everything on the English. Indeed, they admired England's growth and said they wanted to replicate it in Scotland, not demand more from the London government. They produced simple figures showing a thirty-year trend for Scotland's growth at 2.1 per cent lagging behind the UK with 2.4 per cent and the European average of 2.5 per cent. They went on to show how far Scotland had fallen behind and suggested what it could do to catch up.

Then their message turned political and it turned to the right. A low-tax economy, with low corporation taxes, reduced business rates and a competitive general tax rate, could attract business and create growth, they said. The only way to get that, they added, was with independence. What was remarkable was not just the switch from a traditionally negative message of Nationalist politics to something hugely positive, but also the complete change from the socialist, high-tax agenda which the SNP had adopted before the 1999 elections.

Mather recalled later:

> We wanted to set up a dialogue. In one sense it was easy because when you explain the lack of economic powers to people in business, they understand it straightaway. None of them would contemplate running a business that had total power over its spending but zero power over revenue raising because they know they would not be in business for long.
>
> We were suggesting changes that we believed could radically

improve the economy while the Executive would not even talk about it. People in business understand the need for constant evaluation and renewal, yet the Executive were saying, not only that nothing should change, but we should not even talk about suggesting change.

When you have a declining population and low growth that the government wants to do nothing about, business is concerned because none of them would vote for fewer customers with shallower pockets.*

The impetus for the Mather–Wilson charm offensive came from Alex Salmond when the full impact of his party's failed 1999 campaign started to sink in. The SNP leader realised not only that the strategy of outflanking Labour on the left with the higher income tax policy had failed, but also that the party would need to win over the business community if it was to have any chance of seizing power. In 1999, 100 Scottish businesses had signed up to a newspaper advertisement warning of the dangers of independence. Salmond was determined to reverse this, if not by 2003, then definitely by 2007.

The results of the boardroom tour were not immediately evident. Business leaders were generally very wary of the Nationalists after the 1999 election but they wanted to be courteous and open minded, which is why they let Mather and Wilson in. Often, when they finished their presentations, the SNP politicians realised they had made an impression but had no idea how great. There were some business leaders who did not move at all, but there were many others who started to approach the issue of independence as one not of passion and politics, but of business – what would it do for their company?

There is no doubt, though, that Mather and Wilson changed the attitude of business in Scotland from suspicion to acceptance and, in many cases, approval. It took until 2007 for the full impact of their boardroom tour to take effect but when it did, the results were significant.

This was the first part of a major strategy, on several fronts, to turn the SNP from being a rather woolly, left-wing-based movement

---

* See John Penman, 'SNP raring to get down to business', *Sunday Times*, 13 May 2007.

into a modern, effective and ruthless political party that was ready for power. John Swinney realised, when he took over the leadership in 2000, that the SNP had to become a more effective campaigning organisation, and that to compete with the efficient New Labour machine, the Nationalists had to become leaner, tougher and not as wayward as they had been in the past.

Through the 1990s, the SNP seemed to delight in internal battles played out in public. At the heart of most of these divisions was the split between the fundamentalists and the gradualists. Salmond and Swinney were in the latter camp, while Alex Neil, Jim Sillars, Bill Wilson and, to a certain extent Kenny MacAskill, were the leading figures on the fundamentalist wing.

But the SNP, because it was by its very nature a rather loose assembly of people from different backgrounds driven by one common goal, also had traditional political divisions. Party figures such as MSPs Sandra White and Campbell Martin came from a determined left-wing background – completely at odds with the sort of low-tax business-friendly cause being espoused by Mather and Andrew Wilson. If there was a crossover, it was that the funda-mentalists were more likely to be left wing and the gradualists more centrist, but that was no more than a broad rule of thumb.

When Swinney came to power, he took over a party that was in no shape to win an election. He had to find a way of gaining much more control for the leadership: over the messages being sent out from the party, over the way the party selected its candidates and over the activists themselves. It took him three years to put his plans in place, by which time the party was even more divided, but the 2003 elections convinced not just Swinney but other senior figures that something had to be done.

With the vast majority of SNP MSPs elected through the party's eight regional lists, it was vital for any ambitious politician to secure a high position on one of those lists. But the ranking for these lists was not done by secret ballot; it was decided at a series of regional hustings, the delegates at which were mandated by their branches to back particular candidates. This gave significant power to local branches, a power which some on the left and from the fundamentalist wing used to good effect, dominating some branches and swaying the hustings meetings to the benefit of their favoured candidates. This led to the ditching of Wilson and Mike Russell, another high-profile MSP from 1999, who were placed so low on their regional lists for 2003 that they had virtually no chance of re-election.

As soon as the 2003 election was over, Swinney moved against the activists who had driven Wilson and Russell out. His plan to take back control of the party was twin tracked: introducing one-member one-vote elections for candidate selection and leadership elections and centralising party membership records and subscriptions. The first part was vital in preventing some branches from dominating hustings events and picking their favoured candidates but the second part was, if anything, more important. Allowing branches to control all the records, subscriptions and details of their memberships left the party headquarters blind and powerless. Taking charge of the membership records would allow party managers to make sure all the subs were paid, to target membership drives properly and to collate a proper, efficient membership system. Swinney knew this was vital, not just to impose some sort of authority on recalcitrant branches but to grow the party's activist base, which was healthy in some parts of the country but virtually moribund in others.

Swinney also knew he had to do something about the party conference. SNP annual conferences were traditionally fun and frantic affairs. They were old-fashioned events featuring real debates and defeats for the leadership. They also gave activists the chance to air some of the more fanciful grievances which some Nationalists still harboured. But, at a time when all the other main parties – save probably the Liberal Democrats – were turning their conferences from policy-making forums into party political rallies designed for the television, Swinney knew the SNP had to do the same.

By the time Swinney stood down as party leader, the SNP conference had become more stage managed. The kilt-and-sandal brigade, the bearded grumblers and others were being kept more on the fringes and, crucially, major disputes were usually sorted out behind closed doors, not on the conference platform. The SNP conference did still remain the policy-making body for the party and there continued to be serious and important debates, but the leadership team ensured that, as far as the general public was concerned, the SNP was not as wild and unpredictable as it had appeared in the past.

Swinney did all this while fighting for his political survival, seeing off Bill Wilson's challenge in the autumn of 2003 and, in doing so, getting the mandate he needed for his reforms. But the effort and the fight that it took left Swinney weakened. He spent so long trying to turn around the SNP that, when the party failed yet again, in the 2004 European elections, Swinney's time had run out and he resigned.

What he had done was similar to the job Neil Kinnock did for the Labour Party through the 1980s and early 1990s. Kinnock did not survive as leader long enough to enjoy the fruits of the reforms he introduced, driving out Militant and getting the party into a position where it could challenge for power. But he paved the way for Tony Blair's New Labour revolution, the creation of the ruthless campaigning machine and the dropping of Clause IV. Swinney did a similar job in the SNP, getting the party in a healthier shape with much more central control by the time Salmond returned to the leadership in 2004.

But there was still a lot for Salmond to do. Swinney had reformed the party's internal structures but it was still burdened with debts, it had pools of activists in some parts of the country and hardly a presence elsewhere, and it had slipped even further behind Labour in electoral terms since the 1999 election. Salmond came back as a leader with a proven track record and immediately imposed not only his own personal style but also his own brand of leadership on the party. His first move was to declare his unwavering intention to win the 2007 Scottish elections. There was hardly anybody in 2004, either inside the SNP or outside it, who thought the party could actually do that. The SNP was simply too far behind Labour, in every sense. The Nationalists would have to make significant inroads into the traditional Labour areas of west and central Scotland to stand any chance of winning in 2007 and, at that time, it had virtually no presence outside the north and east.

But Salmond was serious. His leadership technique was to set his party apparently impossible targets and then force it to meet them. He said he was going to win the election and he set about getting the party into a shape where it could do just that. After his election in the early summer of 2004, he told the party it had to have 10,000 members by its annual conference in September. It did. That September, he told the party it had to raise £250,000 from scratch to fight the next UK general election, which was expected for spring 2005; it hit that target too.

Salmond told the party it had to win the 2007 election and, to do so, it needed to raise £1 million just for that campaign – more than any other party in Scotland had raised or spent on a single campaign. He also set a target of winning twenty more Scottish parliamentary seats in that election – an extraordinary aim given that this would represent a 75 per cent increase on the twenty-seven seats the party won in 2003.

But to achieve this grand ambition of winning the 2007 election, Salmond knew he needed three different, but interrelated factors to come together. He needed the public endorsement of large sections of the business community, he needed a campaigning organisation to rival and beat Labour's and he needed the political climate to turn against Labour sufficiently to give the SNP a chance. Above all, though, he needed money. So, in 2006, he resurrected his business charm offensive. This time Jim Mather was accompanied by Jennifer Erickson, a new asset for the party. Erickson was an American economic adviser and came not just with solid academic credentials but with strong North American political savvy as well.

It was at one of these events, led by Salmond himself at a hotel on the outskirts of Edinburgh in February 2007, that Salmond secured the backing of one of Scotland's biggest business names, Sir George Mathewson, the former chairman of the Royal Bank of Scotland. Mathewson liked what he heard and wanted to learn more. It was here that Salmond's political skills came to the fore. Aware that securing Mathewson's backing was a major coup for the SNP, Salmond did not want to waste it on an ordinary news day.

Mathewson wanted to declare his general support for independence in a letter to the *Scotsman* but was persuaded by Salmond to hold off until it would have the most effect. Salmond knew that Blair would be coming to Scotland in March on a visit deliberately designed to coincide with, and deflect attention from, the start of the SNP's spring conference. So, with Mathewson's agreement, Salmond kept the former banking leader in the background until that day.

The result was explosive. The Prime Minister arrived on a crusade to launch a major offensive on the economics of independence and to undermine the SNP conference. Instead, he found that day's headlines dominated by Mathewson's conversion. Irritated, all Blair could do was insult Mathewson, describing his views as 'absurd' and nothing more than 'pure self-indulgence'. If Mathewson had been a more modest figure in the Scottish establishment, the Prime Minister's comments might have had some resonance, but he had only just stood down as the chairman of Scotland's most successful company. During his nineteen years at the top of the Royal Bank of Scotland, Mathewson had helped increase annual profits from £32 million to more than £8 billion and had played a key role in the takeover of NatWest in 2000.

Mathewson had given his cautious backing to independence but declared a much more generous endorsement of Salmond. In a letter to the *Scotsman* he had said:

> I do not share the fear of independence which is currently being fostered by those who have the most to lose by a change in the status quo and those who see Scotland as a source of safe seats, thus guaranteeing their rule over the United Kingdom.
>
> Our votes will choose the new First Minister of a parliament which has consistently disappointed since its creation, partially due to the lack of high-quality leadership. The outstanding candidate must be the SNP leader, Alex Salmond.

Blair's personal attack on Mathewson seemed churlish and his assault on the economics of independence never got going. But Salmond had another card to play during that conference. A day after Mathewson's intervention in the debate, Salmond unveiled the biggest donation ever received by the SNP. The bus tycoon Brian Souter had given the SNP £625,000 to fight the 2007 election campaign, an extraordinary amount which pushed the SNP a long, long way towards its £1 million target. Souter's cash allowed the SNP not just to outspend Labour for the first time but also to fund all the detailed campaigning measures which it needed to take on Labour across Scotland.

The interventions of Mathewson and Souter were massively important to the SNP cause in their own right, but they also provided examples of the detailed presentational planning and the long-term strategy which the SNP adopted in the run-up to the 2007 election.

Mathewson was the highest-profile business leader to convert to some form of cautious independence, or at least acceptance that independence was a possible way forward, but he was far from the only one. Ben Thomson, the chief executive of Noble Group, an investment bank with one of its three offices in Edinburgh, said in 2006 he was 'not at all afraid' of independence; Crawford Beveridge, the executive vice-president of Sun Microsystems, with a factory in Linlithgow, claimed early in 2007 that a separate Scottish state could 'focus the minds' of politicians to implement pro-business policies; while Sandy Orr, the owner of City Inn, a hotel chain registered in Edinburgh, described independence as a 'quite exciting' prospect. These individuals gave credibility to the SNP, showing others that senior figures in the business community were not only no longer afraid of nationalism but actually willing to embrace it as a way of improving the Scottish economy.

These interventions gave the SNP a solid base on which to build but it was other business leaders who came with endorsements and cash whose help proved to be the most important. Sir Tom Farmer, the founder of the Kwik-Fit chain, gave the SNP £100,000 and Ian Watson, the Glasgow-born chairman of the mining group Galahad Gold, offered £50,000, but they and all the others paled beneath the Souter donation.

Having succeeded in getting strong business support, giving his party the sort of economic credibility it had lacked in the past, Salmond set about calming the other main fear in Scotland over independence – that it would somehow estrange family members on different sides of Hadrian's Wall. To do this, Salmond toned down his independence message. Almost every time he went on national UK television or radio to talk about the issue, the SNP leader stressed his desire for Scotland to stop being a 'surly lodger' and to become a 'good neighbour'.

He then went further, arguing that while he wanted to end the 1707 Union of the Parliaments, he was keen to retain the 1603 Union of the Crowns, creating a 'social union' between England and Scotland in its place. In doing so, he was trying to paint a picture of Scotland running its own affairs administratively but still being part of the British Isles in a looser, friendlier way, with the same monarch, the same traditions and no guards patrolling the border between the two countries. Salmond also said he wanted to keep the pound, at least until the Scots had been given the opportunity to decide on euro membership. It was a deliberately softer message, designed to allay the fears of those who might like the idea of more autonomy but who hated the idea of England becoming a foreign country.

So, by 2006, the party had the structure to campaign effectively, it had decided on its message, it had the business backers and the leadership, and it was getting the money; the only piece left was the campaign strategy, and this was handled by Angus Robertson. A former television news reporter and editor, Robertson was the SNP MP for Moray and a presentational expert. He had decided to learn all he could from the way the American political parties went about winning elections and then to apply these lessons to the SNP.

At the heart of his strategy was new technology. He realised that the party with the most comprehensive electoral database would be best placed to target the floating voters who would decide the election. With the funds to put his plans into practice, Robertson brought in a new computer system to analyse and target voters all over the country. It took time and money but, by the time the 2007 campaign started, the SNP knew which voters they had to target in which seats and which to leave alone.

Labour had nothing to match it. Part of Labour's problem was that, for years, it had taken some seats and some voters for granted. What was the point in spending money and effort working out where party supporters were in rock-solid safe Labour seats? There seemed little point because there was no threat so Labour had concentrated its resources, quite understandably, in more marginal seats. But what that meant was this: when the SNP started moving into Labour areas, the Labour Party did not have the information it needed to fight back effectively. It was not unusual for Labour candidates in safe seats to send all their activists out to canvass and campaign in marginals. While this helped target resources where they were most needed, it did nothing for information gathering in Labour's safer seats.

The Nationalists out-thought and outplanned Labour in the run-up to the 2007 election. One clear example came over the ballot papers which were to be used in the election. In previous Scottish elections, voters had been given two ballot papers, one for the regional list vote and one for the constituency vote. This had led to the big rise in the smaller parties, first because the smaller parties, like the Greens, had simply targeted the regional list vote with slogans like 'Second vote Green', but also because voters started seeing the regional list vote as a second-choice vote. Members of the public could vote for their preferred party on the constituency, or first, vote, and then have a second vote, which allowed them to experiment with other parties. The SSP, for example, benefited from left-wing Labour voters who dutifully voted Labour in the constituency vote and then Scottish Socialist in the regional list vote.

Labour leaders were determined to counter this so they set out about trying to change the ballot paper design for the 2007 election. They wanted both voting lists on the same piece of paper with the candidates from each party next to one another. In this way, they believed, voters would have much more chance of voting Labour in the constituency vote and then moving their pencils across to the right and voting Labour again, this time on the regional list ballot. After months of wrangling and repeated complaints from the smaller parties, a compromise was hammered out. The two ballots would be on the same piece of paper, but the parties would not necessarily be alongside each other.

However, while Labour politicians were worrying about the order of the party names on the ballot, SNP managers were working out how best to exploit the system. Aware that party names would be ordered alphabetically, they decided to go with the name 'Alex Salmond for First Minister' with an SNP logo, rather than the traditional SNP–Scottish National Party name, on the regional lists. The result was that, on almost every regional list ballot paper, some of which had dozens of parties and individuals on them, the SNP took the top spot courtesy of the A in 'Alex Salmond'. It also meant that voters were given the more subliminal message that the regional list vote was, if anything, more important than the constituency vote, because it would decide who would become First Minister.

All this was being played out through 2006 and showed the meticulous planning of the SNP, under Robertson's direction, towards the 2007 campaign – it marked an astonishing turnaround for the party which had bungled the 1999 election and failed even more spectacularly in 2003.

Every aspect of the campaign was planned and organised. Every

SNP activist in the country received a glossy colour calendar ahead of the campaign, setting out a detailed, day-by-day timetable for the campaign. It showed every event of importance, from each SNP party political broadcast to the deadlines for postal vote applications and the close of nominations. It had five markers, the first of which stated 'win election', with the next four setting out targets that had to be met along the way: 29 constituency seats, 629,000 list votes, 250 ward victories in the council elections and £1 million to raise in a fighting fund.

Six months before the election, a group of strategists, headed by Robertson, met in a back room at SNP headquarters to plan the final week of the campaign. 'What would we do to run the perfect final seven days of the campaign? What would we need to do so, and how were we going to plan it?' one of those who was present said later. They planned a series of newspaper advertisements, each one signed by people from a different group in the community – business leaders, pensioners, professionals and so on – they planned specifically targeted leaflets, each one different for a different group of wavering voters, and they decided to ratchet up the volume of calls from their call centres.

It is undoubtedly true that all this preparation and the campaigning strategy could not have been achieved without the extraordinary amount of money which the party raised for the 2007 campaign. Robertson was able to plan the ideal campaign because he was not limited financially and that was an amazingly privileged position for an SNP election manager to be in.

But that then comes back to Salmond's leadership. Salmond had always had the reputation of a gambler. His love of horse racing was well known and his gambling instinct took over in the run-up to 2007. He knew that it was his last chance to seize power and, if the SNP failed this time, there would be many, inside and outside the party, who would ask whether it would ever achieve power. So Salmond told his party to raise £1 million for the campaign so it could outspend Labour for the first time, and it did. He threw everything at the election campaign. He had made sure it was going to be the best-planned, the best-financed and the best-supported campaign in Scottish political history.

All he had to do was wait for the real battle to begin.

16

It's time

MANUEL Biondi, from Brescia, near Milan, was used to dealing with problems, but they usually concerned exuberant customers or unpaid bills. The 31-year-old deputy manager of the Bella Italia pasta restaurant on Edinburgh's Royal Mile was certainly not prepared for the furore he faced in the middle of January 2007, when reporters, photographers and camera crews appeared at the door of his restaurant demanding to see the ladies' toilets.

January 2007 marked the 300th anniversary of the signing of the Act of Union, the legislation which put the Scottish Parliament into abeyance and joined the Scottish and English administrations under one parliament at Westminster. The anniversary prompted a welter of articles and debates and a number of interesting new theories, one of which suggested that the Act of Union had been signed in the cellar of a Royal Mile townhouse, a house tentatively identified as the one now occupied by the Bella Italia chain.

'The toilets are not such an exciting place to see,' Biondi warned as reporter followed reporter down the stone stairs into the basement. He was certainly right about that but it did not stop the feverish interest in the venue. This was partly because all the news outlets involved knew they had to find something to lighten up the rather dreary story that was the anniversary of the Act of Union but partly because it actually seemed oddly appropriate that such a seminal piece of legislation in Scottish history was actually signed in such an earthy venue.

The story about the Bella Italia toilets also drew attention to the reason why no-one really knew where the act had been signed. It was because the Scottish lords involved were being chased by such a mob that they had to seek refuge somewhere to sign the document.

That sense of estrangement – a political establishment clinging onto power and favours granted by London – and the feelings of the general populace seemed to carry a strong resonance in the early part of 2007, as the Scottish elections drew near.

A series of opinion polls, carried out by ICM for the *Scotsman*, had given the SNP early momentum for the campaign ahead. The first, published on 1 November 2006, showed support for independence at 51 per cent, with just 39 per cent against – the highest level of support for separatism for eight years. It gave the SNP a lead in the constituency vote, at 32 per cent to Labour's 30 per cent, with the two parties tied on 28 per cent in the regional vote. That would still not be enough to give the SNP the most seats (it would have left the party four short of Labour) but it showed that the contest was going to be very tight.

The next ICM poll, published on 27 November, showed that the SNP was making progress. That poll gave the Nationalists a lead in both votes and, if translated into seats, would make the SNP the biggest party at Holyrood. Alex Salmond had to wait until the end of January for the following ICM poll but, when it came, it brought even more good news. The SNP had 33 per cent of the vote in both ballots, with Labour on 31 per cent in the constituencies and 27 per cent in the regions. There were other polls at this time, most of which tended to show the SNP in the lead in the race towards the 2007 election campaign, but ICM was the only major company to poll consistently through this period, allowing politicians from all sides to track the vote, rather than relying on individual samples, any one of which could have been misleading.

The psychological effect of these polls was immense. Through the autumn and winter of 2006–7, the Nationalists actually started to believe they could run Labour close. Salmond used this early impetus to keep up the demand for more money and to cajole and persuade more business leaders to come on board. He was aware of how important positive momentum was and he was determined to carry it through to the campaign itself.

The one party, however, which had the most adjusting to do during this time was the Liberal Democrats. Jim Wallace had stepped down as Scottish Liberal Democrat leader following the 2005 general election. On 9 May 2005, just four days after the election, he

announced he was leaving frontline politics. He had been Deputy
First Minister for six years, dealing with three Labour First Ministers,
two SNP leaders and one Scottish Conservative leader. A veteran of
the Scottish political scene, he had led the Scottish Liberal Democrats
for thirteen years, taking them through the devolution referendum
and the difficult early negotiations with Labour after the 1999 election.

There were two stand-out candidates to replace Wallace: Nicol
Stephen, the Executive's transport minister, and Tavish Scott, the
deputy finance minister. Stephen made it clear almost immediately
that he would stand but Scott, who was in the middle of a divorce,
decided that his personal circumstances would not let him take on
the job at that time.

The contest came down to a straight battle between Stephen, the
45-year-old frontrunner, and Mike Rumbles, a backbench outsider
and one-man 'awkward squad' in the parliamentary party. Rumbles
stood because he wanted a contest and because he wanted to allow
the party to debate its future direction. His consolation was an
impressive 26 per cent of the vote. Stephen took the rest and
assumed Wallace's mantle, not just as party leader but as Deputy First
Minister as well.

Stephen was solid, if uncharismatic. He was not a terribly good
platform speaker but he had served the party for a long time, in both
Westminster and Holyrood, and was respected. He did bring with
him, however, a more sceptical approach to coalitions with Labour.
Rumbles certainly shared that scepticism and Stephen made it clear
he did not enjoy the same easy friendliness with Labour and extreme
caution towards the Nationalists as his predecessor.

Not long after, in January 2006, the Liberal Democrats also lost
their UK leader when Charles Kennedy stood down. The Scottish MP
had suffered from increasingly vocal complaints about his drinking
and he resigned soon after New Year. He was replaced by another
Scottish MP, Sir Menzies Campbell. The party which had been in
the Scottish Executive as a junior partner since 1999 was now being
fronted by two new leaders.

Campbell was similar to Wallace. The two had known each other in
the Commons and came from similar backgrounds. Both distrusted
the Nationalists to an extreme degree and were comfortable with
their friends and colleagues in the Labour Party. Stephen, meanwhile,

was keen not to shut off any avenues, although he made it clear right from his election that he would not go into coalition with the Nationalists if the price of that coalition was a referendum on independence.

Campbell got his leadership off to the best start possible when his party won the Dunfermline & West Fife by-election, called following the death of the sitting MP, Rachel Squire. They snatched a Labour seat right out of Gordon Brown's grasp, and the Liberal Democrats felt they were heading in the right direction as the 2007 elections approached. The Nationalists had their own by-election boost when Richard Lochhead held Moray for the Scottish Parliament, but this was a much more muted success. As in Dunfermline, the by-election was caused by the death of the incumbent, in this case the popular SNP MSP Margaret Ewing, who had built up a sizeable majority over the past seven years. Lochhead increased the SNP majority in the April 2006 contest, which represented an achievement, but it was hardly unexpected.

The Conservatives' preparations for the election were thrown off course by the publication of an embarrassing memo from David Mundell, the party's sole Scottish MP, in which he derided his Holyrood colleagues, claiming there was a 'lack of thinkers' in their ranks. He went on to label Scottish deputy chairman Bill Walker a 'Thatcherite dinosaur' and said Annabel Goldie, the Scottish Conservative leader, showed a 'lack of activity'. The memo's publication was humiliating, both for Mundell and for the Conservative parliamentary party, and the party's Scottish conference soon afterwards was distinctly uncomfortable for all concerned, but they managed to get through it without any further ruptions.

The situation for Labour was rather different. The party had failed in Dunfermline and in Moray the Labour candidate, after he had seen his party's share of the vote fall by half, blamed Tony Blair's ongoing problems for the disappointing result. But its position in the Scottish Parliament was stable and even encouraging. In January 2007, it emerged that the Scottish Executive's inpatient waiting time target of eighteen weeks from GP to treatment had been met a year early. There were still problems with waiting times for cancer but good progress was also being made on outpatient treatment and accident and emergency times. Given the problems the Scottish

Executive had experienced in the past, this did represent remarkable progress.

Jack McConnell was in the process of completing his administration's legislative programme and although it was not too demanding, it did indicate a solid if unspectacular level of achievement. The party was suffering, however, from the backwash of an increasingly unpopular government in London. Everyone knew Blair was going, but no-one knew exactly when.

There were many in the Scottish Labour Party who wanted the Prime Minister to stand down a month or so before the May 2007 Scottish elections. That way, they reasoned, Brown would take over on a wave of goodwill and his honeymoon period would carry Labour to victory in the Scottish elections. The worst-case scenario, they believed, was for Blair to stay stubbornly in office through the elections, reminding every voter of the war in Iraq.

Blair arrived in Scotland in September 2006 and held his first round-table discussion with the Scottish political press pack for many years in an upstairs room in Edinburgh's Caledonian Hotel. It was at this event that he revealed, unexpectedly and almost certainly inadvertently, that he would still be Prime Minister the following May. He insisted he would not go 'on and on' like Margaret Thatcher, but, asked whether he would still be in post for the Scottish elections, Blair replied 'yes'.

Despite their public protestations of support, it was not the news many in the Scottish Labour Party wanted to hear but it delighted the Nationalists. They much preferred the prospect of taking on an embattled and unpopular Blair to a new, popular and Scottish Prime Minister in Brown.

The 300th anniversary of the Act of Union could have provided Labour with a political platform, allowing the party to champion the successes of Scotland's membership of the United Kingdom. Blair certainly thought so, using his final speech to the Scottish Labour conference, in Oban in November 2006, to champion the Union as a bulwark against the politics of 'fear and grievance' of the SNP. But, across Scotland, commemorations for the anniversary were much more muted. The Nationalists had warned, with good reason, that the Scottish Executive should not celebrate the Act of Union too overtly during the election campaign and both ministers and officials then backed off, not wanting to be seen to be doing anything too political on the issue. However, what events there were – and there were public debates, televised discussions and formal commemorations – did tend to draw attention to Scotland's traditional differences with England, rather than anything else.

The constitutional question had already been thrust to the top of the political agenda by the simple fact that the Nationalists appeared, for the first time ever, to be heading for a possible election victory. That in itself lent an interesting context to the Union's anniversary but everyone in politics knew that, however interesting the discussions over Scotland's past were, Scotland's future was in the balance and the five weeks of the election campaign would be crucial in deciding where that future would lie.

As the weeks ticked down towards the 3 May poll, McConnell appeared strangely subdued. He refused to get involved in debates with the other party leaders through February and March and this 'where's Jack?' issue was turning into a problem for Labour, simply because it was allowing the SNP to set the agenda. But on Sunday 18 March, the final day of the SNP's spring conference, all that changed when Alex Salmond published a document setting out what his administration would do in its first 100 days in office. It was meant to show the pace, style and approach of an SNP government but it also revealed how the Nationalists would take their fight for independence to the Westminster government as soon as possible and as often as possible, demanding a whole list of concessions in the first weeks after taking office, including a share of North Sea oil revenues.

For McConnell, it was the moment he had been waiting for. He broke his self-imposed silence, called a press conference for Labour's Glasgow headquarters early on Monday 19 March and strode to the platform without notes, so pumped up was he by the SNP's publication.

'We are angry,' he declared, five times. The First Minister said he was 'angry' at the deception of the SNP, angry at the impact the SNP's plans would have on hard-working families and angry at the turmoil the SNP would create if it got into power. The SNP would spark disputes with Westminster during its first 100 days in office; Labour would spend its first 100 days putting together a package of measures for Scotland's children. 'This weekend we saw a wake-up call for Scotland. This [SNP] document is a reminder of what the SNP really stand for. It sets out in writing the road they would choose – and it is a route to tax and turmoil,' he said.

As he left the stage, McConnell's right hand was balled into a fist like a boxer's. His left hand was on a colleague's shoulder. 'Game on,' he said quietly, a smile on his face for the first time in weeks.

At long last the phoney war was over and battle was joined. It took another ten days for the parliament to be dissolved and for McConnell to head out around Scotland in his battlebus, but that Monday morning press conference not only signalled the start of the campaign for the 2007 election but set its course as well.

Unlike previous contests, which became plebiscites on the record of the incumbent government, the 2007 Scottish Parliament election was all about Salmond and the SNP. The big issue was whether Salmond could be First Minister and what sort of government he would lead, not McConnell's record in charge of the Scottish Executive. There was a backlash against Labour, but it was a weariness with Blair and ten years of New Labour, rather than a rejection of the policies espoused by McConnell. This was partly because many of the policies adopted by McConnell mirrored similar initiatives in London and partly because McConnell had managed Scotland's affairs rather than blazed a new course.

Both Salmond and McConnell knew that the question Scots were asking was: are we ready for an SNP administration? Aware that that was the underlying theme, both parties focused on the same thing.

The Labour messages were almost uniformly negative and directed at the SNP – 'tax and turmoil', 'grudge and grievance', 'an expensive divorce', they declared. As for the Nationalists, their campaign was almost presidential. Not only was Salmond's name on virtually every ballot paper, but when the SNP sent a shortened fold-out version of its manifesto to a million homes in Scotland, it turned into a giant glossy poster of the SNP leader when reversed. The Nationalists knew Salmond was their biggest asset and they did everything possible, and then they did some more, to capitalise on his profile.

Salmond launched his party's campaign in the futuristic setting of the oval main lecture theatre at Edinburgh's Napier University. For the first time since 1999, the SNP leader found he had a global audience for his message. The SNP's lead in the opinion polls had raised the possibility of a Nationalist government in Edinburgh and even independence for Scotland. It was big news, particularly in Europe and Canada, and demand for press access was high.

Salmond was at his conciliatory best, repeating his 'from surly lodger to good neighbour' line and insisting that independence would turn England and Scotland into 'best pals'. He showed his mastery of the sound-bite too. When asked about his plans to pick fights with Westminster and his relationship with Gordon Brown, he replied: 'I confidently predict my relationship with Gordon Brown will be substantially better than his relationship with Tony Blair over the last few years.'

The message for the Scottish people was clear: the SNP had the policies to form a credible government. Trust us with that, Salmond was saying, and we will prove we can govern before moving on to independence. The SNP had been in business for seventy-three years, Salmond said, but this manifesto was of 'particular importance'. It was, for the first time, a 'programme for government'.

There were problems he did his best to get round, notably the 'black hole' in his plans for a local income tax because of the UK government's refusal to hand over £380 million a year in council tax benefit payments. The Nationalists wanted to introduce a local income tax but had been told that, if they scrapped council tax, they would not get funding for whatever replaced council tax benefit, a loss which would deprive the administration of money it needed to fulfil its other manifesto commitments. There were other issues too, such as the lack of detailed costings of all the plans and proposals but, as far as the UK and the world media were concerned, the event simply showed the SNP was more competent, professional and accomplished than it had ever been and, possibly, ready for government.

There was another message from the event, however, and this was aimed purely at the Liberal Democrats. Aware that, even if the SNP did win the election, he would not have enough seats for a majority government, Salmond made a deliberate and public pitch. Nicol Stephen, the Scottish Liberal Democrat leader, had made it clear he would not go into a coalition with the SNP if a condition of that deal was a referendum on independence. So Salmond offered a concession. For the first time, rather than just talking about a yes–no referendum on independence, Salmond said that that was merely his 'preference' and that the issue would be decided in negotiations with other parties. He did not give any more details, but to political observers the signal was clear – he was prepared to have more than one question in a referendum, possibly including one on more powers for the parliament, the position backed by the Liberal Democrats.

McConnell's manifesto launch was very different, deliberately so. The Scottish Labour leader chose the smaller, tighter and more intimate surroundings of a conference room in Glasgow's Royal Concert Hall for his party's event. Everywhere there were pictures of smiling children and the focus was entirely on education and McConnell's plan for an education bill to raise the school leaving age to seventeen, language tuition from Primary 3, an extra 500 modern language teachers and a reduction in class sizes. His 'radical' approach would see a freeze in the budgets of every other department to pay for improvements in education. The money would be spent in Scotland's classrooms, not on picking fights with Westminster.

Labour wanted there to be a contrast in style and tone from the SNP launch and there is no doubt they achieved that. Labour managers simply set out to compare the SNP's focus on the constitution with their own theme of children and education, believing that voters would chose the latter over the former. It was a sensible strategy but it was not that easy to defend, particularly as McConnell then faced the constant question: you have been in power for eight years; why haven't you done this before? For McConnell, though, a former schoolteacher, the issue of education was not only of great personal importance but it was something he could, and did, speak with passion about. It was also a reprise of the 'education, education, education' campaign which Blair had run so successfully for New Labour in 1997.

'I am the underdog,' McConnell declared as he set out on the campaign trail shortly afterwards and, despite having almost twice as many seats as the SNP going into the campaign, he did seem to be speaking the truth. The polls showed that the SNP was ahead and with Labour suffering across the UK, McConnell had every right to feel he was starting from behind. But, rather than falter as a result, McConnell seemed to relish the campaign. After months of being accused of ducking debates and of constitutional wrangles inside and outside the parliament, McConnell enjoyed getting out and meeting the voters. He started to relax and enjoy the process, although he was well aware of the stakes: 'Five weeks left to save devolution,' he declared.

If McConnell was worried, Brown was terrified. The Chancellor knew that he was within months of securing his dream of becoming Prime Minister but he also knew that that inheritance would be tarnished if Scotland was lost to the SNP on the eve of his accession. He decided to intervene, unaware that he no longer had the dominating influence he once enjoyed.

He was in Edinburgh on Easter Day, 8 April, and asked Sir Menzies Campbell for a discreet meeting. Campbell was the Liberal Democrat UK leader but, under his party's federal system, he was not in charge either of the Scottish election campaign or of any subsequent negotiations. However, Brown wanted to do something, anything, with someone he knew and trusted, in an attempt to undermine the SNP's advance.

Campbell described later how he met Brown in secret, without the knowledge of their Scottish parties, to talk about the SNP threat:

> Like me, he was anxious about the possibility of the SNP governing in Scotland, our own backyard. Was there common ground between Labour and the Lib Dems to tackle the SNP? He made a number of suggestions. I told him I would have to discuss them with Nicol Stephen.
>
> He then raised possibilities for a new coalition between the Lib Dems and Labour on the assumption the two parties had enough seats jointly to form a government.

Campbell said there was little he could do to help Brown because he was not in charge of his party's approach, either to the election or to any subsequent coalition negotiations.

As the election grew closer, Brown was in touch again. Campbell stated:

We met at the same discreet place as before. Throughout the campaign, the polls had put the SNP ahead of Labour. Was there scope for an arrangement between our parties? What would be the consequences for Scotland and our parties if the SNP used the £30 billion Scottish Executive budget to build support for independence over the next few years?*

These meetings showed not only how desperate Brown was to do something to keep the Nationalists out of office, but also how powerless he had become. Even as Chancellor and the putative next Prime Minister, there was nothing he could do to stop the SNP. His private meetings with Campbell counted for nothing as the campaign went on, the final proof perhaps that Brown's traditional dominance over Scottish politics had run its course at last.

Nicol Stephen knew that the Liberal Democrats had to forge their own electoral identity, away from the shadow of both the main parties, if they were to have any chance of holding on to the seats they had. In much the same way as every Liberal Democrat campaign press conference in 1999 had been dominated by the issue of tuition fees, so 2007 for the Liberal Democrats became defined by the 'will they, won't they' debate over a referendum on independence.

Stephen himself was prepared to listen to the arguments from the SNP for an independence referendum, particularly as Salmond had made such a blatant overture by suggesting there could be more than one question in the referendum. But he was bitterly opposed by Tavish Scott, his senior lieutenant and the man running the Liberal Democrat campaign. Stephen insisted repeatedly that there would be no deal over an independence referendum, but he left open the possibility of talking about other issues, including a multi-question referendum. At the same time, Scott was briefing a much harder line, making it plain that there would be no discussions with the Nationalists at all unless they dropped their commitment to an independence referendum – something the SNP was never likely to do. This 'good cop–bad cop' routine was not a ploy, it was just a reflection of where the two most powerful figures in the Scottish parliamentary party were coming from.

---

* Menzies Campbell, *My Autobiography* (London: Hodder & Stoughton, 2008).

Both the Liberal Democrats and the Tories knew they were going to have to fight hard to hang on to the seats they held going into the election. The polarisation of the contest into a straight SNP–Labour fight would make it harder for the two smaller parties to make gains.

The Conservatives ran a good campaign, resisting attempts to squeeze them out, thanks to Annabel Goldie. Goldie had not really shone as a parliamentary debater, she had not adopted any radical policies to make the party noticed – she really was conservative, with a small and a capital C. But her rather matronly approach, with a disapproving voice which appeared to have come straight from the front of a classroom in the West End of Glasgow, worked for her party. Goldie also decided that, as a 57-year-old spinster, she could get away with stunts that would seem cheap from younger, more agile politicians. So she went quad-biking and abseiling, getting her photocalls into more newspapers than her party had any right to expect. David Cameron helped by calling her (more than a touch patronisingly) his 'Scottish Auntie' but it was her dry wit that really did the trick. During one live television debate she announced that the one advantage she had over the other leaders was 'sex'. What she meant was that she was the only woman but she knew none of the others would have the guts to come up with a retort.

The reason Goldie succeeded with the voters – if only to the extent that they did not rise up and seek to punish the party, as they had done before – was because she appeared unmanaged; she really appeared as if she did not pay any attention to image makers and party handlers, running her own campaign the way she wanted, and it worked.

The same degree of solidity and success was not evident, however, in the small parties, including the Greens, the SSP and Solidarity. The Socialists were in a mess, riven by infighting, disputes and personality clashes. The formidable SSP machine, which had secured six seats in 2003, had lost its most visible presence in Tommy Sheridan, and although Solidarity now had the most famous socialist in Scotland as its leader, his image had been tarnished by the damaging court case against the *News of the World*.

The main parties had been caught out by the way the smaller parties had targeted the regional vote in 2003 and were determined it should not happen again. They all went after the 'second vote' with a ruthlessness that surprised the Greens and the Socialists. The big parties made it clear that every vote counted for the main battle and none could be 'wasted' on the luxury of a sentimental vote.

There were others who were even more naive and who imagined that simply because the Greens and the Socialists had done so well in 2003, they might achieve some success in 2007. Top of this list was Archie Stirling, the charming, charismatic and hopelessly over-ambitious head of Scottish Voice.

Stirling was without doubt the most colourful figure to land in Scottish politics for decades. The nephew of SAS founder David Stirling, the 63-year-old landowner decided to start his own political movement after becoming depressed by the calibre of the politicians at Holyrood. Stirling himself liked to spend time in the south of France and was fond of horse racing. He served quails' eggs and champagne at his manifesto launch, which promised nothing very much on anything at all, except strong words on health and education.

At the very least, Stirling stood out from the crowd of lawyers, professional politicians and union reps who were standing for election across Scotland in 2007. Unfortunately for him, though, Scottish Voice sank ignominiously with hardly a trace. Stirling and his friends had put up £184,920 to stand candidates across Scotland but received only 8,782 votes in total – spending the equivalent of £21.06 for every vote cast, by far the worst return for any party in the election.

By the eve of the election, Wednesday 2 May, the contest was so tight that no-one could predict which way it was going to go. The last few polls had put the SNP ahead but, given the margin of error in which the pollsters work, they could not be taken for granted.

For all the leaders, the final day fitted the pattern they had set during the rest of the campaign. Alex Salmond spent it in a helicopter, touring Scotland and stopping off at key marginals in the closest thing to a presidential campaign Scotland had ever seen. Jack McConnell went to Donald Dewar's statue in the centre of Glasgow and had an impromptu rally while Gordon Brown was in Edinburgh, out on the streets shaking hands. Nicol Stephen was in Aberdeen-shire, being photographed with Charles Kennedy, and Annabel Goldie abseiled down into her press conference in Edinburgh.

There was drizzle and rain to greet some early morning voters on Thursday 3 May 2007. At the polling stations they were given two ballot papers. The first was split into two coloured sections. The first section, the regional ballot, contained the names of all the candidates and parties standing in the region; the first name on almost all of them was 'Alex Salmond for First Minister'. The second section was for each constituency and listed the names of the candidates standing with their party. Voters were expected to mark a cross against one name on the regional list and another against one name on the constituency list. The second piece of paper, which was white, was for the local elections. It was at about this point that confusion started to set in for many voters. The white piece of paper contained a list of parties standing in the area and voters were asked to mark this one in order of preference: 1, 2, 3 and so on.

Not only were there two different elections being held on the same day with three separate ballots on two pieces of paper but three electoral systems were being used: first-past-the-post for constituency elections, the list system for regional top-up seats and single transferable vote (STV) for council elections. To make matters worse, the ballot papers had been standardised to make sure they fitted the electronic counting machines. Some authorities found they had so many parties standing on the lists that they had to trim the voting advice at the top of each page, so voters were not told exactly what they had to do.

Even more confusing was the decision to make the regional vote the 'first' vote. This was done to counter the Greens, who had campaigned so successfully in 2003 on the 'Second vote Green' slogan, and to make sure the regional list was seen as a proper, important vote in its own right, not a second-chance vote. But what all this meant was that thousands of voters ended up bewildered. Some put crosses on all three ballots, some marked their Scottish Parliament ballots in order of preference and some managed to get the whole thing wrong. As the votes started to pile up through the day, so did the spoiled papers. By the time the polls closed, there were 145,000 spoiled papers for the Holyrood elections, 85,000 constituency votes and 60,000 regional votes, about 3.5 per cent of the total votes cast.

The Scotland Office had introduced electronic counting machines for the first time, principally to cope with the local government elections. It is possible to count STV ballot papers manually but it takes a huge amount of time and effort. The only way to do it quickly is to use machines, so they were brought in for both elections. Some counts were held up by mechanical problems, others because of disputes over papers which had been marked as spoiled. A general sense of disorganisation and confusion built up at counts all over Scotland as the night wore on. The dual nature of the Scottish elections, with the constituencies announced first and the regional results later – only when all the constituencies for the region had been declared – simply added to the sense of uncertainty.

Salmond found himself at a television studio with Stephen soon after the polls closed and the two leaders had a rare chance to talk in private while they were waiting to go on air. Stephen told Salmond he was willing to talk about a coalition, once the results were in. Salmond, aware that a minority government would be extremely difficult, certainly came away from that conversation with the impression that there was room for compromise in the Liberal Democrat attitude to coalition and that an SNP–Lib Dem administration was a very real possibility.

The first results came through from the urban areas in west and central Scotland, Labour's heartlands, but gave no real indication of the overall trend as Labour MSP after Labour MSP was returned. But then the SNP started to make inroads. Bruce Crawford took Stirling from Labour's Sylvia Jackson, Tricia Marwick triumphed over Labour's Christine May in Central Fife and Joe FitzPatrick took Dundee West from Labour, defeating Jill Shimi, the leader of the council. Nicola Sturgeon, the SNP deputy leader, was jubilant after winning Glasgow Govan from Labour's Gordon Jackson – her third attempt to take the seat – and in the north-eastern constituency of Gordon, Salmond triumphed, gaining the seat from the Liberal Democrats. These wins were not going to be enough on their own to secure the twenty or so seats the SNP needed to emerge as the largest party but they indicated a decisive swing in some parts of the country to the Nationalists. Everyone knew that everything would come down to the allocation of seats from the regional lists.

There were two crucial moments over the course of that long election night. The first happened in Ayrshire's Cunninghame North, where Allan Wilson, the Labour MSP, was trying to hold off a strong SNP challenge. When the votes were counted, the SNP's Kenneth Gibson emerged as the winner by just forty-eight votes. Wilson demanded a recount but this was turned down by the returning officer. There were 1,015 spoiled ballot papers in Cunninghame North, more than enough to have swayed the contest either way, but Gibson was named the winner.

The second crucial moment came right at the end of the counting process, at 5 p.m. on Friday 4 May, a full thirty-four hours since the polls had opened. Every result except the Highlands & Islands list result had been decided by this point and Labour had forty-three seats to the SNP's forty-five. With seven seats to be divided up, the entire election result was going to hinge on what happened in Inverness. All the politicians had been up for almost two days without a break, everybody was showing their nerves and no-one knew whether Jack McConnell would hang on or whether Salmond would get his chance to govern at last.

Salmond had arranged to fly in by helicopter to the lawns of Prestonfield House in Edinburgh, hopefully for a victory press conference at 5 p.m. He landed, waved to the press and went into the hotel to consult his aides, who confirmed there was still no result from Highlands & Islands, so there could be no victory or defeat press conference. Instead, Salmond went to the microphone and promised a full inquiry into the spoiled ballots fiasco if he became First Minister. There really was little else he could do.

Meanwhile, in Inverness, the returning officer called the candidates together and told them the regional list votes had been counted and allocated as follows: four to Labour, two to the Conservatives and one to the Greens – with none to the SNP. While the Labour candidates celebrated, Dave Thompson, one of the SNP candidates, intervened. He said:

> I had been doing my own tally and reckoned we had 35 per cent of the vote, which meant we should have five seats [overall, list and constituency]. It did not seem right we should only have the four constituency seats, the same number as Labour. So, just as the returning officer was about to get up on to the podium to announce the results I stood in his way to stop him. The resulting review of

the result showed that the SNP list votes had not been counted and the party ended up with two regional list seats, Labour three and the Conservatives two.

As that review was taking place, Salmond was being driven to central Edinburgh, to the Hub, the converted church at the top of the Royal Mile. While he was in transit, the Highlands & Islands result was announced. The overall result was now clear: the SNP had forty-seven seats to Labour's forty-six. The Conservatives won seventeen, the Liberal Democrats sixteen and the Greens two, and Margo MacDonald, the independent, got in again as well. The margin of victory was tight. The SNP won 1,297,628 votes, 31.97 per cent, to Labour's 1,243,789, 30.64 per cent.

Every senior Nationalist who was heading to the Hub was listening in to the result. John Swinney, the former leader, had to stop his car on Edinburgh's Grassmarket to wipe the tears from his face. Word spread through to the others who were waiting at the Hub, gathered for what was now going to be a victory party. A cheer went up; there were more tears and hugs for party workers, new MSPs and activists.

Salmond arrived to a thunderous ovation but he was deliberately conciliatory in tone. He knew the SNP had beaten Labour by the slimmest of margins. He also knew the parliamentary arithmetic was tight so he would have to seek out a coalition if he was to govern with anything other than great difficulty. So again he sent out a message to the Liberal Democrats. 'I think there is a progressive coalition available which wants to take Scotland forward,' he said.

Salmond added that he would introduce a new style of government:

> It's a difference of attitude and style, a difference of not how we approach the people who agree with us, but the people who remain to be convinced. I don't quite know how we are going to configure that coalition of the progressive forces, but we will go forward with an attitude which will look for the goodwill which I know is there.

It was clear that, at this point, Salmond's favoured option was coalition government with the Liberal Democrats and possibly the Greens.

McConnell quickly conceded defeat, having made it clear during the election campaign that the party which emerged with the most seats would have the moral right to attempt to form an administration first. The former First Minister stressed that while he recognised that the SNP was now the biggest party at Holyrood, this did not give Salmond the mandate to push for independence. He then retreated to be with his wife and family, leaving the Nationalists to celebrate the closest election in Scottish history and the most groundbreaking.

Salmond knew that the nature of his administration, coalition or minority, and its course for the next four years would be decided over the next few days. He had been led to believe by Nicol Stephen, on election night, that there might be room for discussions on a possible SNP–Lib Dem coalition and he was keen to find out if that would work.

There were other senior Liberal Democrats, however, who had very different ideas.

17

Going it alone

ON the evening of Friday 4 May 2007, Sir Menzies Campbell, the Liberal Democrat leader, held a private supper at his elegant Georgian townhouse in Edinburgh's West End for Nicol Stephen, the Scottish Liberal Democrat leader, and Tavish Scott, Stephen's senior lieutenant. There was only one topic under discussion as the politicians and their partners ordered takeaway pizzas. The SNP's victory in the election had only been announced a couple of hours before and the Nationalists' forty-seven seats, combined with the Liberal Democrats' sixteen, would be enough for a majority coalition, but only if the Greens also brought their two MSPs on board too.

Should the Liberal Democrats join forces with the Nationalists? There were arguments in favour: the two parties shared similar domestic agendas, particularly on the scrapping of council tax and its replacement with a local income tax, and a coalition with the SNP would allow the Liberal Democrats to break free from the shadow of Labour. It would also keep them in power and, given their strong bargaining position, might even give them more ministers than they had had before. Against this was the fundamental policy difference – the SNP's determination to hold a referendum on independence. The Liberal Democrats believed in a federal Britain, not an independent Scotland, and, having stood up against this policy for the whole of the campaign, it would look very bad if the party caved in on it now, particularly if they appeared to make that concession just to get their hands on power.

Stephen was prepared to talk to the Nationalists, but Scott was much more cautious, as was Campbell, who said later: 'We sent out for pizzas . . . after two hours we packed away our pizza boxes and any possibility of a coalition with the SNP.'* The prospect of the Liberal Democrats becoming the instrument for the break-up of the UK was too much for him, for Scott and, eventually, for Stephen.

But while the party leadership had reached a decision, it still had to consult the parliamentary party. The sixteen Liberal Democrat MSPs met in Edinburgh's Grosvenor Hotel the following day, Saturday 5 May. They were disappointed and bruised from an election which they had believed could have seen them leap-frog Labour into second place. Instead, they had gone backwards, losing one seat of the seventeen they won in 2003 and ending up behind the Conservatives. The overall feeling was one of despondency.

Stephen asked for the group's views on a coalition with the SNP and the referendum issue. Some MSPs were keen to hear what the Nationalists had to say. Others were much more forthright, arguing that there must be no coalition unless the SNP dropped its insistence on an independence referendum. Once again it was Scott's views that prevailed. He always denied later that he threatened to walk away from the party if the Liberal Democrats went into a coalition with the SNP, but that was the clear impression he left with some of those at the meeting.

Stephen talked to Alex Salmond by telephone that evening, letting him know that there would only be talks if the SNP took the referendum issue off the table, something the SNP leader was never going to do. Nevertheless, Salmond was conciliatory, urging Stephen not to make any ultimatums at this stage. The SNP leader was still keen to get the Liberal Democrats round the table to discuss the issue, at the very least.

That weekend marked Salmond's twenty-sixth wedding anniversary. His aides insisted he would be enjoying a quiet weekend with his wife Moira. He certainly avoided public appearances but his weekend was anything but quiet. While the Liberal Democrats were meeting, so was Salmond with his senior aides, deciding what to do. John Swinney was making preliminary contact with senior civil servants to ease the formal process of government and the SNP spin doctors were also hard at work, selling the message that Salmond was prepared to talk about the referendum issue, maybe postponing

---

* Menzies Campbell, *My Autobiography* (London: Hodder & Stoughton, 2008).

it or putting it out to a commission, but he was not prepared to drop it.

Any possibility that the Liberal Democrats and Labour might try to form another government if the Nationalists failed to find a way through was then ended by Scott, who told the BBC on Sunday 6 May that he was categorically ruling out any coalition with Labour.

The following day Salmond went into discussions with the two Green MSPs, knowing that he had to secure the support of both the Greens and the Liberal Democrats if he was to form a majority administration, so at least the theory of an SNP–Lib Dem deal was still alive. In reality, however, it was so far off it was already virtually dead.

The Greens, like the Liberal Democrats, had been badly bruised by the election. Their band of seven MSPs had been reduced to just two, Patrick Harvie and Robin Harper. They were hurt by their party's failure but were still determined to have an impact. They were very aware that their two votes could be crucial in providing Salmond with a majority so they started making it clear that they had two 'red line' issues, policies they would expect to be implemented by any three-party coalition government: no new nuclear power stations and tough new targets for carbon emissions. The first was already SNP policy so the Nationalists had no trouble with it, but the second was tied in to less road building and stopping the expansion of Scotland's airports, which the SNP did have issues with.

So, on Monday 7 May, when Salmond had hoped to be in formal coalition discussions with the Liberal Democrats, he was instead involved in talks with the two Greens. With the prospect of an SNP–Lib Dem coalition now all but dead, there was not the pressure to get the Greens on board too. Salmond wanted a bigger cushion than the one-seat advantage he enjoyed over Labour and would have like to have tied down the Greens to a deal but the two Green MSPs made it clear they simply could not endorse an administration which wanted to increase capacity at Scotland's airports and on Scotland's roads. After two hours, official talks between the Greens and the SNP broke up with both sides saying they wanted to work more closely together but both admitting a formal coalition deal was impossible.

For the Greens, it was extremely disappointing. The party was on the verge of securing more influence with just two MSPs than it had achieved after 2003 with seven. A 'rainbow coalition' with the SNP and the Liberal Democrats would have allowed the party to salvage something tangible from the wreckage of the 2007 election, so discreet calls were put into the Liberal Democrat leadership to find out whether there was any way of working round the party's objection to a referendum on independence. But the Liberal Democrats did not budge. By this time, the party position had been decided and set in concrete. There would be no going back.

The SNP had emerged as Scotland's largest party on Friday 4 May. By Monday 7 May, Salmond was having to face the prospect not only of surviving as a minority administration but doing so with the leeway of just one seat over his closest rivals. It was not something he had favoured before the election but, as it turned from being a possibility into reality, he came to see its advantages. Minority government had not been tested in Scotland before and no-one knew how it would work. Annabel Goldie, the Scottish Conservative leader, had been calling for it for some time, believing that it would be a way of giving all the parties some influence, with the government having to seek alliances for each of its policies.

When Salmond and his senior colleagues started to plan their strategy for the weeks and months ahead, they realised they could achieve an awful lot, much faster than would have been the case had they had to clear everything with coalition partners. Many people in politics, inside and outside the parliament, had assumed that, because legislation is the basic building block for every major policy, parliamentary votes would always be the key to the success of any administration. But what Salmond discovered – by pure necessity – was that much could be achieved by announcement, proclamation and executive decision making, without even going through the parliament.

Labour's problems were very different. After his party's one-seat defeat, Jack McConnell, the Scottish Labour leader, stepped back and gave Salmond time to try to form a government. There was still some discussion within the party over the possibility of a new Labour–Lib Dem coalition if Salmond failed to form an administration, but nobody really believed it. The most popular theory was that

Salmond would form a minority administration and Labour would have a short time to wait before it collapsed. There was also an assumption that McConnell, having led Labour to defeat, would resign as leader but he showed no sign of doing so, retreating to consider his future but making no moves to stand aside.

On Monday 14 May, Alex Fergusson, a 58-year-old Tory farmer, former Church of Scotland elder and justice of the peace, was elected as the Scottish Parliament's third Presiding Officer, seeing off a late challenge from Margo MacDonald, who decided to stand for the post at the last moment. Then, two days later, Salmond was elected as Scotland's fourth First Minister, the first Nationalist to hold the post and the first to try to lead a minority administration. Salmond's father, Robert, an ardent Nationalist, had refused to enter the House of Commons to hear his son speak because he disapproved of Scotland being part of the institution but he made sure he was there, in the VIP gallery of the Scottish Parliament chamber, for his son's election and maiden speech as First Minister.

'We are not divided. We have a sense of ourselves. A sense of community and above all, a sense of the "common weal" of Scotland,' Salmond declared, carefully invoking the spirit of Donald Dewar's speech to the parliament opening in 1999. He added: 'There is a broad consensus on the need for this parliament to assume greater responsibility for the governance of Scotland and there is an understanding that we are engaged in a process of self-government – and an awareness of the distance already travelled.'

It was a deliberately conciliatory speech from Salmond as he took his first wary steps into the uncertain world of minority politics. He knew he would need the support of at least one of the major parties every time he wanted to get one of his policies through the parliament and he was careful to suggest that the one key theme which linked all the main parties was a desire for greater powers for the parliament.

The new First Minister's speech was courteously received but, as soon as it was over, Salmond showed he was prepared to move fast to start implementing his manifesto. After discussions with Sir John Elvidge, the permanent secretary at the Scottish Executive, Salmond cut the number of departments from nine to six – thereby sticking to one of the first commitments, to scale down the size of government.

He appointed five people to his Cabinet and changed their title from 'minister' to 'secretary', raising the Cabinet's status and profile a notch, one of the many small things which Salmond did to increase the perception of power and influence in his administration. Nicola Sturgeon was appointed Cabinet Secretary for Health and Wellbeing and was made Deputy First Minister, John Swinney was made Cabinet Secretary for Finance and Sustainable Growth, Kenny MacAskill was Cabinet Secretary for Justice, Fiona Hyslop Cabinet Secretary for Education and Lifelong Learning and Richard Lochhead Cabinet Secretary for Rural Affairs and the Environment.

It was a Cabinet very much in Salmond's image. All its members and, indeed, all the junior ministers too, were Salmond loyalists. There was no job for the stalwart SNP MSP and former leadership hopeful Roseanna Cunningham – the candidate who might have won the leadership before Salmond decided to return and stand. There was no job either for Alex Neil, the SNP's best parliamentary debater and firebrand orator, who had opposed Salmond from the fundamentalist wing in the past. Also, there was only a junior ministerial job (minister for the environment) for Michael Russell, the former party chief executive, who had just returned to parliament after a four-year gap.

However, if Labour in Scotland was having trouble getting used to the idea of an SNP government, then it was finding it even more difficult at Westminster. Salmond received a phone call of congratulation from Douglas Alexander, the Scottish secretary, but heard nothing from Downing Street, from either No. 10 or No. 11. The silence from both was possibly understandable given the loathing both Tony Blair and Gordon Brown felt for the Nationalists but it was nevertheless discourteous and actually gave Salmond ammunition which he stored away and used to ridicule the UK government later.

But if the Prime Minister was having trouble acknowledging the SNP victory, then the Queen was not. At just before 5 p.m. on Thursday 24 May, Salmond bowed slightly and shook hands with Her Majesty in one of the grand staterooms at the Palace of Holyroodhouse, receiving his royal warrant of appointment as First Minister. In doing so, Salmond became the first elected leader of any part of the United Kingdom to take office as the head of a democratic parliament on a commitment to break that country apart.

Perhaps showing the sort of long-term political intelligence which has contributed to her longevity as monarch, the Queen was as accommodating as possible to Salmond – in marked contrast to the churlish silence still emanating from Downing Street.

Just a week later Prince Charles followed suit, spending even longer with the new First Minister. They spent an hour together on 31 May, talking about the Prince's Trust, renewables and other issues of interest to the heir to the throne. It was as if the two senior members of the royal family had decided to prepare the ground, just in case Scotland became independent, taking a much more consensual approach than Westminster's policy of outright rejection of the SNP government.

These first few days and weeks of the SNP administration were characterised by a strange sense of unreality in the Scottish Parliament. At each step, as Salmond received his royal warrant and the Great Seal of Scotland, as he named his Cabinet and as he was escorted to meetings in a new, hybrid, ministerial car, so it gradually sank in that Scotland had a Nationalist government. This strange feeling of not-quite-normality was not confined to the opposition, however. The SNP administration, with its new, young team of special advisers, found it just as hard to come to terms with the change. Indeed, later that year when Salmond invited Cabinet members and some senior colleagues to Bute House to watch Scotland's Euro 2008 qualifier against France in Paris, one senior MSP, reduced to tears as Scotland won 1–0, was heard saying: 'Scotland win in Paris, the SNP in government, we're in Bute House – I just can't believe it.'

But Salmond, who had been waiting for this opportunity for the whole of his political life, was determined to move fast, principally because, leading an untried minority administration, he had no idea how long his government would last. He was adamant that his ministers snap out of the sort of day-dreaming listlessness which they were in danger of succumbing to, almost as if by merely becoming a government they had done what they had set out to achieve. Salmond knew that the greater price, of independence, would only come about if the SNP proved itself competent and credible in government. He had set the SNP a demanding 100-day programme for government and he intended to see it through, even if that meant working right the way through the summer recess without a break.

Even before Salmond unveiled his programme for government, on 23 May, he had already initiated two new policies. On 15 May, after talks with the Greens, he announced that the new administration would take steps to prevent controversial ship-to-ship oil transfers from starting in the Firth of Forth. Then, on 22 May, at its first Cabinet meeting, the SNP government decided to implement another key manifesto commitment, scrapping toll charges on the Forth and Tay bridges. In a sign of how competent the SNP's press team was, this announcement was then given to the press that evening for publication in the next morning's newspapers, on the day the programme for government was to be unveiled, giving the administration two days of positive coverage, one for the tolls and the other for the government programme.

Salmond's message was again consensual when he outlined his programme for government – it could not really be called a legislative programme because there would not be much legislation. He said he wanted to usher in 'a new style of government', he wanted the economy to be at the centre of the government's work and he announced the creation of a US-style council of economic advisers, ticking off yet another manifesto commitment.

Yet, even as he was busy deciding on his domestic policy agenda, Salmond was also fulfilling the other, less consensual, part of his 100-day programme: picking fights with Westminster. He made it clear he wanted to revive the joint ministerial committees to arbitrate on disputes between the devolved administrations and Westminster – the procedural mechanism which had fallen into abeyance during the years Labour dominated in Edinburgh and London. And then, to prove his point, Richard Lochhead demanded that Scotland be given control of fisheries negotiations for the UK in Europe because the vast majority of the fishing fleet was based north of the border.

There was more to come. Kenny MacAskill opened discussions with his Westminster counterparts, arguing that Scotland should get control over its firearms legislation; John Swinney made a formal request for the attendance allowance money which Westminster had stopped giving Scotland since free care for the elderly had been introduced in 2002; and Salmond himself asked for Scotland to be given a share of oil and gas revenues – something he had promised to do but which nobody thought would even be listened to in

London. It was all part of a carefully prepared strategy designed to give the impression that Scotland was being short changed, both financially and in terms of power. All the requests were made courteously and formally and each one combined to build up a picture of righteous grievance.

Salmond was waiting for the opportunity to act decisively as Scotland's First Minister and be seen to be standing up to London and it was not long before he got his chance. On 7 June, he made an emergency statement to MSPs just before the parliament rose at the end of its working week. His subject was the Lockerbie bomber, Abdelbaset Ali Mohmed al-Megrahi, who was serving life imprisonment in a Scottish jail for his part in the destruction of the Pan Am airliner in 1988. Salmond claimed, with ill-disguised fury, that the UK government had tried to go behind the back of the Scottish government and do a deal with the Libyan leader, Colonel Muammar al-Gaddafi, which could secure the removal of Megrahi from Scotland to serve out the rest of his sentence in his homeland.

The reason for Salmond's carefully controlled outburst was a confidential memorandum of understanding which Tony Blair signed with Gaddafi on 29 May that year, in which he committed the British government to working together with Libya on a range of fronts, including prisoner transfer. As far as Salmond was concerned, there was only one Libyan prisoner of any notoriety in Britain and that was Megrahi. Libya had stated repeatedly its desire for Megrahi to spend his sentence in Libya so the agreement must mean that Britain was considering a deal. What gave Salmond's arguments weight was the fact that legal affairs in Scotland were devolved and Scottish law could not be superseded by any deal done by the UK Prime Minister.

The speed and style of Salmond's ambush caught everyone by surprise and even his Labour opponents found themselves agreeing with the First Minister's sentiments in the chamber because they had not been given enough notice of the statement to check all the details. The UK government protested over the next few days that no deal had been done and that if any prisoners were to be the subject of any transfers, then the Scottish Parliament, the Scottish government and the Scottish legal authorities would have a veto. But by then the damage had been done and Salmond had scored a notable first success over Westminster. He had appeared rightfully indignant, statesmanlike and also a stout defender of Scotland's interests. For his opponents, particularly those in London who had simply ignored his accession to office, it was a sign of things to come.

In the background, Salmond was preparing another change – yet again something symbolically important and something which could be done without legislation: changing the name of the Scottish Executive to the Scottish Government. Although Henry McLeish had dabbled with this back in 2000, Salmond did it properly, making the change on everything from stationery to podiums, from official papers to the front of the main government buildings. The change was not announced until 2 September but, by then, everything was in place and there was nothing that the opposition or the London government could do about it.

This was one of the many small changes which Salmond instituted to raise the public perception of the Scottish Government to the level of the Westminster government. He wanted the two to be seen as equals, not as one senior and one junior partner. He refused to debate with any other politicians on television unless he was able to go head-to-head with the Prime Minister and he did his best to refer to the Prime Minister as his equal, rather than as some sort of political overlord.

As these changes were being made behind the scenes, so Swinney was working on the SNP's first budget, trying desperately to squeeze all the party's competing priorities and commitments into the finite pot of money that was the Scottish Government's block grant from Westminster.

Every finance minister comes to power believing they can change a lot, using the vast amount of £30 billion or so per year of government money to change Scotland in radical ways. Then they find that their room for manoeuvre is tight. Almost all the money which the Scottish Government is given is already allocated: most to salaries of those working in the public sector – teachers, nurses, police officers, doctors and council workers. The rest is committed on rolling programmes of expenditure which cannot be changed. There is at most 5 per cent of the budget which can be reallocated and only then if efficiency savings or cuts are made elsewhere.

Like most new finance ministers, Swinney came to office with a string of manifesto commitments behind him, pledges he was under pressure to meet. His problems were compounded when the parliament of minorities made its first, telling financial decision, a decision which went against the SNP government's policy agenda and committed the government to spending it felt it could not afford.

Edinburgh City Council, with the backing of the previous Labour–Lib Dem Executive, had been preparing to bring back trams to Scotland's capital. The Nationalists felt the £600 million cost was a waste of money. Edinburgh had toyed with various options to improve its congested transport system for years, including Labour's attempt to introduce a congestion charge in 2001, which was defeated in a public vote. The latest plan involved two ambitious schemes: a rail link to Edinburgh airport, which included a tunnel under the runway and would cost £650 million, and a trams project, the first line of which was scheduled to cost another £600 million. The cost of these two schemes was to be split between the Scottish Government and the city council. The council was in favour and the government was against both plans.

At his debut appearance at First Minister's Questions Salmond tested the temperature inside the chamber by suggesting that his administration might axe both. The Greens threatened to vote against the budget if he did that and the independent MSP Margo MacDonald said such a move – going against the clear wishes of the parliament – could spark a no-confidence motion. When the vote was taken, at the end of June, the parliament voted to continue with the trams and dump the airport rail link, or rather put it out to further consultation, which was the nearest thing to axing it. The SNP administration had to accept the will of the parliament or risk starting a feud which could prevent it from governing. It had no choice. It accepted the decision and allowed the trams project to proceed.

The Scottish Government was therefore committed to finding £500 million for the trams, money it did not want to spend. Swinney accepted the decision grudgingly but made it clear to the city council it would not get a penny more than the agreed amount if the project ran over budget. Any extra would be picked up by the council and the local council taxpayers. It was the first jolt of reality for the government and a clear reminder of the problems of governing without a majority in the parliament.

Salmond, however, was suddenly and unexpectedly confronted with a different side of life as First Minister on the evening of Saturday 30 June. He was looking forward to that Saturday night. To celebrate the end of the parliamentary term, Salmond had commissioned a special performance of the acclaimed National Theatre of Scotland production of *Black Watch* – a brutal and gritty portrayal of life in Iraq for Scottish soldiers. The play has to be performed with the audience on both sides – it is best done in a military drill hall – and the Edinburgh University sports hall at the Pleasance had been turned into a venue for this special performance.

Another feature of the play is that, because the audience sits so tight and close to the action, no-one is allowed to enter the hall once it is underway. That night, when the play started and the lights went down, the guest of honour, Sir Sean Connery, was sitting with his wife Micheline but the seat next to him was vacant. That seat was supposed to be taken by Salmond but he did not appear until after the play was over.

The reason for the First Minister's absence soon became clear, though. A jeep packed with gas cylinders and petrol had been driven into the packed terminal at Glasgow airport late that afternoon and Salmond had been involved in crisis telephone discussions with Cobra, the Downing Street terrorist response committee, ever since. The attack was a shock most of all because Scotland had never really been targeted by terrorists before. It did, however, cut through the rather petty stand-off between Downing Street and Bute House which Tony Blair had perpetuated in the early days after Salmond's victory. Gordon Brown was now the Prime Minister and he and Salmond worked calmly and efficiently together, easing fears of more attacks and coordinating the security response. In political terms, both men benefited from the exposure and the way they reacted to the attack. Both appeared statesmanlike and authoritative although Salmond's stock probably rose higher, simply because he was seen to be operating on the same level as Brown.

Salmond went to Belfast twice in his opening few months as First Minister and once to Brussels before he visited London. Even this was calculated to make the right impression. Salmond was aware of the importance of a Celtic axis – through Edinburgh, Cardiff and Belfast and even through Dublin – in putting pressure on the

Westminster government and he also wanted to make greater use of the European Union, even bypassing Westminster when he could, to further his separatist aims.

Salmond picked up the pace through July and August, aware that the 100-day deadline which he had set before taking office would be coming to an end on 24 August. His government had achieved a great deal of what it had set out to do: tolls on the Forth and Tay bridges had been scrapped, threatened accident and emergency units had been saved from closure, parents had been promised more nursery care, the process of abolishing prescription charges had begun and the graduate endowment for students was being abolished.

There was one glaring omission, however, as the deadline approached – there was not yet a bill to commission a referendum on independence, the cornerstone of SNP government policy. That was rectified on 14 August, when Salmond published a 48-page document titled *Choosing Scotland's Future: A National Conversation*. It was an explanation of the arguments for independence and a call for a nationwide discussion on the issue. Near the back was a short bill, the first ever to be drafted and published by an arm of the UK government, for a referendum on Scottish independence.

Symbolically, this was a huge and decisive moment for the nationalist movement. Salmond promised a three-year cycle of roadshows, ministerial visits and a huge web-based consultation process – aware that he could not command a majority in the parliament for a referendum so he might as well go over the heads of the politicians and appeal to the public directly.

Salmond had gone into the 2007 election hoping to emerge with a strong coalition government and ended up with a wafer-thin lead over Labour and a potentially hazardous minority administration. But it was because he did not have other parties to deal with that he could achieve so much so quickly. He decided to find out what could be done without legislation and went and did it, controlling the direction and speed of government in a way that none of his predecessors as First Minister had been able to do.

The SNP's success was built, in part, on the chaos within the opposition. Labour was fumbling its way through the wreckage of its election defeat. It may only have lost by a single seat but it reacted as if it had lost by two dozen. It was in no position to mount any serious form of opposition to Salmond in his first few months. The Liberal Democrats were in a similar position. They were still feeling the pain of an election which they thought would bring them more and they had dodged around on the question of coalition before retreating to opposition to regroup. The Conservatives were in pretty good spirits but, on their own, were not strong enough to coordinate any sort of sustained campaign against the new government. The sole occasion when the opposition parties came together to defeat the new government concerned trams and that was only because the policy had been decided and agreed by the parties before the election.

On 24 August, the 100-day programme was complete and, as the white paper on independence brought it to a close, it also prompted a wave of interest from Europe and the world. The *Scotsman* asked 100 figures in Scottish society, from the arts to sport and from business to politics, to assess Salmond's first 100 days in office and hardly any thought he could have done better. 'Alex Salmond continues to walk on water,' declared the German newspaper *Die Märkische Allgemeine Zeitung*, while *Der Zürcher Oberländer* in Switzerland declared the First Minister a 'statesman' for his handling of the Glasgow terror attacks. The French news agency AFP predicted that the SNP's continuing success was jeopardising Labour's chances of winning the next UK general election.

For Labour in Scotland, however, the next general election was too far away to worry about. What was of much more concern was who was going to lead the party into the next session of parliament.

18

A takeaway coup and a coronation

IT was really nothing more than an evening in for a group of friends. Six women came together on a Friday evening in Glasgow to have a Chinese takeaway and gossip but, because of who they were and the timing of the get-together, it meant an awful lot more than that. The venue was the flat belonging to Pauline McNeill, a Glasgow Labour MSP. The other guests were Margaret Curran, the former parliament minister, Johann Lamont, the former deputy justice minister, Sarah Boyack, the former transport minister, Jackie Baillie, the former social justice minister, and Karen Gillon, the Labour MSP for Clydesdale. The timing was crucial: the group came together on Friday 11 May 2007, exactly a week after Alex Salmond had celebrated victory in the election.

Everybody, inside and outside the Labour Party, expected Jack McConnell to resign if he lost the election – that's what party leaders were supposed to do, after all. But the former First Minister was not going anywhere, at least not for the time being. All the same, the Scottish Labour Party had got itself into such an anxious and gossipy state following its election defeat that the simple news of such a private get-together was enough to suggest factions were forming, divisions were being exposed and McConnell was being forced out.

A very strong rumour flying around was that Wendy Alexander, a close friend and ally of McNeill's, was considering challenging McConnell for the leadership. One of those present at McNeill's flat insisted afterwards that there had been no talk of a leadership challenge. 'Until the dust settles and until Jack makes clear what he is doing, it is all just speculation,' she said. Indeed, there is no record of the women MSPs discussing any more than the election result. There is certainly no evidence that they were plotting a leadership campaign for Alexander – but there did not need to be.

All the news did, though, was spur McConnell to dig in. 'The First Minister is not even thinking about standing down,' a spokesman said after details of the 'Chinese takeaway coup' had appeared in the papers. McConnell was not unwilling to go, but he was only forty-six at this point and, as the experienced political animal that he was, he did not want to leave without something to go to, maybe a seat in the House of Lords or some other political appointment which would ease the loss of Bute House. So he decided to wait and negotiate for his future before throwing away the only bargaining tool he had left – his leadership of the Scottish Labour Party.

There was a clear expectation that McConnell would have to resign at some point so the potential candidates started canvassing for support behind his back while McConnell started negotiations with his political masters in London for another job. It was a totally understandable stance for McConnell to take but it did not do his party any good. Labour's first defeat in Scotland for fifty years had left the party so shocked it hardly knew what to do or where to go and, to make matters worse, it had a leader whose attention was fixed elsewhere.

The SNP's 100-day programme was designed to give the impression of an administration working hard and changing as much as possible as soon as possible. It was challenged in part, but only in a piecemeal way, by the Labour Party. There was no coordinated, proper assault on the agenda as a whole, which should have happened had Labour been focused on its job. The party nationally was going through the elevation of Gordon Brown to 10 Downing Street and that did deflect attention from the situation in Scotland but there was no doubt the Scottish question needed to be resolved, and quickly.

July came and went with more manoeuvring behind McConnell's back but with still no decision from the former First Minister. By the start of August, however, it was clear that the leadership race to replace McConnell had all but taken place while he was still in charge. All the potential challengers had taken soundings and assessed their support bases and all but one – Alexander – had dropped out of the race. Curran had canvassed support then backed away from a challenge and Andy Kerr, the former health minister, had done the same.

Many in the party believed McConnell was waiting for a peerage in Tony Blair's farewell honours list, but that was not the only reward he was looking for. On 15 August, McConnell held a press conference, announcing he was standing down as Scottish Labour leader and surprising almost everyone by saying he was going to become the next British high commissioner to Malawi. The negotiations with Blair, Brown and the Foreign Office had at last come good and he had been promised the job he wanted and the change of direction he craved.

It was rare but not unusual for someone with no diplomatic experience to take on such an important overseas posting. Helen Liddell, the former Scottish secretary, had become high commissioner to Australia and Paul Boateng, a former Home Office minister, had taken the same post in South Africa.

McConnell did have form as far as Malawi was concerned. He had made the southern African country his top international focus as First Minister, had been there and met President Bingu wa Mutharika in 2005 (see Chapter 12) and had even held a reception for charities and officials in the palatial British high commissioner's residence on the outskirts of Lilongwe. He was delighted but events did not quite pan out as he had hoped. Twelve months went by and still McConnell had not got the contract from the Foreign Office he needed to take over in Lilongwe.

The existing high commissioner, Richard Wildash, was due to leave the posting in February 2009. McConnell was keen to take over but he would have to resign his Scottish parliamentary seat to do so. With the SNP holding only a one-seat lead over Labour in the Scottish Parliament, Labour leaders were reluctant to sanction a by-election in Motherwell & Wishaw — a by-election the Nationalists could win, allowing the SNP to stretch its lead over Labour to a crucial three seats.

In October 2008, Brown acted and told McConnell he would not be getting his Malawi posting as planned, at least not yet. Labour could simply not afford the by-election so Brown created a job for McConnell, making him a 'special envoy' on conflict resolution. It was a grand-sounding title but in reality did not amount to very much. McConnell would be expected to work on conflict resolution for one day a week, unpaid, while his well-paid diplomatic posting, with staff, a grand house and a generous pension, would go to someone else. McConnell was told he would still be going to Malawi as high commissioner in 2011 but, by that time, there was no guarantee that Labour would be in charge at Westminster, nor that any other party would honour the posting.

McConnell insisted he was happy with his new role but everyone in the Scottish Labour Party knew he had lost out. Brown still blamed McConnell not just for losing the 2007 election but also for his constant feuds with Alexander, so his reaction to the prospect of McConnell quitting and forcing a by-election was understandable, if a bit brutal.

However, when McConnell stepped down as leader, in August 2007, all that was to come. Alexander was virtually the leader in waiting. She had the support of her parliamentary colleagues, she had solid if unspectacular union support and she apparently had the backing of Brown, newly ensconced in No. 10 as Labour Prime Minister.

Alexander was already one of the best-known figures in Scottish politics. She was one of the few to be known just by her first name, Wendy. Indeed the term 'you've been Wendied' was common at Holyrood because it described the all too frequent experience of being harangued and verbally assaulted by Alexander without being able to get a word in to respond. Small and full of energy, Alexander had a reputation for being exceptionally bright – she had had her first book published at twenty-four and had a string of awards and academic credentials after her name – but she was also known for being difficult to work with. The reports of phone calls at 3 a.m. and constant demands on all manner of different subjects were well known throughout the civil service and the Labour Party. She came from the nearest thing the Scottish Labour Party had to a political dynasty, with her brother Douglas then the international development secretary in Brown's Cabinet.

Brown had been a loyal supporter of Alexander for some time and she had ridden up through the Scottish Labour Party with his patronage and with the support of Donald Dewar, who had first employed her as a special adviser in the 1990s. Nobody had any reservations about her intelligence or her drive; what was queried, rather, was whether she had the common touch or the parliamentary skills to take on Alex Salmond.

Within a week it became clear that Alexander would not face even a symbolic challenge from the left and that she had become leader in waiting of the parliamentary group of the Scottish Labour Party. She immediately signalled her intention to embrace a radical new approach for the party. Deciding that the party had to come up with a new way of taking the fight to the Nationalists, Alexander suggested more powers for the Scottish Parliament – including new tax powers. She declined to say which powers should come to Scotland but made it clear that this was her way of taking on the constitutional argument, ditching the simple warnings such as 'divorce is an expensive business' which had been the cornerstone of Labour's arguments in the past. 'Taking a fresh look at the [devolution] settlement is not something that holds any anxieties for me,' Alexander said on 21 August, the day she became leader-elect.

Alexander's openness to more powers for the parliament was consistent with her line over the previous ten years, when she had argued, unsuccessfully, for some form of fiscal responsibility for Scotland, for the Scottish Parliament to be more accountable for the money it spent. But her new approach was not favoured by influential colleagues in London. Des Browne, now the Scottish secretary, made it clear he did not believe the devolution settlement needed to be radically redrawn, a view supported by the new Prime Minister. However, Alexander also asserted the right of the Scottish Labour Party to make its own decisions on domestic policy, effectively challenging her political superiors in London to countermand her.

Even though she had no challengers for the leadership, Alexander decided to campaign as if she did have a contest to fight. She raised money from supporters, about £16,000, and used it to tour the country speaking to activists and party members, both to find out what they wanted the party to do and also to raise her own profile. There were some in the party who did not like the idea of a straightforward coronation of the new leader and believed a proper contest would be a better way of exploring new ideas and policies but, by the time Alexander had sewn up the support of her fellow MSPs, there was no-one left of any political weight to stand against her.

Her early rhetoric was promising. She vowed to improve the party's organisation, which had been left trailing by the SNP's investment in top-quality computer databases in the 2007 election, and she promised to review all the party's policies, putting more emphasis on education.

On 17 September, having just been elected formally as leader of the Labour group in the Scottish Parliament, Alexander selected her shadow Cabinet team. Intriguingly, most of those who had come together for that now infamous Chinese takeaway in May were named in the Alexander team. Pauline McNeill, who had hosted the Friday evening gathering, was given the important justice brief – a move which surprised many in the party simply because she had no ministerial experience; Sarah Boyack, who had been transport minister under Dewar and Henry McLeish, was brought back to cover the rural affairs brief; Jackie Baillie, another former minister from the McLeish era, was appointed to the important role of being in charge of policy delivery in the parliament; and Margaret Curran was given health. Rhona Brankin, a former teacher, was handed education; Iain Gray, who had been enterprise minister under McConnell but who lost his seat in 2003, was rewarded with the key finance portfolio; and Andy Kerr was given the finance and public services briefs.

Alexander almost seemed to be turning the clock back. Labour figures who had been in government under McLeish found favour again with Alexander and those who prospered under McConnell were left on the back benches – Tricia Ferguson, Cathy Jamieson and Hugh Henry were three clear examples. By doing this, Alexander appeared to be entrenching the McConnellite/McLeishite split that had dominated Labour politics at Holyrood for so long. It really now appeared as if there were two clear factions, those who were favoured by McConnell and those who supported McLeish and now, by extension, Alexander.

McConnell's allies tended to be based around Labour's Lanark-shire heartlands with the McLeish–Alexander camp more disparate, stretching from Fife to Edinburgh and over to Paisley. There were some figures who managed to skirt both camps and find favour with each, Tom McCabe being a good example. He managed to keep in with both, as did Kerr, but some – notably Baillie, Brankin, Ferguson and Jamieson – were clearly favoured by one side but not the other.

Alexander had wanted the Scottish Labour leadership for some time but even she admitted that the party was hardly in the rudest health when she took over. Membership had fallen 30 per cent in the seven years since 2000, dropping from 26,500 to 18,500. At the same time, SNP membership had risen from 9,450 members in 2003 to 13,585 in August 2007, a rise of 44 per cent in four years. Labour used to be able to rely on a phalanx of local councillors to campaign, fund-raise and canvass on its behalf, but the introduction of proportional representation for council elections had stripped Labour of 161 councillors and given the SNP an extra 182. This changed the balance of political power, not just in town halls across the country but on the doorsteps too, giving the Nationalists more willing volunteers while Labour lost out. In Holyrood and Westminster, Labour was losing representation and resources. In 1999, the party had fifty-six MSPs and fifty-six MPs. By August 2007, Labour had forty-six MSPs and forty MPs, partly owing to boundary changes but mainly because of the SNP's success.

Even though Labour had lost the election by only one seat, it was clear to anyone who looked below the surface that the party had been on the way down for some time. The election defeat was the first public sign of an internal disintegration, caused partly by disillusionment with Tony Blair and the Iraq War and partly by a lack of enthusiasm after ten years in power in London.

The difference between Labour on the way down and the SNP on the way up was clearly illustrated at the party conferences in the spring of 2007. Blair, then still the Prime Minister, arrived in Aviemore to galvanise the Scottish Labour Party ahead of the election but found the 650-seat auditorium barely two-thirds full because not enough Labour constituency delegates had turned up. Stallholders and exhibitors were brought in to hear the Prime Minister to make the hall look full. Even the delegates who were there were overwhelmingly male, middle aged and overweight, mostly from unions and affiliated organisations – a clear sign of a moribund, static and stagnant party.

Soon after that conference, Alex Salmond addressed the SNP at the new conference hall in Perth. He spoke to an audience of 1,200 and there were many more who could not get in to hear him. But probably more important than the size of the audience was its make-up. The usual middle-aged party hacks were there, but they had been joined by hundreds of young people and dozens of pensioners too, representing a real cross-section of Scottish society – many of the kind of people, in fact, who had been attracted to the Labour Party in the past.

Alexander came to the leadership of Scottish Labour when it had lost activists, councillors, MSPs and members but, crucially, also the civil service. Labour had been in power for eight years and all the senior figures had become used to the support of civil servants in drawing up policies, coming up with new ideas and generally keeping the theoretical side of the party alive. In opposition, Labour managers had to find ways of taking on this policy development role on their own, without official back-up, and it would take time for them to come to terms with this.

Also, the party was suffering financially. The Scottish Labour Party accounts had always been linked into the UK Labour Party with central union donations spread around the country. But with the UK party suffering from the cash-for-peerages controversy, mounting debts and a lack of donors, the Scottish party, which had just fought an expensive election campaign, was suffering too.

Alexander's first main policy move was to bring the three main opposition parties together in the common cause of more powers for the parliament. The Conservatives, the Liberal Democrats and Labour all agreed on the need to review the powers of the parliament but they were divided on the direction any such review should take. The Liberal Democrats wanted a fully federal Britain, with Scotland in charge of all tax and spending decisions. Labour was more cautious but felt more powers needed to come north to challenge the SNP arguments, while the Tories were even warier, agreeing to a review but going no further than that.

Alexander was instrumental in getting the new Prime Minister's backing for what she described as a 'Scottish constitutional commission'. Gordon Brown was cautious about more powers for the parliament but was willing to give Alexander the scope to make her own decisions as Scottish party leader, so he gave the commission his blessing, named the Commission on Scottish Devolution when it came into being. When asked about it, Brown did seem to lack enthusiasm, stressing that the review, as he called it, might decide to take powers back from Holyrood as well as granting it new powers, but he did not stand in its way.

Alexander used a set-piece speech at Edinburgh on 30 November, St Andrew's Day, to set out her ideas on the commission. 'We cannot become unthinking unionists,' she said. 'It is legitimate to ask whether that settlement now needs to be adjusted in the interests of all the nations of the United Kingdom.'

Alexander needed the other unionist parties on board to give her new commission the sort of political credibility which the Scottish Constitutional Convention had had when it drew up the devolution plans in the 1980s and 1990s. The Liberal Democrats were willing collaborators in the scheme and the Conservatives, while more cautious, also followed Alexander's lead. Then, on 25 March 2008, Professor Sir Kenneth Calman, chancellor of Glasgow University, was named as the man to lead the commission.

Calman was the ideal candidate. He was a respected academic and was also a unionist and a devolutionist. He was also willing to work for free. Calman was asked to look at all aspects of the devolution settlement, except independence, and come up with recommendations to change it. The Nationalists, who had started their own National Conversation on independence, dismissed the Calman commission as an irrelevant sideshow but, with the backing of 78 of the parliament's 129 MSPs and a wide-ranging remit, it had the potential to become an extremely powerful tool.

The devolution settlement, which Donald Dewar had had to fight so hard to secure in 1998, was being re-examined with the likely outcome of some new powers for the Scottish Parliament. The Calman commission was looking into the handover of powers which were never even considered in 1998, such as the power to change stamp duty or excise duty or control over the expenditure raised by income tax in Scotland. This concept of 'assigned taxes' was a particular favourite of Alexander's. The idea behind them was that the Scottish Government would then have an incentive to grow the tax takes by stimulating the economy in other ways, giving it some form of limited, financial accountability.

Until she took on the job, Alexander's reputation for poor personnel skills had largely been confined to the Holyrood village. The more intense scrutiny of the leader's job, however, soon made sure that that knowledge spread wider and wider. One problem was her inability to keep key press advisers. Her first was Brian Lironi, the former political editor of the *Sunday Mail*. Lironi lasted a month as Alexander's press spokesman before quitting, having been unable to cope with the demands of working for her. The next to go was Matthew Marr. Marr quit after shouting insults at Salmond during the Politician of the Year Awards in 2007 as the First Minister was going up to receive the main award. Marr's departure was not Alexander's fault in any way and he was not her press adviser – he was a party press spokesman – but his departure added to the impression that the new Labour leader was having difficulty holding onto key staff.

A new spin doctor, Gavin Yates, was brought in as head of Labour's press desk at Holyrood but even before he was appointed, he had managed to cause his new employers some embarrassment. In a blog written several months before his appointment he had described Alexander as 'abrasive'. Yates rode through this minor hassle, though, and brought some stability to the Labour spin operation, which was still being beaten at every turn by the much more pro-fessional SNP machine.

In February 2008, Simon Pia, a former *Scotsman* journalist, was recruited as Alexander's new press spokesman. It was a job which everyone in the industry, including Pia, knew would be challenging but even he could not have imagined quite what a difficult time he and his new boss would be in for.

19

Cheques and balances

LIKE any ambitious politician, the Labour MSP Charlie Gordon wanted to be on the side of the winner. In June 2007, when it became clear that Wendy Alexander would be the only serious contender for the Scottish Labour leadership, Gordon joined her campaign team. Keen to show that he had something to offer, Gordon phoned round a number of allies in the business world to solicit donations for Alexander's leadership campaign. One of his contacts was Paul Green, a Jersey-based businessman.

Gordon had got to know Green, then a retail developer, when he had been leader of Glasgow City Council. Gordon asked Green whether he wanted to donate money to the Alexander leadership campaign fund and Green said yes, giving £950. Gordon had done his job, or so he thought, securing money for Alexander's campaign.

There was not a hint of the problems to follow until 11 November 2007, two months after Alexander had been elected leader unopposed. Then came a piece in the *Sunday Herald*, revealing that Alexander had received a number of donations to help her fight for the leadership over the course of that summer, each of which, like Green's, had been just under £1,000. Every donation of £1,000 or more had to be declared to the Electoral Commission so all of Alexander's donations had been just below the limit, the newspaper stated, allowing the donors to remain anonymous and allowing Alexander to keep the donations a secret. At that time, nobody outside the Alexander camp knew how much had been raised and who had given the money. Asked if Alexander would publish the names of all the donors, a spokesman simply replied: 'We have complied with every rule.'

By 25 November, word had leaked out that one of Alexander's donors was a tax exile living in the Channel Islands. This was strictly against the rules. Only those registered to vote in the UK could donate money to UK political parties, but even at this stage, the situation did not appear too damaging to Alexander's cause. However, it did not take long for the press to find out the name of the donor, and Green's identity, which had been so carefully hidden by the decision to donate just £950, was exposed.

By this time it was becoming clear that Alexander had accepted an illegal donation from someone who should not have given money to her campaign. But there were also other questions to be answered – for example, why did she raise £16,000 for a campaign which did not really take place because she was the only candidate? Suddenly Alexander's judgement and probity were being questioned.

The Alexander team turned on Gordon. The Glasgow Cathcart MSP had already secured a donation from Green for his own election campaign and he had gone back to the Jersey-based businessman again, either unaware that Green's donations were illegal or because he did not bother to check. His attempt to help the Alexander campaign had backfired and got the new Scottish Labour leader, and himself, into a lot of trouble.

Gordon admitted that the donation was his fault and resigned as Labour's transport spokesman. Tom McCabe, speaking for the Alexander campaign, said the money had been returned. McCabe insisted that an honest mistake had been made because the campaign team believed the money had come from a UK-based company, not from Green personally.

Team Alexander hoped that, by putting all the blame on Gordon, they could escape further problems. 'Wendy, like everyone else on the campaign, was on the receiving end of the assurances and assumptions that Mr Gordon gave,' said McCabe, quite pointedly blaming Gordon at the press conference where Gordon resigned.

That might have been the end of the matter had it not been for two other oversights. First, the money had not come from one of Green's UK-based companies, it had come from him, in the form of a personal cheque. It was sent from Green, complete with a covering letter from his house in Jersey, and Alexander had written a personal reply to thank him. Also, Alexander had failed to approach anybody in the Scottish Parliament to ask whether she should declare the donations in the Holyrood register of members' interests – a register which operated under quite different rules from the Electoral Commission. The parliament rules were clear that MSPs should err on the side of caution: they should declare any gifts over £540 if they had any doubts about them and should seek advice at the earliest opportunity. Alexander did seek advice from the clerks to the Standards Committee about whether she should have declared her leadership donations in the members' register, but not until November, more than a month after the arrival of the first donation.

As December started, the Alexander donations story became unstoppable. The media was in a feeding frenzy with every lead being followed up, however tenuous, and every avenue explored. The SNP rode in on the back of this as well, with activists and other party members complaining to every possible investigative body in the hope of pursuing the embarrassment and discomfort of Alexander as long as possible. It hardly helped that Labour nationally was going through an even more tortuous investigation into donations, this time over the use of so-called 'phantom' donors, who were used to disguise the identities of real donors.

The whole affair was handed over to the Electoral Commission to investigate at the start of December 2007. Alexander said she would like to explain herself but could not say anything until the commission had reported and decided whether to refer the matter to the police. But for a new leader who was already struggling in other areas – she was having great difficulty coping with Alex Salmond's jibes, taunts and debating skills at First Minister's Questions – the Electoral Commission investigation made her look weak and embattled.

As far as Gordon Brown was concerned, already having to cope with police investigations and donation problems of his own, Alexander had to stay on. There were those close to the Prime Minister who believed in a 'domino' effect: if Alexander resigned over a donations scandal it could lead to the fall of others closer to Brown in London and could endanger the government.

Alexander went to Brown for advice and was told to hang on and ride out the storm. For her part, she did not want to resign because she did not believe she had done anything which she felt was worthy of resignation. She had only been in the job two months and she wanted to fight on and win through.

On 6 December Salmond intervened to increase the pressure on Alexander. The First Minister said a police inquiry was now 'inevitable' and Alexander should step aside as leader until that investigation had finished. With the whole matter effectively on hold until the Electoral Commission reported, Salmond's comments were clearly designed to keep the Alexander issue at the top of the political agenda for as long as possible. Salmond kept the pressure up over Alexander's donations at the start of 2008, telling the BBC on 13 January that the Electoral Commission would lose credibility if it failed to take action against the Labour Party over illegal donations, north and south of the border.

There was another controversy, however, which would cause Alexander more problems, this time of a political nature. In November 2007, Andy Kerr, Labour's finance spokesman in the Scottish Parliament, raised the possibility of Labour backing a referendum on independence. The idea was to 'lance the boil' of independence by holding a snap poll, defeating the Nationalists and putting the constitutional question away indefinitely. The argument was put forward by Allan Wilson, a former MSP and a key ally of Kerr's. Kerr then went on television to say it should be discussed within the party.

Kerr knew that Alexander had been talking to Brown about the issue for several months. Alexander was taken by the radical suggestion. She wanted to do something to seize the agenda back from the SNP and this appeared a bold but risky strategy. Brown did not give his backing to it but listened and made it clear he was considering the policy.

The Kerr–Wilson suggestion was merely a bit of 'kite flying' from the Labour duo. They wanted to see if the idea would take off so placed it in the public domain to see what happened. There was no outright rejection but the issue of Labour's backing for a referendum disappeared again until Monday 21 April 2008, when Brown went to Inverness to address the Scottish Trades Union Congress.

After his speech, he was chatting in private to a small number of senior trade unionists when he mentioned that he had discussed the idea of backing a referendum with Alexander. Brown did not say he supported the idea but the story that he was considering the policy found its way, from one of the trade unionists, into the *Sunday Mail* on 4 May. Alexander went on to the BBC's *Politics Show* that same day, aware that Brown had not backed the policy shift but also aware that the idea was now out in the open. 'Bring it on,' she declared, insisting she was not scared of a referendum on independence and challenging the SNP to introduce one as soon as possible. Alexander's comments were remarkable because she had basically announced a complete U-turn in party policy in three short words, taking Labour from outright opposition to a referendum to supporting it.

Two days later, on Tuesday 6 May, Alexander was asked on the BBC's *Newsnight Scotland* whether she had the backing of the Prime Minister for her U-turn. She claimed, hesitantly, that Brown had 'endorsed' her decision. This was a careful attempt to try to say that the Prime Minister had allowed her to make the decision without backing it himself but all it looked like was a statement claiming that Brown supported the decision, which he did not. This left the Prime Minister in an extremely difficult position, one he got out of simply by disowning his Scottish leader. Asked by David Cameron at Prime Minister's Questions whether he supported Alexander's referendum call, the Prime Minister refused to back her, leaving her cast adrift on her own.

At the same time, Alexander was facing a reaction from her own parliamentary party, with many MSPs uncomfortable at such a radical and risky change of policy being made without their backing. With the SNP government insisting that it would not change its timings for a planned referendum in 2010, Alexander's policy change, far from 'lancing the boil', actually appeared to give the Nationalists the support they needed to hold a referendum when they wanted it. Labour had to bring the policy change back and it did. On 13 May 2008, the Labour group in the Scottish Parliament decided to postpone any decision on the referendum until the bill paving the way for it was brought forward. The party would then decide its position and might well oppose the bill if it thought that the right approach.

After two weeks of extraordinary policy U-turns and intrigue, the party was pretty much back where it had started. The only change was that Alexander's leadership had been weakened, her authority undermined and her backing from Brown diminished. Her party had lost out too, appearing muddled, hesitant and uncertain.

On 4 February 2008, there was a further blow for Alexander.

Jim Dyer, the standards commissioner for the Scottish Parliament, had decided that Alexander should after all have declared her donations in the register of members' interests at Holyrood. This opened up the issue on a whole new front for the Scottish Labour leader. Up until this point, the controversy had revolved entirely around the 'illegal' donation from Paul Green and the Electoral Commission investigation into that donation. Now, here was Dyer saying that Alexander broke parliamentary rules by not declaring all the donations in the register of interests. Dyer's view was extremely contentious given that the clerks to the Standards Committee had already ruled that Alexander did not need to declare the donations.

Many in the Holyrood Labour Party were outraged that Dyer should not only accuse Alexander of breaking rules which she had already taken advice on, but that he should then refer her to the procurator fiscal. This actually had the effect of hardening the wavering Labour MSPs behind Alexander. Many were privately starting to question her future, aware that the donations row was bringing the whole party down, but some were so outraged by Dyer's behaviour that they gave her their unequivocal support in return.

There was good news to follow for Alexander soon afterwards, however. The dozen short paragraphs which revealed the Electoral Commission's decision on the illegal donation appeared as an email on computer screens all over the parliament at the same time, at 2.30 p.m. on Thursday 7 February. There were whoops of delight all along the Labour MSPs' corridor at the parliament as the email dropped.

The commission had decided it was 'not appropriate or in the public interest' to report the Scottish Labour leader to the procurator fiscal. Alexander was rebuked for not doing enough to check the legality of the Green donation but she was effectively given the all-clear to remain in her job.

Alexander was buoyant and felt vindicated.

You get tested in the tough times, not in the easy times. I have admitted a mistake was made and I think the public rather like politicians who admit they make mistakes sometimes.

This statement clears me of any intentional wrong-doing. My honesty and integrity have been confirmed by this judgement.

She had been slapped on the wrist but otherwise cleared, as had Charlie Gordon, the MSP who started the process by soliciting the illegal donation. He was effectively given the all-clear too, so there would not be a difficult by-election for Labour to worry about either. At last it appeared as if the whole donations controversy was easing and the party – and its leader – could move on.

There was one nagging problem, however, which remained outstanding. Dyer's decision to accuse Alexander of breaking the parliamentary rules never went anywhere with the procurator fiscal but it was handed to the Holyrood Standards Committee to look into. Nobody at the top of the Labour Party really gave this much thought. Surely, they believed, Alexander had got through the worst of it. After all, she had coped with a full Electoral Commission investigation; surely the Standards Committee could not do any worse, particularly as Alexander had followed the advice she had been given over the register of members' interests?

For the four months after the February decision of the Electoral Commission, Alexander tried to reassert her control over the party, gradually improving her previously poor performances at First Minister's Questions and presiding over a Scottish Labour conference in Aviemore which brought some stability to the party. 'At least we didn't go backwards, we would have taken that at the start of the conference,' one Labour MSP said afterwards.

But then, on 26 June, all that good work was undone when the donations row came back. The Scottish Parliament's Standards Committee had been discussing Dyer's report on Alexander's failure to register the donations in private for some time. That day – the final day of the parliamentary term before recess – the committee made its decision on the report. In a ruling which reverberated around the parliament, the committee decided that Alexander should be suspended for one day for breaking the rules.

It was a massively contentious and political decision. The one-day suspension was the least the committee could impose. It was intended to be symbolic, passing down a punishment which would be seen as such but which would not mean all that much in practice. But it was devastating. It meant that Alexander would become the first party leader in British history to face suspension from the parliament of which she was a member.

The Standards Committee was supposed to be impartial and above party politics but it became clear when its MSPs came to explain their reasons for taking the decision that it was anything but. The committee was made up of three SNP MSPs, including the convener, Keith Brown, two Labour MSPs, one Conservative and one Liberal Democrat.

The two Labour MSPs were understandably against any sanction for Alexander and they were joined in this position by the Tory, Jamie McGrigor. Besides Brown, this left the other two SNP MSPs and the Liberal Democrat, Hugh O'Donnell, to call for a suspension, with the casting vote going to Brown, who also backed the call. Not only did the committee divide on party lines but all those who lined up to demand punishment for Alexander did so using the same arguments as the others, giving the appearance of a party political campaign to suspend the Labour leader.

There was a theory circulating in SNP circles that Alexander would never resign over this issue and more political capital could be gained from having her damaged and hanging on than having a new leader in place – hence the decision to suspend her. But this theory was blown apart just forty-eight hours later when Alexander quit.

The committee's decision to suspend Alexander still had to be ratified by the full parliament and there was a good chance that it would reject the committee's call for suspension. But, with the committee making its decision on the last day of the parliamentary term, there was simply no time for the full parliament to discuss it. This meant that Alexander went into the summer recess with the threat of suspension – and the ongoing donations row – hanging over her.

Had the parliament made its decision and voted down the suspension before the recess, Alexander would have stayed in her job but the prospect of another two months of uncertainty was just too much. On Friday 27 June, Alexander met with her closest aides and advisers and told them she could not take any more. She had been pushed that way by her husband, who saw what the controversy and the leadership struggles were doing to her, and, at the end of those meetings, when she had faced repeated appeals to stay, she took the decision to quit.

The following morning, shortly before midday, Alexander

delivered a short statement to the press at John Smith House, Labour's headquarters in Glasgow, announcing her decision to quit after only nine months in charge of the Scottish Labour Party. She was clearly angry and hurt at the way she had been treated, accusing her opponents of denying her 'natural justice' and claiming that the Standards Committee had made a 'partisan decision'.

> My pursuers have sought the prize of political victory with little thought to the standing of the parliament. Some may feel they have achieved a political victory, but wiser heads will surely question: 'At what price?'
>
> It is clear that vexatious complaints will continue to dominate the headlines as long as I remain Scottish parliamentary leader. I cannot ask Labour supporters in Scotland for further forbearance.

Alexander's resignation came on the same day as another, less high-profile, figure decided to stand down. David Marshall had been the Labour MP for Glasgow East (in its various guises) since 1979 but persistent health problems forced him to quit. The Scottish Labour Party, which had only just managed to get itself up and fighting again after a year of turmoil since the election, was now facing two contests of equal magnitude and equal danger: a by-election in Glasgow East and the race to become the fifth party leader since devolution.

20

Divide and rule

IT was while they were watching Alex Salmond jump around in delight, dressed in a light tan suit to ward off the sticky Sri Lankan heat, that some Labour activists started asking whether anything would ever go right for them again. The First Minister had gone to Colombo to do the sort of last-minute lobbying that had worked so well for Tony Blair when London secured the 2012 Olympic Games two years before. This time the prize was the Commonwealth Games of 2014 and the battle was a straight fight between Glasgow and Abuja in Nigeria.

Much of the hard work on Glasgow's behalf had been done by Glasgow's Labour council leaders and Jack McConnell when he was First Minister. Yet it was Salmond, who had only been in office for six months, who was there in Sri Lanka to celebrate with the winning team. McConnell was back home in Scotland as his successor cavorted in Glasgow's moment of triumph.

It was perfect for the SNP. Glasgow had won the right to host one of the major world sporting events, one of the few in which Scotland competes on its own. The saltires were everywhere and it really did appear as if the new wave of nationalism, which the SNP victory had ushered in six months before, was starting to have an effect.

Salmond's honeymoon was going on and on. The First Minister did not really bother going to London; instead, he went to Sri Lanka to help land the Commonwealth Games, having been to New York the month before to preach his message of a new 'Celtic Lion' economy to receptive American audiences. Salmond also followed up his government's 100-day programme with a declaration that he would light a bonfire of the quangos, completing what Henry McLeish had promised to do seven years before but never achieved.

The Scottish Government's legislative programme for the 2007/8 parliamentary year was modest. There were two high-profile measures, the abolition of tolls on the Forth and Tay bridges and the abolition of the graduate endowment, for both of which the government had enough cross-party support. There was one bill, however, which was crucial for the Scottish Government's survival – the budget bill. John Swinney, the finance secretary, had spent the whole of the summer cajoling and browbeating his fellow ministers until they brought their spending plans into line. But even then, there was very little latitude in the plans. Swinney was relying on savings across government to make his plans work and there was no contingency fund.

At the heart of the budget were two key measures designed to win over so-called 'middle Scotland' – a freeze in council tax and cuts in business rates. These tax-cutting policies were clearly pushing the SNP to the middle ground of politics if not towards the right.

The council tax freeze had been bought from generally sceptical councils, both with extra money and with the introduction of a complicated concordat with local authorities. Swinney had agreed to free up more council money, ending the ring-fencing on some issues which had forced councils to spend money on particular projects. He had also changed the way councils were assessed, moving from monitoring of money going in to a system of monitoring the performance of the outcomes which councils achieved. These were fairly intricate changes but Scotland's councils, some of them still run by Labour, liked the way the SNP government was approaching local government – and the extra money he was promising – and gave Swinney his council tax freeze in return.

But even with the support of the councils, Swinney knew he had to secure the backing of at least one of the main parties in the parliament to get the budget through and that meant negotiation. The Conservatives had been calling for minority government for some time in the hope that they might get just this sort of chance to influence policy. They stepped in to help, but only in return for major concessions.

In its manifesto, the SNP had promised to create 1,000 extra police officers. By the time the party got into government and had a look at the finances, it decided to downgrade this to 500 new officers. In return for their support for the budget, the Tories demanded that the original pledge for 1,000 new, additional officers be honoured, so Swinney agreed. He cut money from prisons, road maintenance and health to find the £10 million he needed for the police.

Swinney then found another £4.3 million for a climate challenge fund, in an attempt to get the Greens on board. But the Tories still held out for more. They asked for the cuts in business rates, which the Scottish Government was phasing in over three years, to be accelerated, helping more businesses more quickly, and they also asked for more money for the fight against drugs.

On 5 February 2008, when Cabinet met on the eve of the final budget vote in the parliament, there was still no agreement. The Tories were demanding more, as were the Greens, and Swinney did not have the votes he needed to get the bill through. It was just the sort of brinkmanship which minority government was supposed to be about but which was completely new to Scotland's MSPs.

Salmond then intervened, giving Kevin Pringle, his press spokesman, permission to slip into his post-Cabinet briefing for the press a warning that the First Minister would quit and force another election if his budget was defeated. Pringle did this in as calm and understated a way as he could, aware that he had created a great pre-budget story ahead of the key vote the following day. As expected, Salmond got the headlines he wanted. 'I'll quit, warns Salmond' screamed the front pages on budget day, 6 February 2008.

On the day of the budget, Swinney held final talks with the Conservatives and the Greens and secured the support of the former and the neutrality of the latter, with a couple of extra concessions: the Tories got the extra money they wanted for drug rehabilitation and the accelerated business rates tax relief scheme, while the Greens secured additional funding for bus operators. There was even new money for Edinburgh, enough to bring independent MSP Margo MacDonald on board.

The Tories were delighted. They had actually achieved something concrete in policy terms after nine years in the Scottish Parliament and they could point to the budget, and their decision to vote for it, as a definite success. But for Labour, the result was simply baffling. The party had not opposed the budget, it had proposed an anodyne amendment which had been accepted but which meant almost nothing, so it could not claim any credit for anything and its decision to abstain on the main budget vote had allowed the SNP to coast through virtually unchallenged in what was supposed to be the Scottish Government's toughest fight. The Labour approach reflected badly on the already weakened leadership of Wendy Alexander and the party's continuing woes were captured in the central image which was carried by newspapers right across Scotland the following morning of a joyful Salmond, leaning back in his parliamentary desk, laughing and slapping his leg in mirth with Alexander just off to his left sitting in glum silence.

Part of the unstated SNP strategy was to show how much better Scotland could do if it had independence. This was couched in terms of 'Standing up for Scotland' but really it meant taking issue with Westminster on a whole range of different fronts, demanding more power and responsibility for the Scottish Parliament. The SNP's opponents called it 'picking fights with Westminster' and it was easy to see why.

First it was nuclear power. Salmond made it clear there would be no new nuclear power stations in Scotland, just when the UK government was giving the go-ahead for a new generation of such power stations in England. Then it was nuclear weapons. Not content just to oppose the nuclear submarines stationed on the Clyde, Salmond convened a 'Trident summit', bringing together church groups, anti-nuclear campaigners and environmentalists, to plot ways of opposing Trident through the devolution settlement. He then went one stage further, writing to all the signatories of the Nuclear Non-Proliferation Treaty, committing Scotland to an anti-nuclear policy and asking for their support. This backfired, though, when it emerged not only that Salmond had written to the governments of Iran and Zimbabwe asking for their help, but that very few of the others had even bothered to reply.

Some of the Scottish Government's initiatives had more credence than that, however. The autumn of 2007 brought with it an outbreak of foot and mouth disease, although thankfully not on the same scale as the crisis of 2001. Officials on both sides of the border moved quickly to shut down all animal movements and the outbreak was brought under control within a few days. But the movement restrictions remained in place, causing severe hardship for Scottish farmers in particular who had lambs destined for the southern European markets but which were stuck on hillsides around Scotland.

Richard Lochhead, the rural affairs secretary, tried to get hold of Hilary Benn, the UK environment secretary, to work out an urgent compensation scheme. The Scottish Government's treatment of this episode showed how much had changed since the days of the Labour-led Scottish Executive.

With Labour in charge in both Westminster and Holyrood, any problems between ministers would have been worked out in private, but when Lochhead found his phone calls to Benn were going unanswered, he went public to embarrass the UK minister. Lochhead let it be known he had rung Benn three times to work out a compensation scheme, but his calls had never been returned, leaving the impression of ignored Post-it notes stuck all over Benn's desk with the words 'Richard Lochhead called again' scrawled on them. But the farmers eventually got the compensation scheme and Lochhead scored a political victory over London.

As the inquest continued into the fiasco of the 140,000 spoiled ballot papers from the 2007 election, so this also turned into a battle for control between Holyrood and Westminster. The Scottish Parliament controlled Scotland's local elections but its own elections were the responsibility of Westminster. UK ministers argued this was sensible but Scottish ministers claimed it was absurd for a parliament not to be in charge of its own elections.

Ron Gould, the Canadian expert brought in to find out what went wrong in the 2007 poll, called for one body to be put in charge of the Scottish elections, and MSPs claimed that body should be the Scottish Parliament. This led to another row with London, with the Scottish Parliament voting to endorse the Gould recommendations and, by implication, calling for Holyrood to have control over its own elections, and the Westminster government refusing to contemplate such a transfer.

Then there was local income tax. This was a flagship SNP policy. The Nationalists had come to power promising to scrap the council tax and replace it with a local income tax, set nationally at 3p in the pound. They had the limited support of the Liberal Democrats who wanted a local income tax but wanted it set locally, by councils. The plans were published by Swinney in early March 2008 and immediately ran into a storm of controversy as they were attacked by some unions, the Tories, Labour, the business community and students.

Swinney had calculated his tax plans on the basis of getting back the £400 million a year the UK government paid out in council tax benefit to Scots. The UK Treasury simply stated that council tax benefit was tied to council tax and if council tax was abolished in Scotland, there would be no more council tax benefit. Swinney argued that money should still come to Scotland, regardless of council tax, but he was turned down at every attempt by Labour ministers in London.

This row then escalated when Yvette Cooper, the chief secretary to the Treasury in London, wrote to Swinney warning of a potential £750 million black hole in his tax plans. It was unprecedented for UK ministers to attack devolved policies being pursued by the Holyrood government but Cooper argued that the Treasury had a right to intervene because Westminster would need to legislate to allow Her Majesty's Revenue and Customs to collect the tax. But Cooper's letter was such a deliberately political intervention that it plunged relations between the two administrations – in public at least – to a new low.

Even the global economic meltdown of October 2008 failed to bring the two administrations together. First, Salmond was angered by the Treasury's intervention, which paved the way for the takeover of HBOS by Lloyds TSB. Then he claimed the UK government did not respond as quickly or as effectively as the Irish government – the sort of small, independent government Salmond would have liked to be running. He also demanded £1 billion in extra resources from the UK Treasury to help Scotland ride through the recession, money which Salmond claimed was already allocated to Scotland but which was being kept back by the Treasury.

The picture all through 2007 and 2008, as far as SNP ministers were concerned, was very clear. Scotland was being short-changed and undermined by Westminster and it was their job to stand up for Scotland's interests.

Under the surface, the situation was a bit more complicated. The two administrations had to cooperate and liaise on routine matters every day. This meant an exchange of information, discussions about approaches, campaigns and policies by officials and ministers and, for the most part, this went on without impediment and without dispute. Indeed, most of the officials had been in place from before the 2007 election and knew their counterparts well so there were many good working relationships in many different departments. It was only when ministers on either side decided they needed to make a point, for political or departmental reasons, that they went public and attacked their counterparts. These rows did damage relations at the top level but did little to harm those further down the chain.

Despite this, Salmond felt there had to be a formal mechanism for sorting out disputes. He called repeatedly for the resumption of the joint ministerial committees, which had been set up under the Scotland Act but which fell into abeyance because they were hardly used. Eventually he got his way but this really appeared to be no more than yet another political point being made by the First Minister.

By bringing together the main Joint Ministerial Council, which was attended by the heads of the devolved administrations and senior figures from the UK government, Salmond could appear to be on the same level as the UK ministers, which was something he wanted. The council met for the first time in its reconstituted form on 25 June 2008, bringing together the First Ministers of Scotland, Wales (Rhodri Morgan) and Northern Ireland (Peter Robinson) with Jack Straw, the UK justice secretary, and the secretaries of state for Scotland, Wales and Northern Ireland. The agenda was fairly uncontentious but the symbolism was important for the SNP government.

However, the Scottish Government did not have a totally calm and untroubled time. There were problems which threatened to knock it off course. The first came in the unlikely shape of Donald Trump, the high-profile American property tycoon who was known to millions from his role in the American television series *The Apprentice*. Trump, whose mother was from the Isle of Lewis, announced plans to build a £1 billion golf development on the Menie estate in Aberdeenshire, a proposal which divided the council and the country. Many thought the development, which included hotels and houses, would be fantastic for the local economy, whereas others thought the local environment would be ruined.

The proposal was first accepted, but then rejected by committees on Aberdeenshire Council which appeared both split and confused over the plans. So the Scottish Government 'called in' the application, effectively stripping the council of its right to decide and taking on that role itself. That decision was taken by Swinney as the lead minister, but Salmond was also deeply involved in the affair as the local MP for Banff & Buchan, the constituency which included the area Trump wanted to develop. The row became an intricate parliamentary issue, with opposition politicians demanding to know what role, if any, Salmond had played in the decision to call in the application, because, as the local MP, he should have stayed out.

The First Minister was brought before the Local Government and Communities Committee on two occasions. Every meeting he had attended and every phone call he had made on the issue was dissected and debated to see if there was any link between Salmond – who had publicly supported the Trump plan in the past – and the Scottish Government's decision.

By the time the committee had finished deliberating, the MSPs were no further forward. The committee issued a report on 13 March 2008 which was divided on party lines. Opposition politicians described him as 'cavalier' in his attitudes to the Trump development, of showing 'exceptionally poor judgement' and a 'worrying lack of awareness' of the consequences of his actions. But the SNP members of the committee refused to sign up to the report, leaving Salmond with nothing more than a mild censure from his political opponents, which amounted to very, very little in parliamentary or political terms.

What the Trump controversy did was give the opposition parties the first scent of a possible comeback against the Nationalists. Up until that point, Salmond had been able to dictate the pace and the direction of politics in Scotland. Then, for the first time, the First Minister had been on the defensive. It was clear that the opposition parties had failed to make any real impression on him but they had seized the agenda at last, which was an encouraging start.

There was more to follow, however, when responses started coming in to the Scottish Government's consultation paper on local income tax. The plans had been heavily criticised when they were published in March but worse was to follow as organisation after organisation lined up to submit detailed critiques of the tax plan.

Another major plank of the SNP's plans for Scottish government was the creation of a Scottish Futures Trust to replace the controversial

Private Finance Initiative (PFI). The PFI scheme had been introduced by the Conservative governments under Margaret Thatcher and John Major and refined by Labour under Tony Blair to the Public–Private Partnership (PPP) scheme. In its broadest sense it was a way of spreading the cost of capital projects over many years, allowing authorities to take out the equivalent of a mortgage with private companies which would then build and run the school or hospital involved. But, like a mortgage, the eventual cost to the buyer ended up being considerably more than the cost of buying it outright at the start. The SNP believed that the PPP could be reformed and turned into a not-for-profit trust, with the Scottish Government issuing bonds to finance major projects at the same time.

But problems soon arose. First, the Scottish Government ran into trouble with bonds, receiving a warning from the Treasury that it could not issue them for national projects. Then it emerged that the not-for-profit trust model was not actually 'not for profit', but 'not for quite as much profit'. The SNP's scheme still allowed companies to make money from public sector deals, but not as much as they would under PPP schemes. This presented the Scottish Government with difficulties because, in the open market of PPP schemes, companies would hardly gravitate towards Scottish 'not-for-profit' schemes if they could get a better deal in England. Ministers did continue to pursue their plans for a Scottish Futures Trust company but it was drastically scaled down from the grand plans for bonds and a whole-sale revamp of the PFI method which Salmond had promised before the election. When the Scottish Government announced its plans for a replacement Forth Road Bridge in December 2008, and declared that the £2 billion structure would be built using the Scottish block grant, and not the Scottish Futures Trust model, that also appeared to knock a major dent in the much-heralded new public finance scheme.

Then there were class sizes. The Scottish Government had come to power on a commitment to reduce the size of all Primary 1, 2 and 3 classes to eighteen. First, councils demanded more classroom space, more teachers and more money, warning they would be unable to fulfil the pledge without that extra help. Then Fiona Hyslop, the education secretary, admitted in a question and answer session with headteachers that the eighteen target was 'flexible' and she would not be forcing schools to bring all classes down to that level if it was logistically difficult to do so. This was on top of the SNP's pledges to write off all student debt and to give first-time buyers a grant of £2,000 to get them on the housing ladder, both of which were dropped as impractical and expensive.

Labour leaders did chase this list of broken promises but it hardly seemed to make any difference to the SNP's poll lead. The Scottish Government was reneging on promises made in its manifesto but it was keeping many more. Also, Salmond recognised that high-profile populist policies tended to carry more weight with the public than opposition accusations of broken promises. Every time anybody drove over the Forth Road Bridge after February 2008, they passed the gaps where the toll booths used to be – a clear reminder of the SNP's decision to scrap the tolls. This was also true of the decisions to retain threatened accident and emergency departments and start the process of abolishing car-parking charges at most Scottish hospitals, rectifying another couple of grievances.

Salmond's inclination and his style of government were undoubtedly populist. He played hard with Westminster, mainly because he believed Scotland should have more power but also because it went down well with the electorate. He goaded and taunted his political opponents in the chamber because he was a good and confident enough politician to do it and because it galvanised his own MSPs, and he ran a ruthless and professional spin machine, headed by Kevin Pringle, which was the best in Scotland by a comfortable distance.

But as the first year in charge melted into year two, it became clear that there was a gap between the populist and the weighty, as far as the minority SNP administration was concerned. It could handle the quick and easy decisions, like bridge tolls and hospital parking, but it was having much more trouble with the big ticket items, like local income tax and the Scottish Futures Trust. By the time the consultations were collated on both these latter issues, it became clear that the Scottish Government had to convince a far wider audience than just the MSPs in the Scottish Parliament of the efficacy of these proposals. But more than that, there appeared to be so many holes in both policies that neither looked particularly well grounded or researched.

In August 2008, Britain's successful Olympians returned from the Beijing Games triumphant with nineteen gold medals and an extraordinary fourth place on the medals table. The UK was buoyed up by the success of the athletes from all parts of the Kingdom and this upsurge in British national pride was difficult for the Scottish Government to cope with. Inevitably, because of the SNP's determination to win Scottish independence and because of Salmond's stated desire for a Scottish Olympic team – whether or not Scotland was independent – the political focus turned to sport.

The contrast between the governmental joy at the saltire-waving celebrations of less than a year before when Glasgow had been awarded the Commonwealth Games and the rather muted response to the success of Britain's Olympians could hardly have been more marked. Salmond welcomed the Scottish Olympians with a reception at Edinburgh Castle but such a great British success was not something the SNP government was comfortable dealing with. However, the First Minister and his aides knew that, in 2010, when the referendum on independence was due to be held, there would be Commonwealth Games success in Delhi to celebrate and that would be Scottish, and not British, success. So they could afford to wait. What the Olympian controversy did do, however, was show that both the country and the government had moved on from the heady, overtly nationalistic days of 2007, when it really seemed as if Salmond and his government could do no wrong.

A year later, Salmond and the SNP were still very much in control, both in the parliament and outside. Opposition was limited and the SNP was still setting the political agenda. What had changed, however, was that not everything was going its way. There were now occasional, quite fierce, patches of turbulence to disrupt the Scottish Government's progress.

21

Uncharted territory

THERE are some by-elections which take off as political battlegrounds as soon as they are announced, local contests which become significant national events, polls which help determine the fate of political leaders and Prime Ministers. The Glasgow East contest, scheduled for 24 July 2008, was one of those.

David Marshall's decision to stand down as the Labour MP for Glasgow East on health grounds came just after two calamitous English by-elections for Labour. The party had lost the safe seat of Crewe & Nantwich on 22 May after a mammoth 17 per cent swing to the Tories, despite an attempt by Gordon Brown to sway the contest with a giveaway Budget just the week before which gave every taxpayer a £120 boost. Labour had then suffered further humiliation at the Henley by-election on 26 June. This was a solid Conservative seat and no-one expected Labour to do well but the party came in fifth, behind even the British National Party, and the candidate lost his deposit. It marked a grim first anniversary for Brown, who really needed time to rally his party. What he did not need was another by-election, but when Marshall resigned just two days after the disastrous Henley poll, that was what he got.

Marshall's resignation coincided with the departure of Wendy Alexander as Scottish Labour leader, but it was a sign of the growing awareness that Glasgow East would be a seminal contest that it soon overtook Alexander's departure as the focus for political interest in Scotland.

The parliamentary recess had just started in Scotland and Alex Salmond was about to head off on holiday. He immediately cancelled his travel plans and declared his intention to spend the two weeks campaigning in Glasgow, upping the pressure on Labour. Salmond deliberately set the tone and encouraged his fellow MSPs and activists to follow. Party workers, MSPs and activists did just what he asked, cancelling holiday plans and heading over to the depressed East End of Glasgow for a by-election which they thought could help decide the Prime Minister's fate.

Labour had held Glasgow East at the 2005 election with a majority of 13,507, making it one of the safest Labour seats in the country. Glasgow East had been Labour territory for generations. No other party had ever got close to winning the seat but it was a sign of the problems that Labour was in that the SNP, far behind in second place, actually felt it had a chance.

Salmond recognised this possibility early, announcing that it would be a 'political earthquake' if the SNP was to win. He was right. It was because it was such a safe Labour seat that Labour had so much to lose. If it lost Glasgow East, it would show that the party was in deep, deep trouble. Not only was this safe Labour territory – and one of the most deprived constituencies in the United Kingdom – but it was seen in London as being in the Prime Minister's fiefdom of Scotland, if not actually in his backyard.

For the Nationalists, the implications of victory were equally important. Not only would they deal a damaging blow to the Prime Minister; they would prove that they could take seats throughout the whole of Scotland, that their appeal was universal across the country and not just confined to their traditional pockets in the north-east and the Highlands and Islands. But, more importantly, the Glasgow East by-election brought Salmond into direct confrontation with the UK government – Holyrood and Westminster merged just for this campaign. Salmond led from the front, on the ground in the East End of Glasgow, while Brown stayed in London, insisting that the Prime Minister never campaigned in by-elections.

Here was a Scottish Prime Minister facing the prospect of being fatally wounded politically in a Westminster by-election by a Scottish National Party led by the First Minister of the Scottish Parliament. For the first time the implications of the SNP's victory in 2007 were hitting home to Labour MPs in England and they were starting to feel it.

The SNP had hardly any sort of campaigning network on the ground in Glasgow East but it had hundreds of willing volunteers and a new and responsive computer system which allowed it to make the best use of its resources. Although Labour had won the seat for decades, the party had not bothered to do much research in the area because it was never seen as important. Now Labour had to fight and it had difficulty getting activists out onto the streets. How do you persuade party workers to spend evenings canvassing on rain-swept streets when the Prime Minister refuses to do the same?

Salmond used the same tactic he had during the 2007 election. He told his party it was going to win and then forced it to work so hard that it had a chance of turning this forecast into reality. What Salmond could not have foreseen, however, was how Labour's bungling attempts to select a candidate would give the SNP a fillip right at the start of the campaign, a boost that was to prove crucial.

At 7 p.m. on Friday 4 July, local Labour activists gathered at the Tollcross Leisure Centre in Glasgow for what was supposed to be a routine selection meeting. George Ryan, a local Labour councillor, had been vetted and approved by the party hierarchy. All he needed was the formal go-ahead from his local party to be selected as the Labour candidate.

With the activists, councillors and party managers all sitting waiting for him, Ryan failed to turn up. He had faced allegations of housing benefit fraud ten years before and although he had been completely exonerated, when a journalist contacted him on this same issue before the selection meeting, he decided he did not want to put his family through the controversy again. Ryan decided not to stand but rather than go to the selection meeting and explain, he simply stayed away. The party could have continued with the meeting and chosen somebody else, but that did not fit with the central control being exercised within the Labour Party, which made sure that whoever was chosen had to have official approval. So, amid scenes of utter chaos, selection was postponed until a suitable candidate could be found.

Over the weekend, desperate party managers then approached Lesley Quinn, the outgoing general secretary of the Scottish Labour Party, but she did not want to stand. The party asked Steven Purcell, the leader of Glasgow City Council, but he did not want to stand either. It could have hardly have been worse for Labour. The party was derided and ridiculed for not even managing to choose a candidate for such a crucial contest. Eventually, Margaret Curran, the feisty

MSP for Glasgow Baillieston (which was part of the bigger Glasgow East Westminster constituency) agreed to let her name go forward, but by that time, word had leaked out of the other refusals.

'Labour's lost weekend' was how a gleeful Salmond described Labour's by-election preparations on Monday 7 July. Not only did it appear as if no-one wanted to stand for the party in the by-election, which was bad enough, but the whole candidacy muddle made the party appear incompetent.

Labour managers started to get to grips with the contest by postponing the Scottish Labour leadership battle until after polling day. Curran, with her sharp, combative style and deep knowledge of the East End, appeared to be a good choice – even though her party had stumbled upon her by accident – and at last the Labour campaigning machine lumbered into gear.

But that delay and those early problems gave the Nationalists an advantage they never looked like losing. They were helped by Curran's embarrassment when she claimed she had lived in the East End 'all my life' – in fact she had lived in the more affluent South Side for many years. It hardly seemed to matter that John Mason, the SNP candidate, was hardly exciting – he was dismissingly described by A. A. Gill in the *Sunday Times* as having a voice like 'like rain falling on derelict carpet' – but he was solid and uncontroversial and that seemed enough.

In the approach to polling day, it was clear that the result was going to be very tight. As the booths closed, both Labour and the SNP believed they could win the seat but the early momentum built up by the Nationalists, plus their better and more enthusiastic campaigning methods, looked like it would prove to be crucial. The decision went to a recount and it was Mason who won through, delighting his cheering, saltire-waving supporters when he was declared the victor in the battle for Glasgow East in the early morning of Friday 25 July by just 365 votes.

The margin was slight but the implications were huge. The SNP had recorded a 22 per cent swing against Labour. If carried through to a general election, it would have left Labour with just one MP in Scotland. It was, as Salmond had forecast, a 'political earthquake'. Glasgow East was, in some ways, more important than the SNP's groundbreaking by-election victories in Govan in 1973 and 1988 because both those were achieved when the Tories were in power, not Labour. Glasgow East was actually more like the Hamilton by-election of 1967, when Winnie Ewing became an MP, because that was contested against the backdrop of a Labour government.

Suddenly Salmond's target of twenty SNP seats from Scotland's total of fifty-nine MPs did not seem too far fetched and Brown's hold on Downing Street was looking very shaky. The Glasgow East result did not bring down the Prime Minister. It did not even precipitate a direct UK Labour leadership challenge, but it left both Brown and his party weakened.

What Glasgow East also showed was that Labour had lost touch with its own supporters in one of its most traditional strongholds. Party managers in London started asking the question: if the party could not hold on to Glasgow East, then where could it win? True, it was a by-election, and by-elections are different from general elections – they encourage protest votes and opposition parties always tend to do well – but it was impossible for Labour to ignore the growing feeling that it was floundering, particularly in Scotland.

It was with that dismal loss in the background that the contest for the Scottish Labour leadership began. For the first time since devolution, the party was going to have a real contest, decided by all its branches in the way that party managers had envisaged, but which had never been tried before.

The electoral college system, which involved party members, the trade unions and elected representatives, had been in place for years but this was the first time it had been used. When Donald Dewar died, the system was dropped because the party needed to elect a leader as soon as possible. Jack McConnell was elected leader unopposed a year later, as was Wendy Alexander in 2007, so there had been no need for the electoral college system until 2008. This time the Scottish Labour Party had the time for a proper contest to decide where the party should go and three candidates to contest it: Iain Gray, the former enterprise minister, Andy Kerr, the former health minister, and Cathy Jamieson, the deputy party leader and former justice minister.

Gray seized the initiative early on. Within hours of Alexander's departure, he let it be known from his sun lounger in Spain, where he was enjoying an early summer holiday, that he would be contesting the leadership. Jamieson was slightly slower to make her announcement but she was unofficially in the race within a couple of days. Kerr was hesitant. He had young children and was not sure he wanted to put his family through the rigours of party leadership. He also realised, rightly, that the Labour Party in Scotland was still on the way down and this might be a foolish time to take on the leadership. He did decide to enter the race, though. Unfortunately for him, he was too late to combat the early leads established by Gray and Jamieson. He had lost both the early momentum and many high-profile backers to his rivals and this left him trailing.

Gray had spent the four years between 2003 and 2007 as a special adviser in Westminster and he had cultivated the support of his MP colleagues. Soon he had signed most of them up as well as a sizeable chunk of the Labour group in the Scottish Parliament. His leadership bid was based on working with Westminster, a more pragmatic approach to politics and a return to solid, safe Labour policies. He was said to have the support of Brown (he certainly had the backing of Alistair Darling, the Chancellor) but the Prime Minister's support was never officially declared.

Jamieson came at the contest from the left, demanding taxes on the profits of the privatised utilities and a higher minimum wage. She quickly won the support of Unison, the local government union, USDAW, the shopworkers' union, and what was left of the National Union of Mineworkers in Scotland. When the union endorsements were divided up, Jamieson had slightly more than Gray, but Gray had done better than expected. Kerr's decision to leave it late to join the race meant he had no union backers and only one affiliate, Scottish Labour Students.

Kerr's campaign was based on confronting and taking on Salmond and securing more autonomy for the Scottish Labour Party from its UK parent. The title the three MSPs were fighting for was officially leader of the Labour group in the Scottish Parliament and, when elected, the new leader would only actually lead the MSPs' group. But, given that the electorate deciding the new leader was the entire Scottish Labour Party, there was some sense in widening the role – even though this would tread on the remit and responsibilities of the UK Labour leader, the Prime Minister.

The contest did not really take off in the way many in the party hoped it would. There were new ideas being debated but nothing really radical or controversial enough to fire up a real discussion about the future direction of the party. When the result was announced, on Saturday 13 September, it came as no real surprise that Gray had won. He had secured 46 per cent of the first vote, while Jamieson had won 33 per cent and Kerr 20 per cent. Kerr was then eliminated and his second-choice votes were reallocated. After that process, Gray emerged as the winner with 58 per cent of the vote to Jamieson's 42 per cent. Johann Lamont, another former minister and a Glasgow MSP, was elected deputy leader, defeating Bill Butler, the candidate from the left, with 60 per cent of the vote to Butler's 40 per cent.

As Gray was being unveiled as Labour's new leader in Scotland, another Scottish MSP was heading down to Bournemouth for his party's national conference, the first he would attend as his party's Scottish leader. This MSP was Tavish Scott. On 26 August 2008 he had been elected as leader of the Scottish Liberal Democrats in a contest which took place, almost unnoticed, during the summer.

Nicol Stephen, the leader of the Scottish Liberal Democrats from 2005, resigned suddenly and unexpectedly at the start of the 2008 summer recess. He had been Deputy First Minister in the Lab–Lib Dem Scottish Executive under McConnell's leadership for two years. He had lost power in 2007 and with it he seemed to lose some impetus too.

There was some sniping from inside the party as the Liberal Democrats, now fourth among the Holyrood parties, seemed to go backwards after the 2007 election. Stephen performed well at First Minister's Questions, regularly striking solid debating points off Salmond, but even most of these appeared to have been worked up for him in advance and he was just the person delivering them. Outside the parliament, the Liberal Democrats lacked visibility and privately Stephen was being blamed for that too. He also had young children in Aberdeen and the strain of spending so much time on party business at Holyrood was affecting his family life.

Stephen had planned to resign on Thursday 3 July 2008 but word of his decision leaked out the night before, which left him with no option but to deliver a hasty statement to the press late that evening. It was not quite the departure he would have wanted and he immediately disappeared on holiday, leaving his MSP colleagues to scramble for his inheritance.

Scott was the clear frontrunner from the start. He had been tipped for the leadership in 2005 when Jim Wallace stood down, but had family problems at that time so moved aside and let Stephen take the leadership. Everybody in the party knew it was really Scott's turn now, particularly as many thought he would have made a better leader over the last three years anyway. Scott was a solid, thoughtful debater, and had the enthusiasm and drive that some in the party felt Stephen lacked. He was antagonistic towards the Nationalists, though, and it was his defiant opposition to a referendum on independence which had pushed the Liberal Democrats away from a possible coalition with the SNP after the 2007 election.

The Liberal Democrats also had a three-cornered fight for the leadership. Scott was challenged by Mike Rumbles, the maverick MSP for West Aberdeenshire & Kincardine, who had run against Stephen in 2005 and received 26 per cent of the vote. Ross Finnie, the former rural affairs minister, was the other candidate but no-one really expected him to do well. He was well liked and respected in the party but was not seen as a dynamic future leader.

Rumbles reasoned, not unnaturally, that if he could up his share to 35 per cent, he would be in with a chance of getting the leadership, particularly as it would be decided by single transferable vote. But when the votes were counted, there was huge disappointment for him. His share of the vote fell to 18 per cent and he was beaten by Finnie, who got 23 per cent. But Scott was way out in front, securing 59 per cent of the first-choice votes, well over the 50 per cent mark which he needed to make sure the second-choice votes did not have to be counted.

As for Gray, he was delighted with his win but was sanguine enough to know that it came within the context of the steady decline of the UK Labour Party. One opinion poll a few days earlier had suggested a massive 150-seat majority for the Conservatives in a UK general election and, on the day Gray was elected, a junior Labour whip in the Commons, Siobhain McDonagh, was sacked for calling openly for Brown to face a leadership election.

The Prime Minister went into the Labour Party conference in Manchester in September 2008 with senior colleagues openly advocating a leadership challenge but with no-one willing to stand up against him. Brown's commanding speech, warning of the dangers of the growing economic meltdown and arguing it was no time for 'novices' (either from inside the party or from without) earned him a little more time, to revive both his own political fortune and that of the Labour Party.

But as the global economic slump deepened and banks all over the world were taken to the edge of collapse, so Brown managed to achieve a most astonishing political resurrection. He not only led the partial nationalisation of Britain's main high street banks but persuaded the rest of Europe and then America to follow his lead, restoring some shaky confidence in the banking system and stability to the money markets.

In Scotland, the effect of this turnaround was two-fold. First, Brown suddenly looked like the wise, experienced politician his allies always claimed he had been. In the first few days after the bank rescue, he was being hailed as nothing less than the saviour of the global economy. This was enough to stabilise the Labour vote and stop it falling across the country as a whole. But it also dealt a blow to the Nationalists.

With Scotland's two biggest companies, RBS and HBOS, now effectively part owned by the UK government and with the Treasury having found £37 billion to fund the package (money which no-one believed an independent Scottish government could have secured), the economic arguments in favour of independence looked shakier than they had for several years. Added to this were the severe problems being experienced by Iceland (a wholesale banking collapse) and Ireland (entering a recession); Salmond's praise for the 'arc of prosperity', which included both those countries and which he wanted an independent Scotland to join, was starting to look fragile.

Brown's remarkable turnaround from the depths of British unpopularity to apparent international economic saviour was extraordinary and showed how quickly the fortunes of political parties can change. It also seemed to give him the confidence he had lacked before. He appointed a new Scottish secretary, Jim Murphy, replacing the friendly but almost invisible Des Browne, who had done the job on a part-time basis alongside his duties as defence secretary. Murphy's appointment gave Labour the boost in Scotland it needed.

Together with John McTernan, a rather waspish but sharp special adviser, Murphy went on the sort of anti-nationalist crusade which Labour had not really mounted since the SNP came to power. With Murphy and McTernan on one side and Gray on the other, Labour started to take issues to the Nationalists with some effect.

Brown's next decision was to be his riskiest. John MacDougall, the Labour MP for Glenrothes, died on 13 August 2008 after a long battle with cancer. His seat adjoined Brown's Kirkcaldy & Cowdenbeath constituency and the politicians had been close friends. Indeed, after his death, Brown came to Glenrothes to hold surgeries on MacDougall's behalf. The decision Brown faced was this: should he break with the 'convention' he had hidden behind in Glasgow East that Prime Ministers do not campaign in by-elections and come to the constituency to campaign?

There was no doubt that Brown had a personal following in Fife that he did not have in Glasgow. There was a chance the Prime Minister could swing the by-election Labour's way. If he did so, he would cement his own future as party leader and kick-start a Labour revival. However, if he campaigned in the contest and Labour lost, the blame would be pinned on him.

With his stock rising as the economy plummeted, Brown decided to gamble on his personal support in Fife and to lead the campaign in the by-election, set for 6 November 2008. So he went to the constituency twice on high-profile visits and his wife Sarah went many more times to help her husband and his party. Salmond went a dozen times and, once again, he predicted a 'political earthquake' and a Nationalist victory. The bookmakers certainly believed that Salmond was right, at least at the start of the campaign, but as the contest entered its final week and Brown's appearances started to have an effect, so the bookies' odds were split, with neither party favourite.

By the time the media, the party hacks and the officials gathered in a large sports hall on the edge of Glenrothes after the polls closed on 6 November, it looked as though the SNP had won again. The Nationalists were quietly confident and Labour managers appeared resigned to losing. But, by 11.30 p.m., an hour and a half after the polls closed, it became clear that the piles of ballot papers stacking up for Lindsay Roy, the Labour candidate, were higher than those for Peter Grant, the SNP candidate – substantially higher. Something was happening which no-one had expected: the Labour vote was going up. By midnight, some SNP strategists were hunched over laptops, grim faced, while others were in tears.

The result, when it was announced to triumphant and relieved Labour cheers, was emphatic. Roy had won by 6,737 votes over his SNP rival. There had been a 5 per cent swing to the SNP; indeed, the SNP got as many votes as they expected to get, a total they believed would be enough to win them the seat. But Labour voters came out in far bigger numbers.

It was a triumph for Brown. He had put his political credibility on the line and he had delivered a victory which had appeared nothing more than a hopeless dream at the start of the campaign.

With Labour on a high from Glenrothes, the party went into December 2008 waiting for the interim report of the Calman commission, which had been set up on Wendy Alexander's instigation to look into the devolution settlement. In many ways it was a huge anti-climax, principally because it did not actually recommend anything; all it did was set out the areas it would be looking into in more depth before reaching its final conclusions the following year. But one important finding was its decision to rule out full fiscal autonomy for Scotland. This would have involved handing over all Scotland's tax revenues and complete control of tax powers to the Scottish Parliament, which would then send back to the Treasury a set amount to cover reserved areas such as defence and foreign affairs. This was at the far end of the fiscal accountability spectrum and the Calman commission decided that its core belief in the Union was incompatible with the sort of sweeping changes which would flow from full fiscal autonomy.

The commission left all other tax powers on the table to be considered later. It did suggest, though, that it was moving towards 'assigned taxes', rather than the handover of tax powers. This would see the Scottish Government given the amounts raised by VAT, excise duty, national insurance contributions, income tax and corporation tax but without the ability to change the rates.

The Calman commission was not due to report until mid-2009 at the earliest but, by the end of 2008, there were already signs that it was going to be much more cautious and conservative than the

Liberal Democrats had wanted and also than some other unionists had hoped for as well.

As this was going on, the Scottish Government's National Conversation on independence was also coming towards the end of its long consultation exercise, although this had been a very different sort of process. Where the Calman commission had taken evidence from experts and studied detailed submissions from interested organisations to find a way forward, the National Conversation had started from the other end. It began with the premise that independence was the best way forward and it set out the Scottish Government's arguments in favour. It then asked for responses to that and sought to persuade people and organisations to back its original premise.

There was sniping from the SNP at the Calman commission and jibes from the commission's supporters at the National Conversation. Each side seemed to resent the presence of the other but actually they complemented each other. They were both examining Scotland's position within the UK constitution, one from the point of view of Scotland staying within the Union and the other wanting Scotland to break away. Given that the political landscape of Scotland encompassed not only both these views but also a multitude of attitudes within them, it seemed sensible that all these options were being explored.

So as the tenth anniversary of the 1999 elections approached, so it was clear that the political atmosphere in Scotland had changed from the days of 2007, when the SNP was untouchable.

Salmond was finding his second year in charge harder than the first. He had taken the politically difficult decision to ditch his much-criticised plan for a local income tax, aware that he would never get it through the parliament, and he had suffered from damning press coverage of his U-turn as a result. There were also problems with the other big domestic change advocated by the SNP, the Scottish Futures Trust. Meanwhile, Kenny MacAskill, the justice secretary, was having difficulty with the series of tough new measures he had proposed to crack down on binge drinking, one of which was to ban under-21s from buying alcohol from shops and supermarkets. The opposition parties united to reject this plan after a wave of criticism from outside the parliament, including from Nationalist students, who did not like the idea of becoming criminalised for buying a bottle of wine to take home, forcing MacAskill to reassess his controversial proposals. These were all big, important domestic issues and on these, at least, Salmond was starting to find life a little more difficult than before. Added to this were the damage that the bank bailout had done to the economics of independence, the Prime Minister's political revival following his success in dealing with the economic crisis and the Glenrothes by-election.

Yet, despite all these problems, the Scottish Nationalists continued to prosper, if not quite to the extent that they had in the first year. Everybody inside Holyrood had expected minority government to be so difficult for the SNP that it would struggle to remain in power for a year or more. But as the tenth anniversary of devolution in 2009 approached, a combination of luck, political judgement and external circumstances appeared to have come together to keep the SNP popular. A clear example of this came with the budget for 2009/10, which was rejected by the parliament at the end of January 2009, a move which appeared to leave the SNP government in serious trouble. But, after some remarkable U-turns by his opponents and more than a slice of luck, Salmond got a slightly revised budget through just a week later with a massive majority.

For Salmond, it was all more than an adequate recompense for those days back in 1999 when he had had to endure a resounding defeat at the hands of Donald Dewar's Labour Party. What the SNP's continuing success did show, though, was that, more than anything in politics, success is about mood and momentum.

Dewar came to power in 1999 on the shoulder of Tony Blair's successful New Labour machine. The UK, particularly Scotland, had become desperate for an alternative to the tired end to eighteen years of Conservative government and New Labour capitalised on that mood for change. Eight years on, in 2007, there was a similar mood for change, this time a rejection of the Labour–Lib Dem Executive, and it was the SNP which benefited. For its first-ever term in office, SNP leaders were helped by the Labour Party's failure to cope with opposition, at least for the first eighteen months after the 2007 election. They were helped too by propitious events and one hugely successful and triumphant by-election, allowing them to maintain momentum, even when some of their key policies were faltering in parliament.

As the Scottish Parliament started to gear up for its tenth anniversary, Labour was on its fifth leader, the Liberal Democrats were on their third, the Tories on only their second. The Scottish Socialists had come and gone and so had most of the Greens. But some things remained constant. Salmond had been there at the start, leading the SNP into the Scottish Parliament as the official opposition in 1999, and he was back, this time as First Minister, as the 2009 tenth anniversary loomed. He, of all people, would probably have been the first to acknowledge that it had been quite some decade, not just for himself and the SNP but for Scottish politics as a whole.

Epilogue

THERE were many critics when the first designs for the Scottish Parliament building were unveiled in 1998. Ten years later, it had become so much a part of the fabric of the Royal Mile that it looked natural, comfortable – almost as if it had always been there.

Enric Miralles, the lead architect, wanted his signature building to melt into the parkland around Arthur's Seat so he designed meadows which were to be sculptured along subtle concrete curves, spanning out from the parliament into the park. Their wild grasses and flowers were planted when the parliament was built and left to grow unhindered. There were also young trees, new, fragile and awkward when first planted in 2004, but by 2009 carrying enough weight and stature to make them look and feel part of the landscape. And because it too had been weathered, ten years on from Donald Dewar's dream, the building looked settled. It had been affected by circumstances outside its control but appeared to become more an intrinsic part of the Royal Mile with every passing month and year.

The Scottish Parliament as an institution developed along similar lines. It did appear immature and uncomfortable when it was first created but it too settled into the political landscape, even helping to reshape the way politics was perceived and conducted, not just in Scotland but throughout the United Kingdom.

When Dewar was wrestling with the Scotland Bill in 1997 and 1998, the key battle he fought was over the extent of the Scottish Parliament's powers. It was given some freedom, but not enough to do its watchful parent any lasting damage, or so the Labour Cabinet believed at the time. Ten years on the core of the debate remained the same – the powers of the parliament. But the breadth and scale of that discussion had changed dramatically.

In 1999 the Scottish Executive had been given the power to raise or lower income tax by up to 3p in the pound – the so-called 'tartan tax'. No First Minister during that initial decade ever considered using so blunt a tool, aware of the serious fiscal and political repercussions of such a move. But by 2009 the argument had moved on. It was now about taxes transferred and taxes assigned, of allocating the whole of Scotland's tax take to the Scottish Government and passing a portion of it back to Westminster for benefits, defence and foreign affairs.

The debate had become more complex, more competent and more realistic. It had travelled a considerable distance from the days when everybody in Scotland could be defined by the simple labels of 'unionist' or 'nationalist'. By 2009, that apparently clear demarcation had become blurred. Instead of two straightforward categories, people in Scotland were more willing to place themselves along a spectrum from unwavering unionist at one end to fundamentalist separatist republican on the other, with most Scots finding themselves somewhere along a rather hazy line between the two. Some believed Scotland should have control over abortion or firearms; others believed strongly in the Union but wanted Scotland to have control of corporation tax, to create a much more business-friendly environment. Still others wanted to see Scotland have more power, but with equal responsibility handed to the other countries of the UK and a massive decentralisation of power from Westminster outwards.

As ever with Scottish politics, it was all about power. The constitution had lain at the heart of political debate in Scotland since the late 1980s and, in 2009, it looked as though it would continue there for the foreseeable future. As the politicians at Holyrood prepared to celebrate the tenth anniversary of their institution in 2009, the Scottish Government was finalising plans for a referendum on independence for the following year. The National Conversation, launched in the summer of 2007, was reaching its conclusion, as was the Commission on Scottish Devolution under Sir Kenneth Calman, set up by the unionist parties as a direct counter to the National Conversation and with a remit to look into more powers for the Scottish Parliament.

So will Scotland become independent? Certainly, by 2009, the country was nearer to independence than at any time since 1707: the election of a Nationalist government – and a popular and successful administration as well – provided clear evidence of that. What was missing was the sort of huge groundswell of popular opinion to drive the agenda towards independence, the type of national mood which propelled the Scottish Parliament into being in 1997. But public opinion can change quickly. The re-election of the SNP government for a second term in 2011 would certainly shift the centre of gravity in Scotland decisively away from the Union and towards separation. The possible election of a Conservative government at Westminster would also create a new dynamic in Scottish politics.

Yet despite these imponderables, there were some certainties. By early 2009 it was clear that, with the unionist parties all edging towards more powers for the Scottish Parliament, Holyrood was going to become more and more powerful over time. There was also a reasonable argument to be made that, if the parliament was given complete control to spend in Scotland tax revenues raised in Scotland, if it had more control over setting different tax rates, if it could lower business rates to attract new business, ban firearms and control all broadcasting, then what exactly was independence anyway?

Dewar's Scotland Act was designed to preserve the Union and give Scotland a degree of home rule. Ten years later, the extent of that home rule deal was being challenged from all sides and it appeared almost inevitable that it was going to lead to more power for Holyrood and less for Westminster. Would Scotland get full-blooded independence following a referendum victory for the SNP? Possibly. Or would it just experience the gradual redrawing of the economic and governmental boundaries with England to such an extent that it became independent in all but name? More likely.

The ten years of Scottish home rule from 1999 set Scotland on a path of political change which, by 2009, had yet to be resolved. Devolution's first decade was momentous, exciting, extraordinary and riven with enough scandals and controversies to keep political editors happy for a lifetime. As for the next decade: well, already it is promising to be even better than the first.

Appendix

Election results in Scotland 1999–2007

Scottish Parliament election, 6 May 1999

	Seats
Labour	56
Scottish National Party	35
Conservative	18
Liberal Democrat	17
Green	1
Scottish Socialist Party	1
Independent	1
TOTAL	**129**

UK general election, 7 June 2001

	Seats
Labour	55
Liberal Democrat	10
Scottish National Party	5
Conservative	1
Speaker	1
TOTAL	**72**

Scottish Parliament election, 1 May 2003

	Seats
Labour	50
Scottish National Party	27
Conservative	18
Liberal Democrat	17
Green	7
Scottish Socialist Party	6
Independent	3
Scottish Senior Citizens Unity Party	1
TOTAL	**129**

UK general election, 5 May 2005

	Seats
Labour	40
Liberal Democrat	11
Scottish National Party	6
Conservative	1
Speaker	1
TOTAL	**59**

Scottish Parliament election, 3 May 2007

	Seats
Scottish National Party	47
Labour	46
Conservative	17
Liberal Democrat	16
Green	2
Independent	1
TOTAL	**129**

Index

abortion 21, 31
Act of Union (1707) 181, 185, 189–90
Agricultural Holdings (Scotland) Act
  (2003) 58
airguns 166
alcohol, purchase by under-21s 258–9
Alexander, Douglas 208
Alexander, Wendy
  becomes Scottish Labour leader
    217, 218, 220–23
  character and background 220,
    225–6
  declines to contest Scottish Labour
    leadership 91–2
  and Holyrood building 75
  leadership campaign donations
    227–30, 232–5
  ministerial posts 13, 45, 93, 96–7
  referendum on independence
    230–31
  resignation as Scottish Labour
    leader 234–5
  and Scottish Parliament powers
    171, 224–5
  and Section 28 23–6
Andrew, Anthony 73
Annan, Kofi 147
Armstrong, Bill 77, 78–9
asylum seekers 166–7
attendance allowances 51–2, 165, 210
Ayr by-election 23

Baillie, Jackie 45–6, 69, 92, 217, 222
ballot papers 182–3, 198–9, 200, 240
Barnett formula 167–9
Barr, Alex 14–15
Beattie Media 14–15
Benn, Hilary 240
Beveridge, Crawford 181
Biondi, Manuel 185
Black Watch (play) 214

Blackford, Ian 41
Blair, Tony
  and Act of Union 189
  and devolution xiii, 32
  London bombings 148
  and Jack McConnell 144–5
  and Henry McLeish 42–3, 63
  and Alex Salmond 6–7, 208
  and Scottish independence 179–80
  and Scottish press 27–9, 189
Blunkett, David 31
Boateng, Paul 219
Bono 147
Bovis 78–9, 80
Boyack, Sarah 13, 92, 217, 222
Brankin, Rhona 222
Brown, Gordon
  and Wendy Alexander 220, 229
  and Calman commission 224–5
  and devolution 32
  and football 163
  and G8 summit 145
  Glasgow airport attack 214
  Glenrothes by-election 256–7
  influence in Scotland 7–8, 170,
    194–5
  and McConnell's resignation
    219–20
  and McLeish office rental 69, 70
  referendum on independence
    230–31
  revival of political fortune 254–7
  and Alex Salmond 208
  Scottish roots 29
Brown, Keith 234
budgets 212–13, 237–9, 259
Bush, President George W. 146, 147
business community 173–5, 179–81,
  238, 262
Butler, Bill 253
by-elections

Index

House of Commons 22–3, 155, 188, 247–51, 256–7
    Scottish Parliament 23, 154–5, 188
Byrne, Rosemary 109, 135

Calman, Sir Kenneth 225
Calman commission 224–5, 257–8
Cameron, David 167, 196
Campbell, Alastair 63
Campbell, Colin 98
Campbell, John, QC 82, 88
Campbell, Sir Menzies 187–8, 194–5, 203
Canavan, Dennis 10, 109
care for the elderly 49–52, 165
Chalmers, Philip 22
Charles, Prince of Wales 209
Chisholm, Malcolm 46, 51, 101–2, 166
Clement, John 73
Clinton, Bill 142–3
Clooney, George 147
Commission on Scottish Devolution (Calman) 224–5, 257–8
Commonwealth Games 236, 246
Connery, Sir Sean 214
Conservative Party 60
    see also Scottish Conservative Party
construction industry 7–8, 243–4
contraception 21
Cook, Robin 170
Cooper, Yvette 241
council taxes 192, 237, 241
Crawford, Robert 127
Cubie, Andrew 3
Cubie report, student finance 14–16
Cunningham, Roseanna 113, 117–18, 119–20, 208
Curran, Frances 136
Curran, Margaret
    Anti-social Behaviour Bill 107
    candidate in Glasgow East 249–51
    health minister 222
    Iraq War 102
    and party leadership 217, 218

D-Day landings commemoration 124
Daily Record, Malawi appeal 141–2

Dalyell, Tam xiii, 169
Darling, Alistair 31, 170
Davidson, Neil 92–3
Davis Langdon and Everest 83, 85
Deacon, Susan
    and abortion 21
    appointed minister 13
    dismissed by McConnell 92
    and free care for the elderly 49–51
    health budget 39–40
    and Section 28 25
dental health 106
devolution
    Calman commission 224–5, 257–8
    Devolution to Scotland, Wales and the Regions Committee (DSWR) 30–33
    'a process, not an event' 33–4
    trend to nationalism 171–2
Dewar, Donald
    apparent lack of strong leadership 14
    character and personality 8, 20, 21–2, 30
    devolution 'a process, not an event' 33–4
    and Devolution to Scotland, Wales and the Regions Committee 30–33
    Dublin visit 12–13
    first Cabinet 13
    ill health and death 38, 40, 41–2
    opening ceremony speech 18–20
    parliament building 74–8, 81, 82–3
    and John Reid 15
    and Section 28 23–6
Dickson, Malcolm 150
Digby Brown 64, 65, 68
Dimbleby, David 66–7
Dismore, Andrew 168
Doig, Barbara 78–80, 81–2, 88–9
DSWR (Devolution to Scotland, Wales and the Regions Committee) 30–33
Duncan, Peter 61
Dunfermline & West Fife by-election 188
Dunion, Kevin 157, 158

Durward, Bob 98
Dyer, Jim 232–3

economic crisis 241, 255
Edinburgh, trams 213
education 193
    see also schools; student finance
Elder, Murray 29
elderly people, care 49–52, 165
elections 265–6
    see also by-elections; European
        elections; general elections; Scottish
        elections
electoral systems
    ballot papers 182–3, 198–9, 200, 240
    importance of 'second vote' 196–7
    local government 95–6, 106, 127
    Scottish Parliament 10, 35, 97–100
Elizabeth II, Queen 18–20, 87, 94–5,
        137, 208–9
Elvidge, Sir John 207
Erickson, Jennifer 179
European elections 116
Ewing, Annabelle 23
Ewing, Fergus 82, 120
Ewing, Margaret 188
examinations system 46–7

Fairlie, Jim 113
farm tenancies 58
Farmer, Sir Tom 181
Ferguson, Alex 207
Ferguson, Tricia 44, 93
Finnie, Ross 13, 25, 56, 254
firearms laws 166, 210
Fisher, Hugh 83
fishing industry 58–9, 126, 210
Fitzpatrick, Brian 45
foot and mouth disease 56, 239–40
football 53, 95, 99, 163–4
Forsyth, Michael 28
Forth Road Bridge 210, 245
Fox, Colin 109, 130, 135–6
fox hunting 55, 57–8
Fraser, Adrian 152–3
Fraser, Murdo 158, 171
Fraser inquiry 87, 88

Freedom of Information (Scotland)
        Act (2002) 158, 161
Fulton, Julie 42–3, 70

G8 summit 144–9
al-Gaddafi, Muammar 211
Galbraith, Sam 13, 25, 46–7, 50, 68
Gallie, Phil 61
Gardham, Magnus 122, 141–2
gas revenues 210–11
Geldof, Bob 145, 147
general elections 59–61, 265–6
Gibbons, John 76, 89
Gibson, Kenneth 200
Gill, Charan 155
Gillon, Karen 217
Glasgow airport attack 214
Glasgow Cathcart by-election 154–5
Glasgow East by-election 247–51
Gleneagles summit 144–9
Glenrothes by-election 256–7
GM crops 55–6
Goldie, Annabel 158–9, 188, 196, 197,
        206
golf 53–4, 242–3
Gordon, Charlie 154–5, 227–8, 233
Gordon, Robert 81–2, 88
Gould, Ron 240
Grahame, Christine 120
Gray, Iain 97, 222, 251–3, 254
Green, Paul 227–8
Griffiths, Nigel 71

Hamilton, Duncan 99, 111
Hamilton South by-election 22–3
Harding, Keith 98
Harper, Robin 10, 205
Harvie, Patrick 205
HBOS 241, 253
health service, in Malawi 140–41, 143
Hillhouse, Sir Russell 34
Hinchliffe, David 49
Holyrood building
    choice of site 73–5, 84–5
    construction 78–81
    costs 75, 80, 81–4, 87
    debating chamber 84

design   40, 76–8, 79, 84–6, 88, 89
Dewar's vision   34
inquiries and investigations   82, 87,
   104
landscape   261
McAlpine bid and legal suit   78, 80,
   88
oak beam repairs   87–8
homosexuality, 'promotion' in schools
   23–6
hospitals
   in Malawi   140–41, 143
   waiting lists   54, 188
House of Commons
   by-elections   22–3, 155, 188, 247–51,
      256–7
   office rentals   65–71
   West Lothian question   169–70
Hu Jintao   147
Hunter, Tom   143–4
Hyslop, Fiona   208, 244–5

immigration policy   166–7
independence
   economic arguments for   255
   likely future developments   263
   referendum   192–3, 195, 203–4,
      215–16, 230–31
Information Commissioner   157, 158
Iraq War   101–2
Ireland   12–13, 121–2
Irvine of Lairg, Lord   30, 31–2
Izzard, Eddie   147

Jackson, Gordon   110–11
Jamieson, Cathy   92, 93, 102, 105–6,
   107, 251–3
Johnston, Nick   61
joint ministerial committees (JMCs)
   36, 210, 242
Joint Ministerial Council   36, 242
Jones, Mike   133

Kane, Rosie   109, 130, 135, 136–7
Kaylor, John   163–4
Keen, Richard, QC   132
Kennedy, Charles   187, 199

Kerr, Andy   93, 107, 218, 222, 230, 251–3
Khan, Anvar   129, 132, 133
Kinnock, Neil   178
Knowles, Matthew   64
Kosovo   4

Labour Party   22–3, 139
   see also Scottish Labour Party
Ladyman, Stephen   165
Lamont, Johann   217, 253
Land Reform (Scotland) Act (2003)   58
Leckie, Carolyn   135, 136
Liberal Democratic Party   187–8
   see also Scottish Liberal Democrats
Libya, prisoner transfers   211
Liddell, Helen   31, 60, 219
Lipsey, Lord   49
Lironi, Brian   226
Little, Tom   68
Livingston by-election   155
Lloyds TSB   241
local government, electoral system
   95–6, 106, 127
Lochhead, Richard   188, 208, 210, 240
London bombings   148

McAllion, John   92
McAlpine construction   78, 80, 88
MacAskill, Kenny   176, 208, 210,
   258–9
McAveety, Frank   107
McCabe, Jim   107–8
McCabe, Tom
   Alexander's campaign funds   228
   appointed minister   13
   dismissed by McConnell   92
   McLeish office sub-letting   64–9,
      70, 71
   and Section 28   26
McCartney, Ian   126
McCombes, Alan   131
McConnell, Bridget   90–91
McConnell, Jack
   2007 election   190–91, 193–4, 197,
      201–2
   and asylum seekers   166–7
   and Tony Blair   144–5

McConnell, Jack *cont.*
  and David Cameron 167
  character and personality 90, 125
  confirmed as leader 91–2
  constituency accounts 102–4
  D-Day landings commemoration
    124
  divided Labour group 93–4
  education minister 45, 46–8
  extra-marital affair 90–91
  finance minister 13, 39–40
  First Minister 92–3, 102, 107
  football 95, 163–5
  and G8 summit 144–5, 146–7,
    148–9
  Glasgow Cathcart by-election 154–5
  and Holyrood building 84
  leadership challenge (2000) 42–5
  lobby access 14–15
  and Malawi 138–43, 165, 219–20
  resignation 217–18, 219–20
  smoking ban 121–3
  US Tartan Week 124–5
  and Kirsty Wark 128
  and whisky industry 166
McCrone committee 47–8
MacDonald, Margo 99, 104, 109–10,
    201, 207
MacDougall, John 256
McGowan, Alasdair 50
McGrigor, Jamie 234
McGugan, Irene 99–100
McGuire, Fiona 130, 132–3
McIntosh, Lyndsay 98
Mack, Alan 85–6
MacKay, Angus 45, 50, 92
Mackie, Kathrine 154
McLaren, John 68
McLeish, Henry
  acting deputy First Minister 39
  background and character 52–3
  and devolution 31–2
  elected Scottish Labour leader 42–5
  and football 52–3
  free care for the elderly 48–52
  office sub-letting 65–71
  parliamentary building 74, 80

  and John Reid 60–61
  resignation 63–4, 70–71
  Ryder Cup campaign 53–4
Macleod, Fiona 100
McLetchie, David
  background 9, 158
  and McLeish office rental 65, 66
  Scottish Conservative leadership
    61–2
  travel expenses 156–8
MacMahon, Peter 63, 68, 70
McNeil, Duncan 117
McNeill, Pauline 96, 217, 222
McNulty, Tony 166–7
McTernan, John 68, 256
Major, John 28
Make Poverty History 145
Malawi 138–43, 165, 219–20
Marr, Matthew 226
Marshall, Christina 14, 15, 103
Marshall, David 235
Marshall, Kathleen 166
Martin, Campbell 112, 116, 176
Martin, Micheál 121–2
Mason, John 250
Mather, Jim 173–5, 179
Mathewson, Sir George 179–81
Mbeki, Thabo 147
media
  and Tony Blair 27–9
  and G8 summit 146, 147, 148
  and Malawi 141–2
  scrutiny of Scottish Parliament
    16–17, 72, 128, 161–2
al Megrahi, Abdelbaset Ali Mohmed
    211
mental health 13–14
Miralles, Enric 40, 77–8, 79, 84–5, 86
MMR vaccine 54
Monteith, Brian 156, 171
Moray by-election 188
MSPs
  allowances 16
  independents 109–10
  medals 17
  travel expenses 156–8, 159–60
  women 35

Mundell, David 188
Munro, John Farquhar 3
Murphy, Jim 255–6
Murray, Elaine 102

National Conversation 258
Neil, Alex 41, 112, 148, 176, 208
News of the World, and Tommy Sheridan
    129–30, 131–5
nuclear power 239
nuclear weapons 239

O'Donnell, Hugh 234
oil revenues 210–11
Olympic Games 246
optician service 106
Orr, Sandy 181

Pia, Simon 226
police officers 237–8
Prescott, John 31
press *see* media
Pringle, Kevin 238
Private Finance Initiative 7–8, 75,
    243–4
proportional representation (PR)
    local government elections 95–6,
        106, 127
    Scottish Parliament 35, 97–100
Protection of Wild Mammals (Scotland)
    Act (2002) 57–8
Pryce, Jonathan 50
public expenditure, Barnett formula
    167–9
Purcell, Steven 249

Question Time 66–8
Quigley, Elizabeth 111
Quinn, Lesley 249

Raffan, Keith 159–61
Rafferty, John 20–22
RBS *see* Royal Bank of Scotland
referendums
    Clause 28 25
    Scottish devolution xiii
    Scottish independence 192–3, 195,

    203–4, 215–16, 230–31
Reid, George 87, 110
Reid, John 15, 60–61, 123, 170
Reid, Kevin 14–15
Robertson, Angus 182, 183–4
Robertson, George xiii, 22, 29
Robertson, John 167
Ross, Fiona 33
Rowley, Alex 20–21
Roy, Frank 44
Roy, Lindsay 256–7
Royal Bank of Scotland 180, 255
Rumbles, Mike 187, 254
Russell, Mike (Michael) 4–5, 99, 111,
    115, 118, 119, 208
Russell, Sir Muir 82, 88
Ryan, George 249
Ryder Cup tournament 53–4

Salmond, Alex
    and Alexander donations 230
    and Tony Blair 6–7
    budget resignation threat 238
    and business community 175
    coalition with Liberal Democrats
        199, 202
    elected SNP leader (2004) 115,
        118–20
    election campaign (2007) 191–3,
        197, 200, 201
    election targets 120, 178–9, 184
    failure of coalition negotiations
        204–6
    Glasgow airport attack 214
    Glasgow East by-election 247–9,
        250–51
    golf development 243
    and Joint Ministerial Council 36,
        242
    and Kosovo 4
    and McLeish office rental 67–8
    minority government 206, 207–8,
        209–16
    populist style 245
    referendum on independence 192–3
    Scottish independence 181–2
    SNP finances 120, 178–9

Salmond, Alex *cont.*
  stands down as SNP leader 40–41,
    61
  travel expenses 156
  Westminster MP 100
Salmond, Robert 207
schools
  class sizes 106, 244–5
  examinations system 46–7
  in Malawi 141, 143
  Section 28 23–6, 28
Schroeder, Gerhard 146
Scotch whisky industry 166
Scotland's Parliament (white paper) 32
Scotland's Voice (newspaper) 5–6
Scott, John 23
Scott, Tavish
  coalition with Labour 105–6
  coalition with SNP 203–4
  declines leadership challenge 187
  elected Scottish Liberal Democrat
    leader 254
  and fishing industry 59, 126
  referendum on independence 195
Scottish Conservative Party
  1999 election 9–10
  2001 election 59, 61
  2003 election 97–8
  2007 election 196
  budget negotiations 237–8
  internal battles 104
  Mundell memo 188
  policy differences 61–2
Scottish elections 265–6
  1999 4–10
  2003 97–100, 101–2, 105, 108–11
  2007 136, 182–4, 197–202
  control by Westminster 240
  small parties 182–3
  see also electoral systems
Scottish Executive
  civil service 127, 224
  and development aid 138–9, 140, 143
  Dewar Cabinet 13
  G8 summit security costs 144–5, 149
  McConnell Cabinet 92–3, 107
  McLeish Cabinet 45–6

parliamentary defeat 102
  renamed 212
  Salmond Cabinet 207–8
  special advisers 20–22
  and Westminster 139, 143, 165–7
Scottish Futures Trust 243–4
Scottish Government 212, 239–42, 258
Scottish Green Party 10, 108, 198,
  205–6, 238
Scottish Labour Party
  1999 election 7–8
  2007 election 182–3, 190–91,
    193–4, 199–201
  and Tony Blair 188–9
  by-elections 249–51, 256–7
  coalition governments 1–3, 96,
    105–7, 126
  declining membership 222
  electoral system 35
  financial problems 224
  and Iraq War 101–2
  leadership 42–5, 220–21, 251–3
  leadership election system 43, 44,
    251
  shadow Cabinet 222
  women MSPs 35
Scottish Liberal Democrats
  1999 election 8–9
  coalition governments 1–3, 96,
    105–7, 126
  and fiscal federalism 172
  PR for local elections 96, 106
  referendum on independence
    192–3, 195, 203–4
  SNP coalition negotiations 199,
    202, 203–4
  Stephen elected leader 187
Scottish Nationalists *see* SNP (Scottish
  National Party)
Scottish Natural Heritage 127
Scottish Parliament
  building *see* Holyrood building
  by-elections 23, 154–5, 188
  debating chamber 84
  electoral system 10, 35, 97–100
  fiscal powers 4, 62, 171–2, 225, 257,
    258

Golden Jubilee address 94–5
legislative procedures 57–8
Local Government and
  Communities Committee 243
media scrutiny 16–17, 72, 128,
  161–2
opening ceremony 17–20, 87
Presiding Officers 11, 94
register of members' interests
  228–9, 232–4
reputation 161
review of powers 224–5, 262
sitting hours 35, 57–8
Standards Committee 15, 233–4
temporary home 10–11, 17
and Westminster 126, 165–7
see also MSPs; Scottish elections
Scottish People's Alliance 98
Scottish Politician of the Year 150
Scottish Qualifications Authority 46–7
Scottish Socialist Party 10, 108–9,
  129–30, 135–6, 196
Scottish Voice (party) 197
Sheridan, Gail 131–2, 133, 135
Sheridan, Tommy
  background 131
  defamation court case 131–4
  elected as MSP 10
  McLeish office sub-letting 69
  and *News of the World* 129–30
  perjury charges 134–6
  SSP leader 109
shipping industry, oil transfers 210
Sillars, Jim 113, 176
Simpson, James 84
Simpson, Richard 102
Skye Bridge tolls 2, 106
Smith, Maureen 90
smoking ban 121–3
SNP (Scottish National Party)
  1999 election 4–7
  2001 election 59–60, 61
  2003 election 97, 98–100, 108,
    110–11
  2007 election 182–4, 186, 190,
    191–3, 199–202
  budgets 212–13, 237–9, 259

and business community 173–5,
  179–81, 186
by-elections 22–3, 247–9, 250–51,
  256–7
failure of coalition negotiations
  199, 202, 204–6
finances 120, 178–81
and G8 summit 148
internal battles 104, 176
internal reforms 112–13, 114, 176–8
leadership 40–41, 117–20
membership 222–3
minority government 206, 207–8,
  209–16
party conferences 177
referendum on independence
  192–3, 215–16
and Scottish independence 5, 101
taxation proposals 101, 192, 240–41,
  243, 258
Solidarity 135–6, 196
Souter, Brian 24–5, 180
SPA *see* Scottish People's Alliance
Spencely report 82
sport *see* football; golf
SQA *see* Scottish Qualifications
  Authority
SSP *see* Scottish Socialist Party
Starkey, Phyllis 169
Steel, Sir David (Lord Steel of
  Aikwood) 9, 11, 84
Steel commission 172
Stephen, Nicol
  2007 election 197
  coalition with Liberal Democrats
    199, 202, 203–4
  elected Scottish Liberal Democrat
    leader 187–8
  referendum on independence 195,
    203–4
  resignation 253
  transport minister 107
Stewart, Brian 86–7, 89
Stirling, Archie 197
Stirling Prize 88
Straw, Jack 30–31
student finance 2, 3, 9, 15–16, 37

Sturgeon, Nicola 110–11, 118, 119–20,
    199, 208
Sun, Malawi appeal 141–2
Sutherland commission 49, 50
Swinburne, John 110
Swinney, John
    2007 election 201
    budgets 212–13, 237–8
    Cabinet post 208, 210
    challenged for leadership 111–14
    internal SNP reforms 112–13, 114,
        176–8
    resignation 115–17, 178
    SNP leader 41, 100–101

Tagliabue, Benedetta 86, 89
Tartan Army 163–4
taxation
    'assigned taxes' 225, 257, 262
    council tax 192, 237, 241
    income tax proposals 101, 192,
        240–41, 243, 258
Taylor, Brian 69
teachers' pay 47–8
terrorism 148, 214
Thompson, Dave 200–201
Thomson, Ben 181
toll charges 210, 245
Tosh, Murray 61, 94
trade unions 7–8
trams 213
Trolle, Katrine 132, 133
Trump, Donald 242–3
tuition fees 2, 3, 9, 15–16, 37
Turnbull, Lord 134
Turner, Dr Jean 110
Tynan, Bill 22–3

Union of the Crowns (1603) 181
Union of the Parliaments (1707) 181,
    185, 189–90

vaccines 54

Walker, Bill 188
Walker, Graeme 140
Wallace, Ben 61
Wallace, Jim
    Deputy First Minister 1–2, 39
    and economic policy 126–7
    enterprise minister 107
    justice minister 13
    resignation 186–7
Wark, Kirsty 128
Watson, Alistair 66
Watson, Ian 181
Watson of Invergowrie, Lord 57, 93,
    150–54
Welsh, Ian 23
West Lothian question 169–70
Westminster
    and Scotland 34, 36, 37
    and Scottish Executive/Goverment
        139, 143, 239–42
    Scottish influence in Cabinet 170
    and Scottish Parliament 126, 165–7,
        240
whisky industry 166
White, Sandra 100, 176
Whitefield, Karen 44
Whitton, David 21, 41–2, 45
Wildash, Richard 219
Wilson, Professor Alan 148
Wilson, Allan 200, 230
Wilson, Andrew 99, 111, 173–5
Wilson, Bill 111–14, 176
Winning, Cardinal Thomas 24
women, MSPs 35
Wyllie, Alastair 75–6

Yates, Gavin 226
Young, John 61
youth crime 106, 127